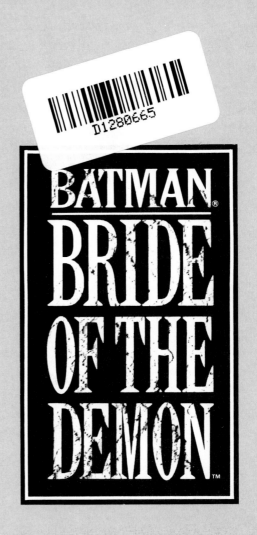

BATMAN®

BRIDE OF THE DEMON™

DC COMICS INC.

DC COMICS INC.

JENETTE KAHN
PRESIDENT & EDITOR-IN-CHIEF

DICK GIORDANO
VP-EDITORIAL DIRECTOR

DENNY O'NEIL
EDITOR

KELLEY PUCKETT
ASSISTANT EDITOR

JIM CHADWICK
DIRECTOR—DESIGN SERVICES

DALE CRAIN
ART DIRECTOR

JOE ORLANDO
VP—CREATIVE DIRECTOR

PAUL LEVITZ
EXECUTIVE VICE PRESIDENT
& PUBLISHER

BRUCE BRISTOW
VP—SALES & MARKETING

PATRICK CALDON
VP & CONTROLLER

TERRI CUNNINGHAM
DIRECTOR—EDITORIAL ADMINISTRATION

CHANTAL D'AULNIS
VP—BUSINESS AFFAIRS

LILLIAN LASERSON
VP—LEGAL AFFAIRS

MATTHEW RAGONE
CIRCULATION DIRECTOR

BOB ROZAKIS
PRODUCTION DIRECTOR

TO BILL FINGER ...
AND TO DENNY & NEAL—
WHO SIRED THE DEMON AND HIS DAUGHTER.

MIKE W. BARR

FOR EVA AND OUR FIRSTBORN

TOM GRINDBERG

BOOK DESIGN BY KEITH WILSON

DC COMICS INC., 666 FIFTH AVENUE, NEW YORK, NY 10103
A WARNER BROS. INC. COMPANY
PRINTED AND BOUND IN CANADA
FIRST PRINTING
10 9 8 7 6 5 4 3 2 1

BATMAN®
BRIDE OF THE DEMON™

MIKE W. BARR
WRITER

TOM GRINDBERG
ILLUSTRATOR

EVA GRINDBERG
COLOR ARTIST

GASPAR SALADINO
LETTERER

BATMAN CREATED BY
BOB KANE

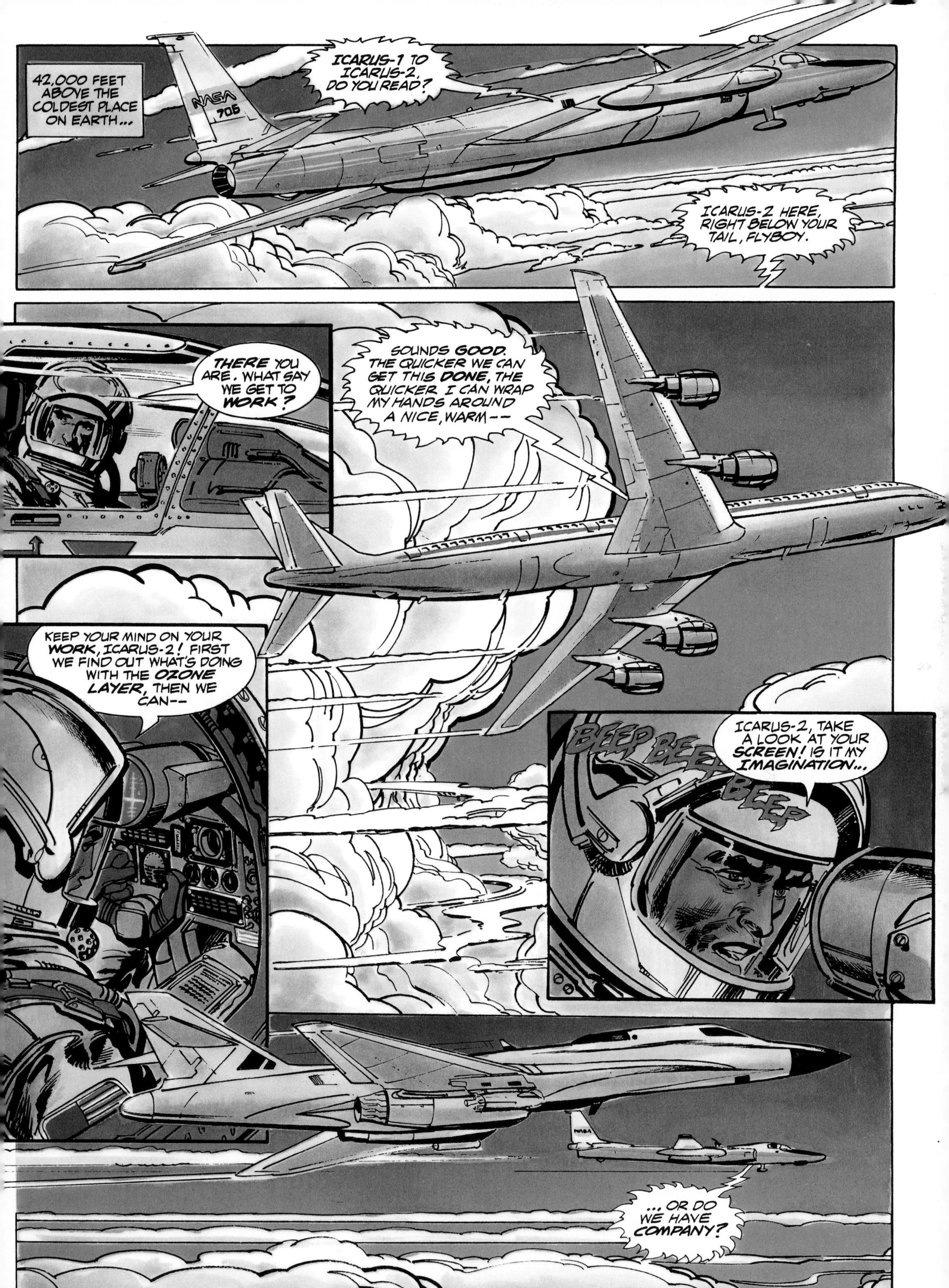

42,000 FEET ABOVE THE COLDEST PLACE ON EARTH...
ICARUS-1 TO ICARUS-2, DO YOU READ?
NASA 706
ICARUS-2 HERE, RIGHT BELOW YOUR TAIL, FLYBOY.
THERE YOU ARE. WHAT SAY WE GET TO WORK?
SOUNDS GOOD. THE QUICKER WE CAN GET THIS DONE, THE QUICKER I CAN WRAP MY HANDS AROUND A NICE, WARM--
KEEP YOUR MIND ON YOUR WORK, ICARUS-2! FIRST WE FIND OUT WHAT'S DOING WITH THE OZONE LAYER, THEN WE CAN--
BEEP BEEP BEEP
ICARUS-2, TAKE A LOOK AT YOUR SCREEN! IS IT MY IMAGINATION...
...OR DO WE HAVE COMPANY?

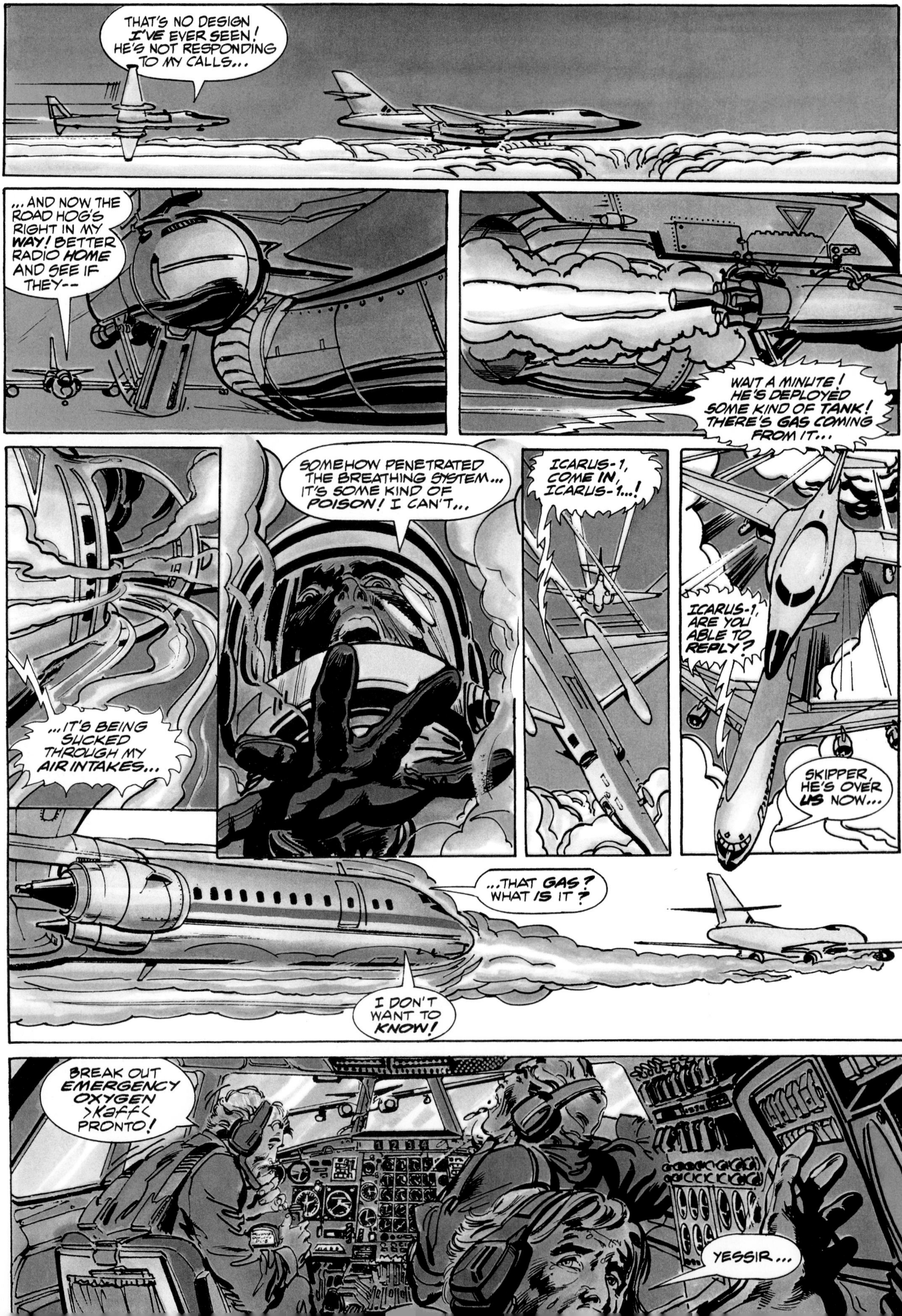
THAT'S NO DESIGN I'VE EVER SEEN! HE'S NOT RESPONDING TO MY CALLS...
...AND NOW THE ROAD HOG'S RIGHT IN MY WAY! BETTER RADIO HOME AND SEE IF THEY--
WAIT A MINUTE! HE'S DEPLOYED SOME KIND OF TANK! THERE'S GAS COMING FROM IT...
...IT'S BEING SUCKED THROUGH MY AIR INTAKES...
SOMEHOW PENETRATED THE BREATHING SYSTEM... IT'S SOME KIND OF POISON! I CAN'T...
ICARUS-1, COME IN, ICARUS-1...!
ICARUS-1, ARE YOU ABLE TO REPLY?
SKIPPER, HE'S OVER US NOW...
...THAT GAS? WHAT IS IT?
I DON'T WANT TO KNOW!
BREAK OUT EMERGENCY OXYGEN >Kaff< PRONTO!
YESSIR...

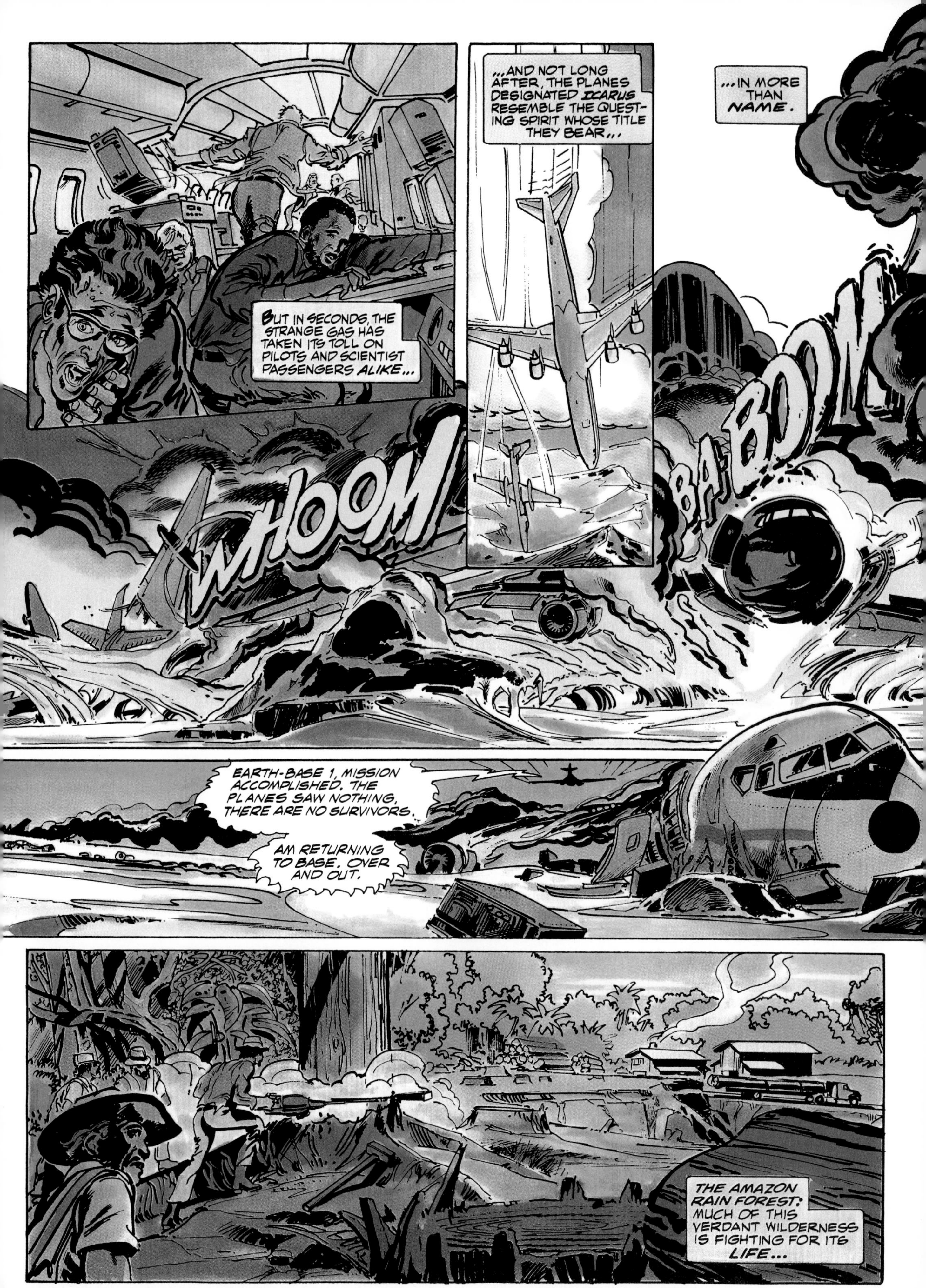
BUT IN SECONDS, THE STRANGE GAS HAS TAKEN ITS TOLL ON PILOTS AND SCIENTIST PASSENGERS ALIKE...
...AND NOT LONG AFTER, THE PLANES DESIGNATED ICARUS RESEMBLE THE QUESTING SPIRIT WHOSE TITLE THEY BEAR...
...IN MORE THAN NAME.
WHOOM
BA-BOOM
EARTH-BASE 1, MISSION ACCOMPLISHED. THE PLANES SAW NOTHING, THERE ARE NO SURVIVORS.
AM RETURNING TO BASE. OVER AND OUT.
THE AMAZON RAIN FOREST: MUCH OF THIS VERDANT WILDERNESS IS FIGHTING FOR ITS LIFE...

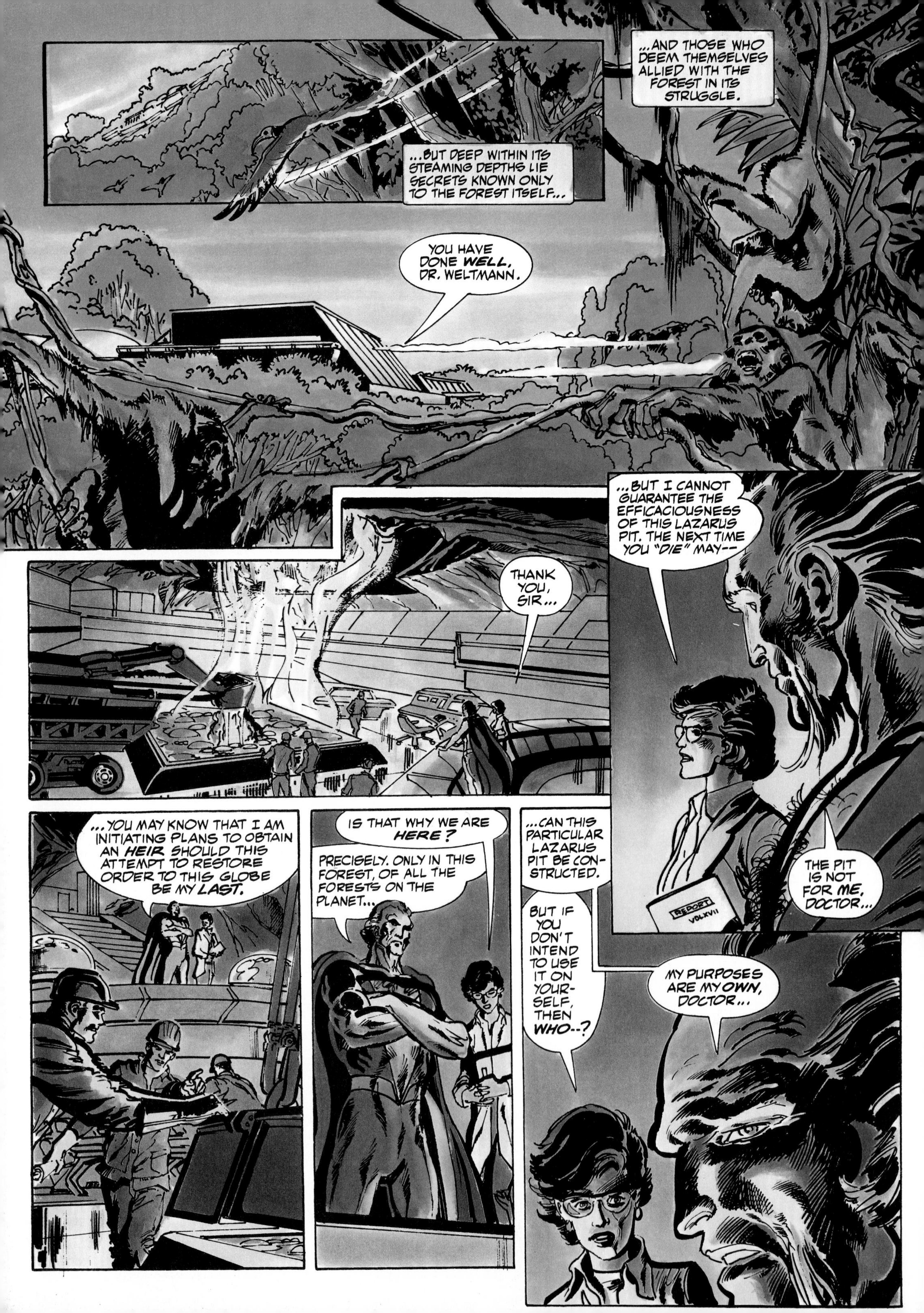

...AND THOSE WHO DEEM THEMSELVES ALLIED WITH THE FOREST IN ITS STRUGGLE.
...BUT DEEP WITHIN ITS STEAMING DEPTHS LIE SECRETS KNOWN ONLY TO THE FOREST ITSELF...
YOU HAVE DONE WELL, DR. WELTMANN.
THANK YOU, SIR...
...BUT I CANNOT GUARANTEE THE EFFICACIOUSNESS OF THIS LAZARUS PIT. THE NEXT TIME YOU "DIE" MAY--
THE PIT IS NOT FOR ME, DOCTOR...
REPORT VOL XVII
...YOU MAY KNOW THAT I AM INITIATING PLANS TO OBTAIN AN HEIR SHOULD THIS ATTEMPT TO RESTORE ORDER TO THIS GLOBE BE MY LAST.
IS THAT WHY WE ARE HERE?
PRECISELY. ONLY IN THIS FOREST, OF ALL THE FORESTS ON THE PLANET...
...CAN THIS PARTICULAR LAZARUS PIT BE CONSTRUCTED.
BUT IF YOU DON'T INTEND TO USE IT ON YOURSELF, THEN WHO--?
MY PURPOSES ARE MY OWN, DOCTOR...

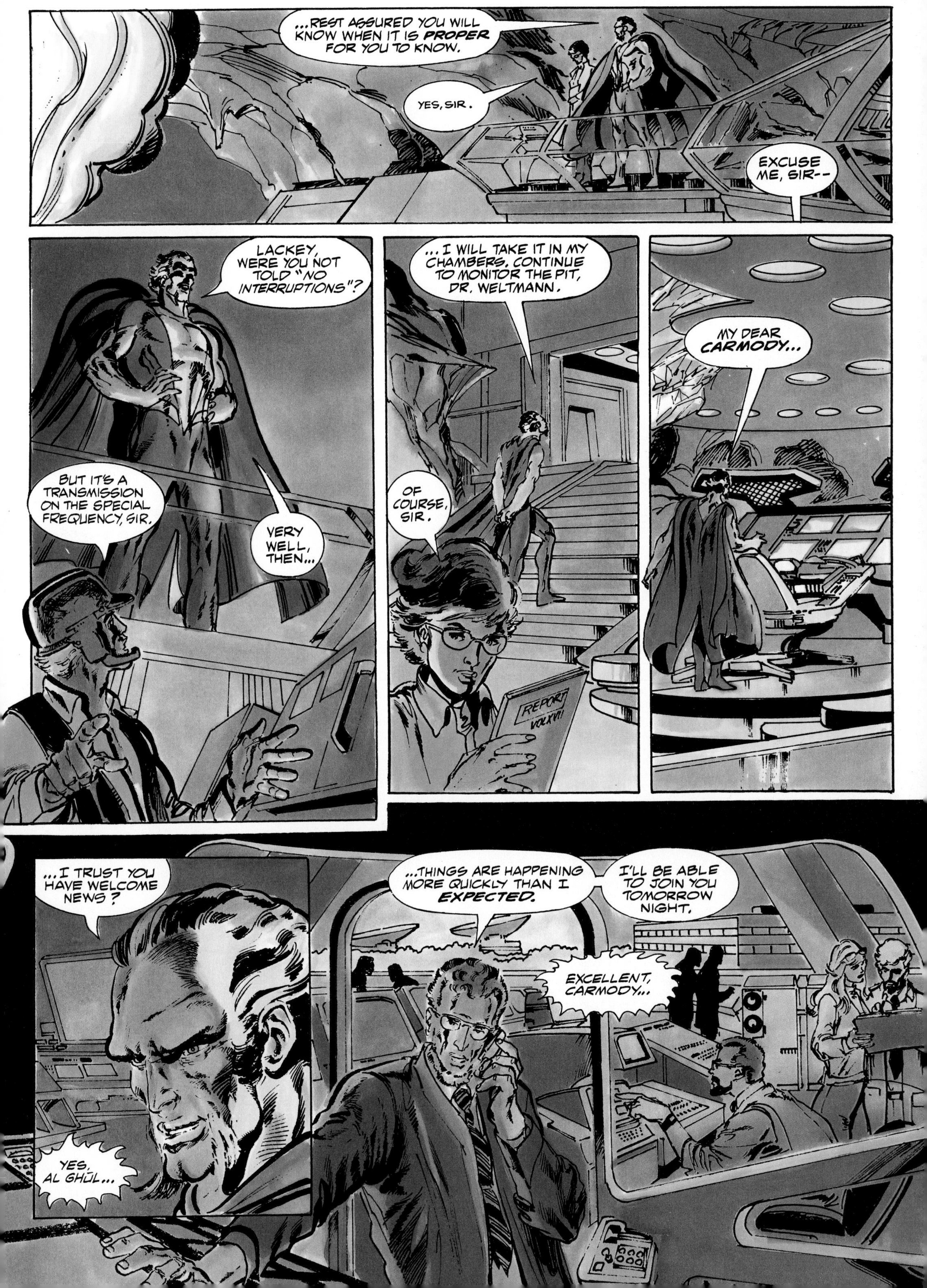
...REST ASSURED YOU WILL KNOW WHEN IT IS PROPER FOR YOU TO KNOW.
YES, SIR.
EXCUSE ME, SIR--
LACKEY, WERE YOU NOT TOLD "NO INTERRUPTIONS"?
BUT IT'S A TRANSMISSION ON THE SPECIAL FREQUENCY, SIR.
VERY WELL, THEN...
...I WILL TAKE IT IN MY CHAMBERS. CONTINUE TO MONITOR THE PIT, DR. WELTMANN.
OF COURSE, SIR.
REPORT
MY DEAR CARMODY...
...I TRUST YOU HAVE WELCOME NEWS?
YES, AL GHŪL...
...THINGS ARE HAPPENING MORE QUICKLY THAN I EXPECTED.
I'LL BE ABLE TO JOIN YOU TOMORROW NIGHT.
EXCELLENT, CARMODY...

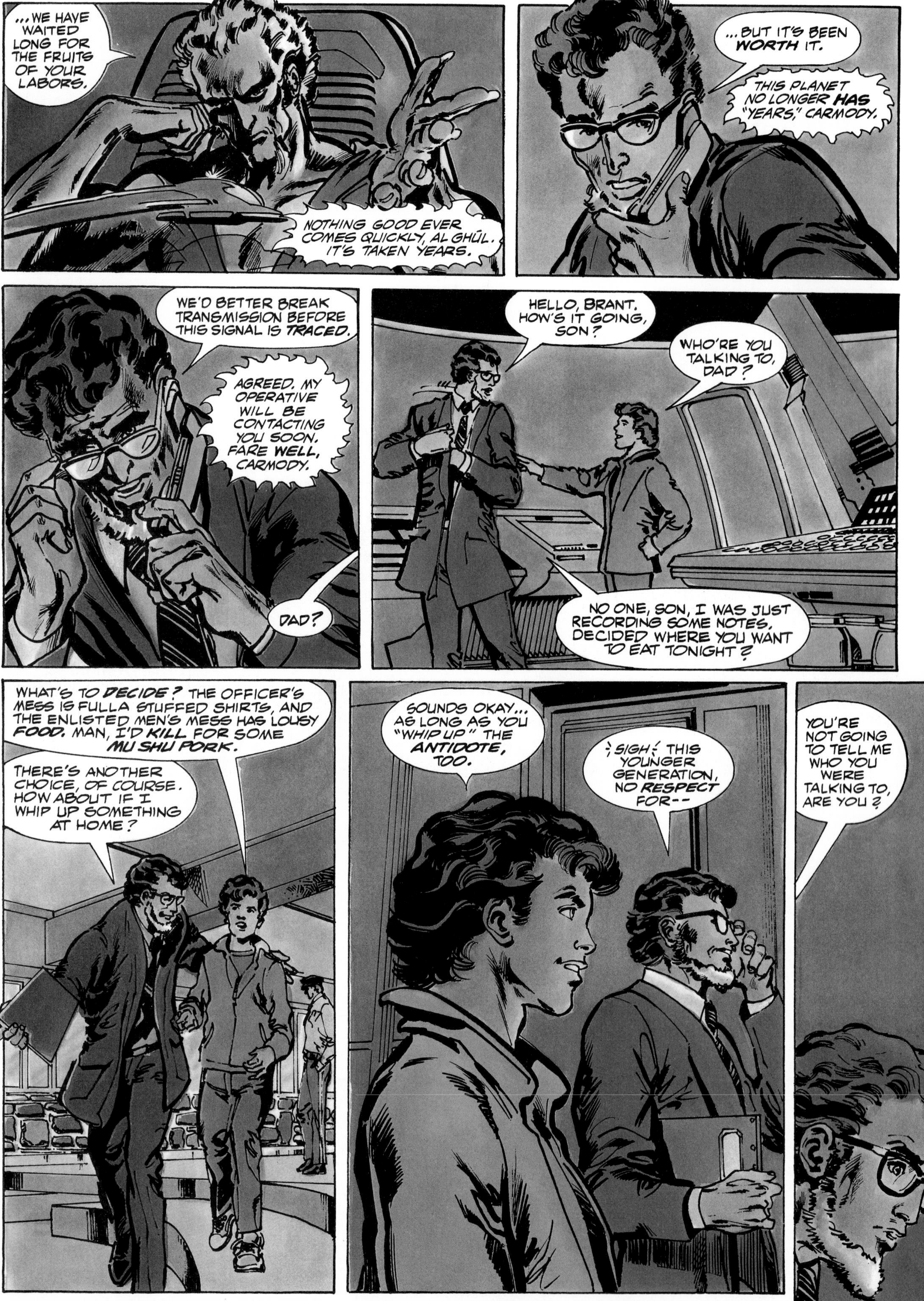
...WE HAVE WAITED LONG FOR THE FRUITS OF YOUR LABORS.
NOTHING GOOD EVER COMES QUICKLY, AL GHŪL. IT'S TAKEN YEARS.
...BUT IT'S BEEN WORTH IT.
THIS PLANET NO LONGER HAS "YEARS," CARMODY.
WE'D BETTER BREAK TRANSMISSION BEFORE THIS SIGNAL IS TRACED.
AGREED. MY OPERATIVE WILL BE CONTACTING YOU SOON. FARE WELL, CARMODY.
DAD?
HELLO, BRANT. HOW'S IT GOING, SON?
WHO'RE YOU TALKING TO, DAD?
NO ONE, SON, I WAS JUST RECORDING SOME NOTES. DECIDED WHERE YOU WANT TO EAT TONIGHT?
WHAT'S TO DECIDE? THE OFFICER'S MESS IS FULLA STUFFED SHIRTS, AND THE ENLISTED MEN'S MESS HAS LOUSY FOOD. MAN, I'D KILL FOR SOME MU SHU PORK.
THERE'S ANOTHER CHOICE, OF COURSE. HOW ABOUT IF I WHIP UP SOMETHING AT HOME?
SOUNDS OKAY... AS LONG AS YOU "WHIP UP" THE ANTIDOTE, TOO.
-SIGH- THIS YOUNGER GENERATION, NO RESPECT FOR--
YOU'RE NOT GOING TO TELL ME WHO YOU WERE TALKING TO, ARE YOU?

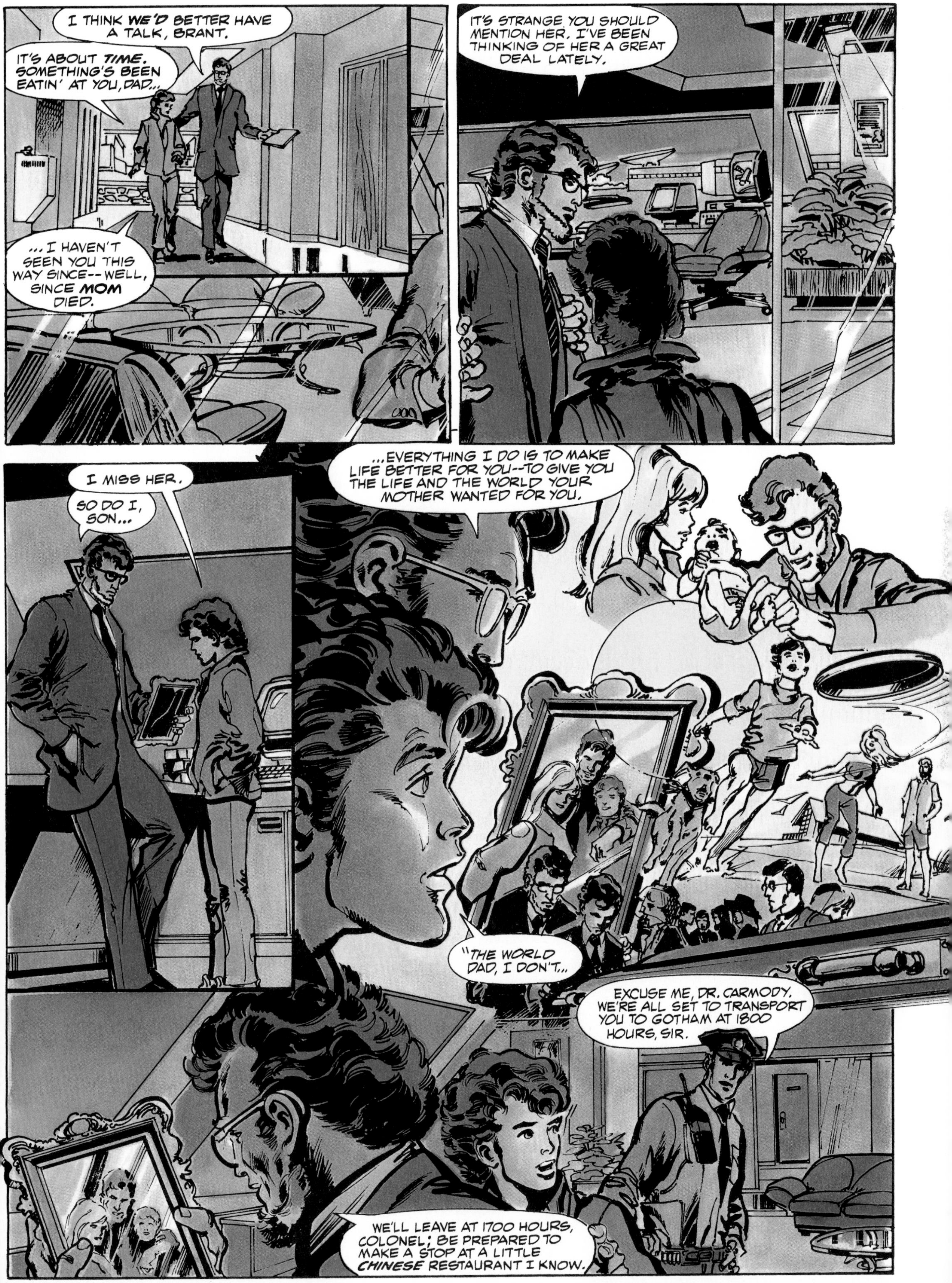
I THINK *WE'D* BETTER HAVE A TALK, BRANT.
IT'S ABOUT *TIME.* SOMETHING'S BEEN EATIN' AT YOU, DAD...
...I HAVEN'T SEEN YOU THIS WAY SINCE--WELL, SINCE *MOM* DIED.
IT'S STRANGE YOU SHOULD MENTION HER. I'VE BEEN THINKING OF HER A GREAT DEAL LATELY.
I MISS HER.
SO DO I, SON...
...EVERYTHING I DO IS TO MAKE LIFE BETTER FOR YOU--TO GIVE YOU THE LIFE AND THE WORLD YOUR MOTHER WANTED FOR YOU.
"THE WORLD" DAD, I DON'T...
EXCUSE ME, DR. CARMODY. WE'RE ALL SET TO TRANSPORT YOU TO GOTHAM AT 1800 HOURS, SIR.
WE'LL LEAVE AT 1700 HOURS, COLONEL; BE PREPARED TO MAKE A STOP AT A LITTLE *CHINESE* RESTAURANT I KNOW.

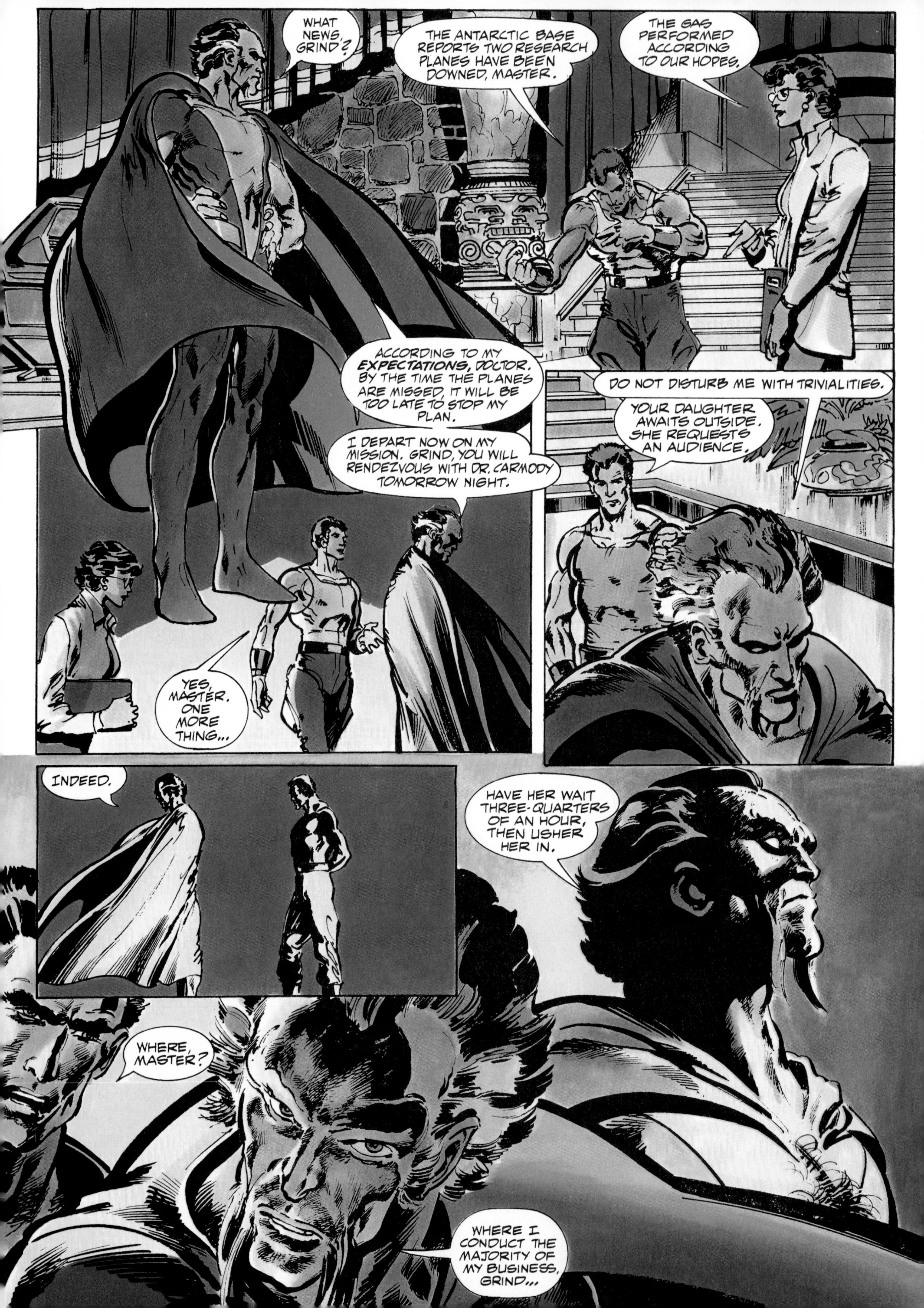
WHAT NEWS, GRIND?
THE ANTARCTIC BASE REPORTS TWO RESEARCH PLANES HAVE BEEN DOWNED, MASTER.
THE GAS PERFORMED ACCORDING TO OUR HOPES.
ACCORDING TO MY EXPECTATIONS, DOCTOR. BY THE TIME THE PLANES ARE MISSED, IT WILL BE TOO LATE TO STOP MY PLAN.
I DEPART NOW ON MY MISSION. GRIND, YOU WILL RENDEZVOUS WITH DR. CARMODY TOMORROW NIGHT.
YES, MASTER. ONE MORE THING...
YOUR DAUGHTER AWAITS OUTSIDE. SHE REQUESTS AN AUDIENCE.
DO NOT DISTURB ME WITH TRIVIALITIES.
INDEED.
HAVE HER WAIT THREE-QUARTERS OF AN HOUR, THEN USHER HER IN.
WHERE, MASTER?
WHERE I CONDUCT THE MAJORITY OF MY BUSINESS, GRIND...

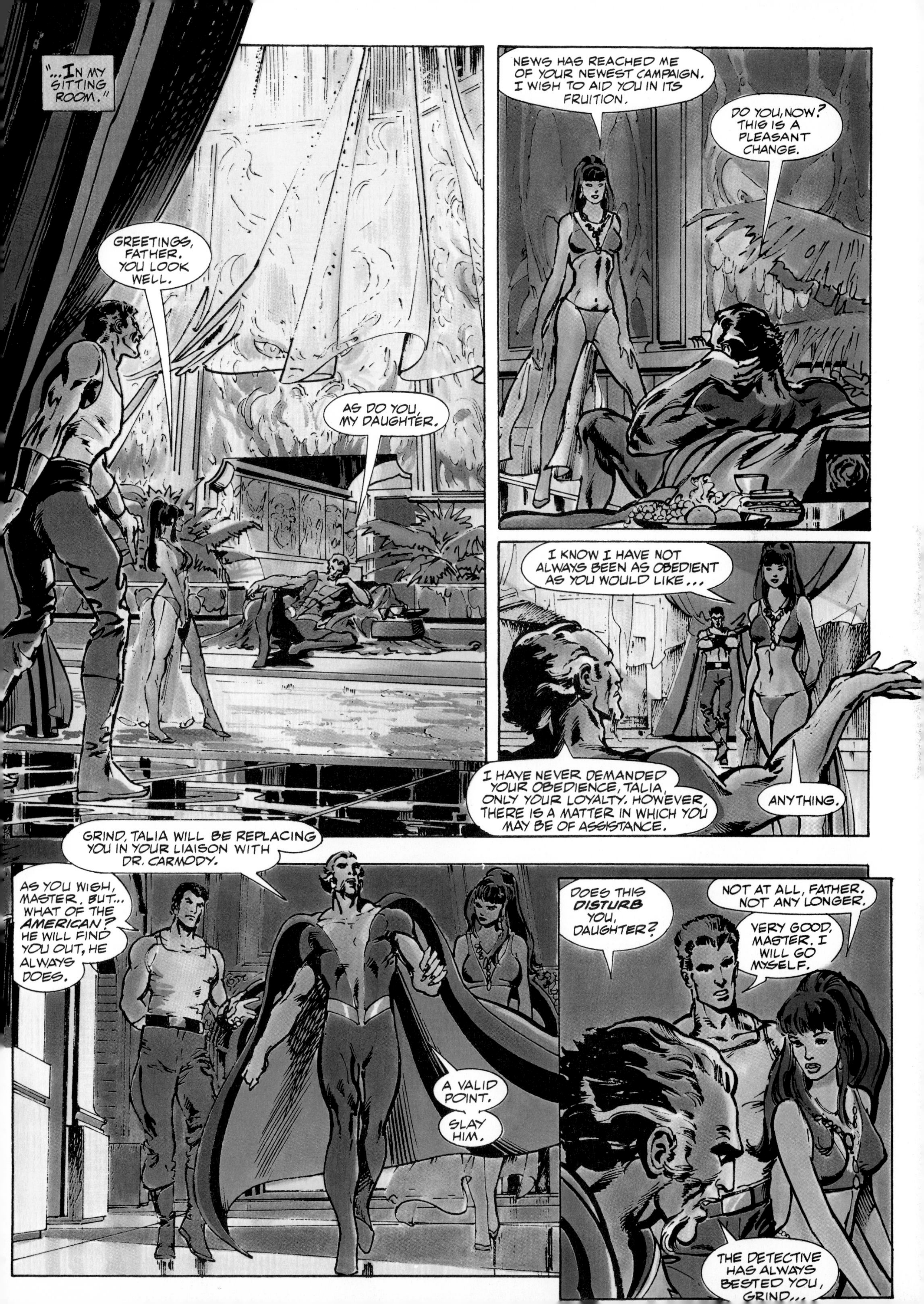
"...IN MY SITTING ROOM."
GREETINGS, FATHER. YOU LOOK WELL.
AS DO YOU, MY DAUGHTER.
NEWS HAS REACHED ME OF YOUR NEWEST CAMPAIGN. I WISH TO AID YOU IN ITS FRUITION.
DO YOU, NOW? THIS IS A PLEASANT CHANGE.
I KNOW I HAVE NOT ALWAYS BEEN AS OBEDIENT AS YOU WOULD LIKE...
I HAVE NEVER DEMANDED YOUR OBEDIENCE, TALIA, ONLY YOUR LOYALTY. HOWEVER, THERE IS A MATTER IN WHICH YOU MAY BE OF ASSISTANCE.
ANYTHING.
GRIND, TALIA WILL BE REPLACING YOU IN YOUR LIAISON WITH DR. CARMODY.
AS YOU WISH, MASTER. BUT... WHAT OF THE AMERICAN? HE WILL FIND YOU OUT, HE ALWAYS DOES.
A VALID POINT.
SLAY HIM.
DOES THIS DISTURB YOU, DAUGHTER?
NOT AT ALL, FATHER. NOT ANY LONGER.
VERY GOOD, MASTER. I WILL GO MYSELF.
THE DETECTIVE HAS ALWAYS BESTED YOU, GRIND...

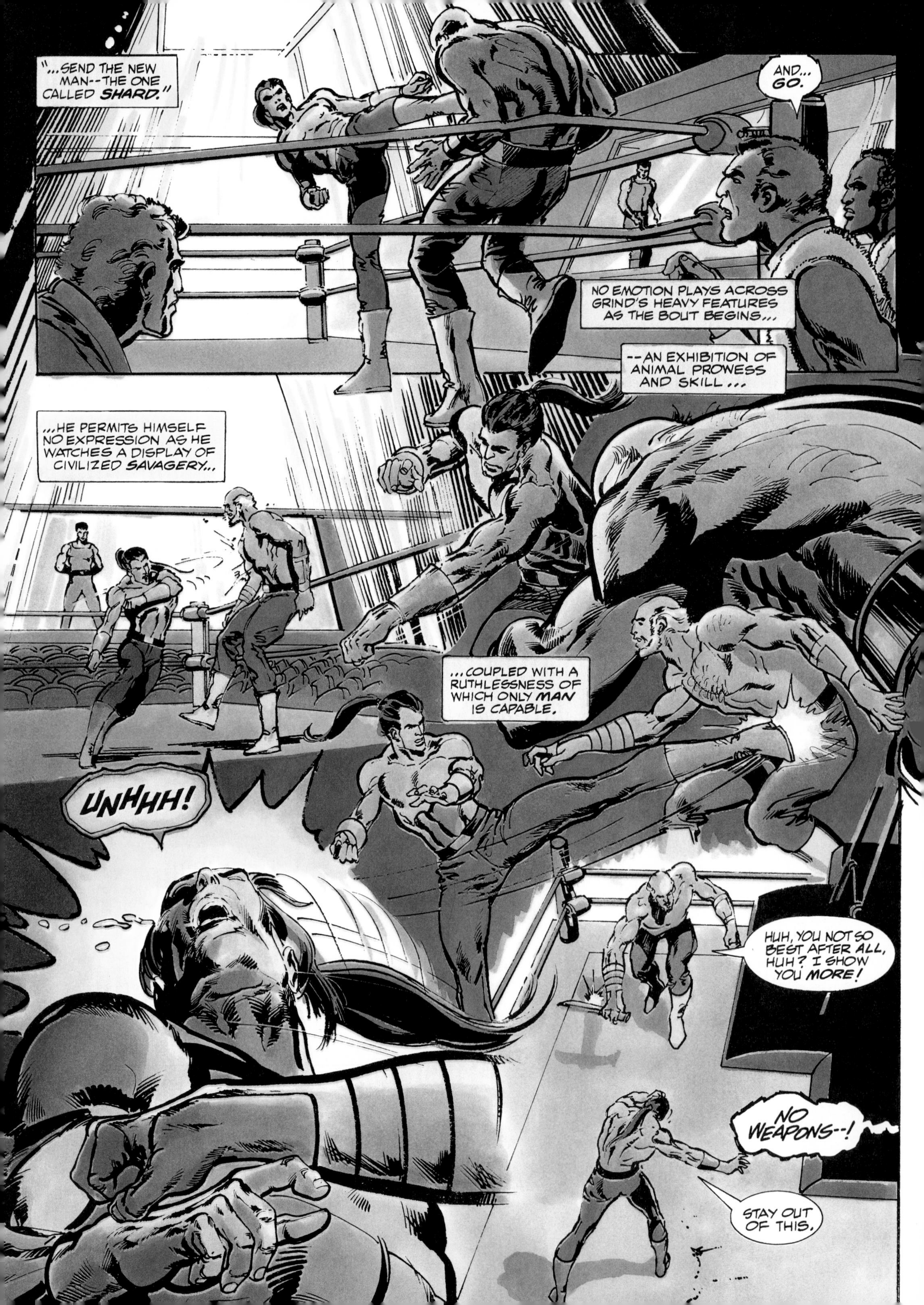
"...SEND THE NEW MAN--THE ONE CALLED SHARD."
AND... GO.
NO EMOTION PLAYS ACROSS GRIND'S HEAVY FEATURES AS THE BOUT BEGINS...
--AN EXHIBITION OF ANIMAL PROWESS AND SKILL...
...HE PERMITS HIMSELF NO EXPRESSION AS HE WATCHES A DISPLAY OF CIVILIZED SAVAGERY...
...COUPLED WITH A RUTHLESSNESS OF WHICH ONLY MAN IS CAPABLE.
UNHHH!
HUH, YOU NOT SO BEST AFTER ALL, HUH? I SHOW YOU MORE!
NO WEAPONS--!
STAY OUT OF THIS.

I TEACH YOU SOMETHING *NOW*, HUH--

HUH?

I'M NEVER TOO OLD TO *LEARN*, COMRADE...

...BUT I THINK I GRADUATED *AHEAD* OF YOUR CLASS!

AGGGGH!

MY *HAND*...! I CANNOT *RELEASE* KNIFE...!

I THOUGHT YOU DESERVED A LITTLE *TASTE*...

...OF YOUR *OWN* MEDICINE!

NO! PLEASE! I *YIELD*...

...I *SURRENDER*!

"*SURRENDER*..?"

...*THAT'S* A WORD I NEVER LEARNED!

GHHHH--!

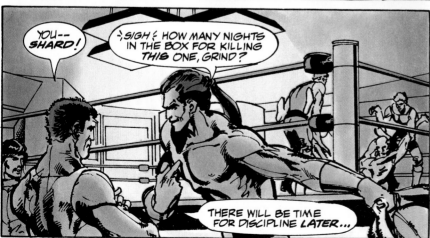

YOU-- *SHARD!*

≥SIGH≥ HOW MANY NIGHTS IN THE BOX FOR KILLING *THIS* ONE, GRIND?

THERE WILL BE TIME FOR DISCIPLINE *LATER*...

...YOU ARE TO LEAVE IMMEDIATELY FOR *AMERICA*--TO KILL THE *DETECTIVE!*

I'LL BE SURE TO GIVE HIM YOUR *BEST.*

DO NOT SMILE SO!

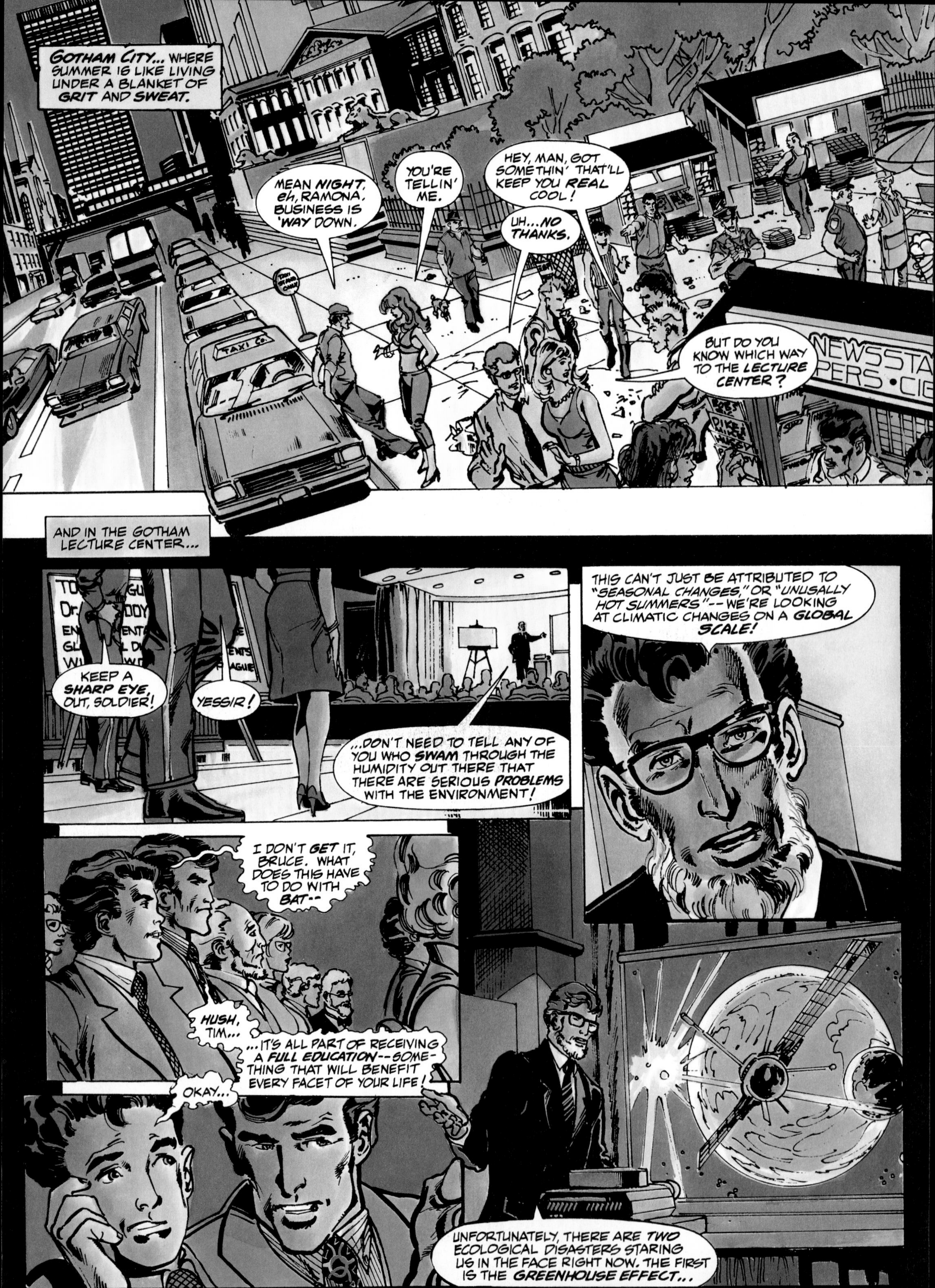

GOTHAM CITY... WHERE SUMMER IS LIKE LIVING UNDER A BLANKET OF GRIT AND SWEAT.
MEAN NIGHT, eh, RAMONA. BUSINESS IS 'WAY DOWN.
YOU'RE TELLIN' ME.
HEY, MAN, GOT SOMETHIN' THAT'LL KEEP YOU REAL COOL!
UH...NO THANKS.
BUT DO YOU KNOW WHICH WAY TO THE LECTURE CENTER?
TAXI CO.
NEWSSTA
PERS • CIG
AND IN THE GOTHAM LECTURE CENTER...
KEEP A SHARP EYE OUT, SOLDIER!
YESSIR!
...DON'T NEED TO TELL ANY OF YOU WHO SWAM THROUGH THE HUMIDITY OUT THERE THAT THERE ARE SERIOUS PROBLEMS WITH THE ENVIRONMENT!
THIS CAN'T JUST BE ATTRIBUTED TO "SEASONAL CHANGES," OR "UNUSALLY HOT SUMMERS"-- WE'RE LOOKING AT CLIMATIC CHANGES ON A GLOBAL SCALE!
I DON'T GET IT, BRUCE. WHAT DOES THIS HAVE TO DO WITH BAT--
HUSH, TIM...
...IT'S ALL PART OF RECEIVING A FULL EDUCATION--SOMETHING THAT WILL BENEFIT EVERY FACET OF YOUR LIFE!
OKAY...
UNFORTUNATELY, THERE ARE TWO ECOLOGICAL DISASTERS STARING US IN THE FACE RIGHT NOW. THE FIRST IS THE GREENHOUSE EFFECT...

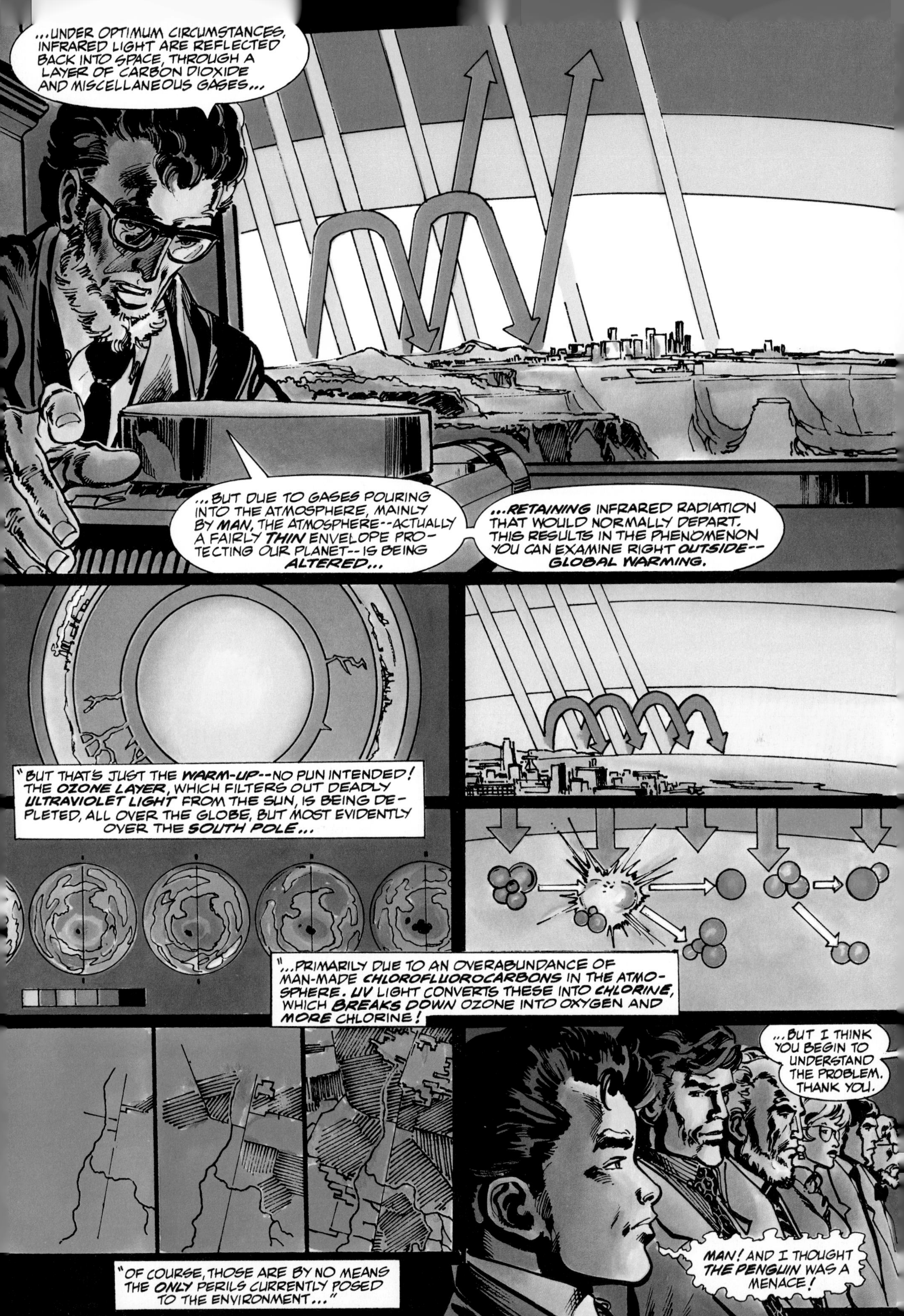

...UNDER OPTIMUM CIRCUMSTANCES, INFRARED LIGHT ARE REFLECTED BACK INTO SPACE, THROUGH A LAYER OF CARBON DIOXIDE AND MISCELLANEOUS GASES...
...BUT DUE TO GASES POURING INTO THE ATMOSPHERE, MAINLY BY MAN, THE ATMOSPHERE--ACTUALLY A FAIRLY THIN ENVELOPE PROTECTING OUR PLANET--IS BEING ALTERED...
...RETAINING INFRARED RADIATION THAT WOULD NORMALLY DEPART. THIS RESULTS IN THE PHENOMENON YOU CAN EXAMINE RIGHT OUTSIDE--GLOBAL WARMING.
"BUT THAT'S JUST THE WARM-UP--NO PUN INTENDED! THE OZONE LAYER, WHICH FILTERS OUT DEADLY ULTRAVIOLET LIGHT FROM THE SUN, IS BEING DEPLETED, ALL OVER THE GLOBE, BUT MOST EVIDENTLY OVER THE SOUTH POLE...
"...PRIMARILY DUE TO AN OVERABUNDANCE OF MAN-MADE CHLOROFLUOROCARBONS IN THE ATMOSPHERE. UV LIGHT CONVERTS THESE INTO CHLORINE, WHICH BREAKS DOWN OZONE INTO OXYGEN AND MORE CHLORINE!
"OF COURSE, THOSE ARE BY NO MEANS THE ONLY PERILS CURRENTLY POSED TO THE ENVIRONMENT..."
...BUT I THINK YOU BEGIN TO UNDERSTAND THE PROBLEM. THANK YOU.
MAN! AND I THOUGHT THE PENGUIN WAS A MENACE!

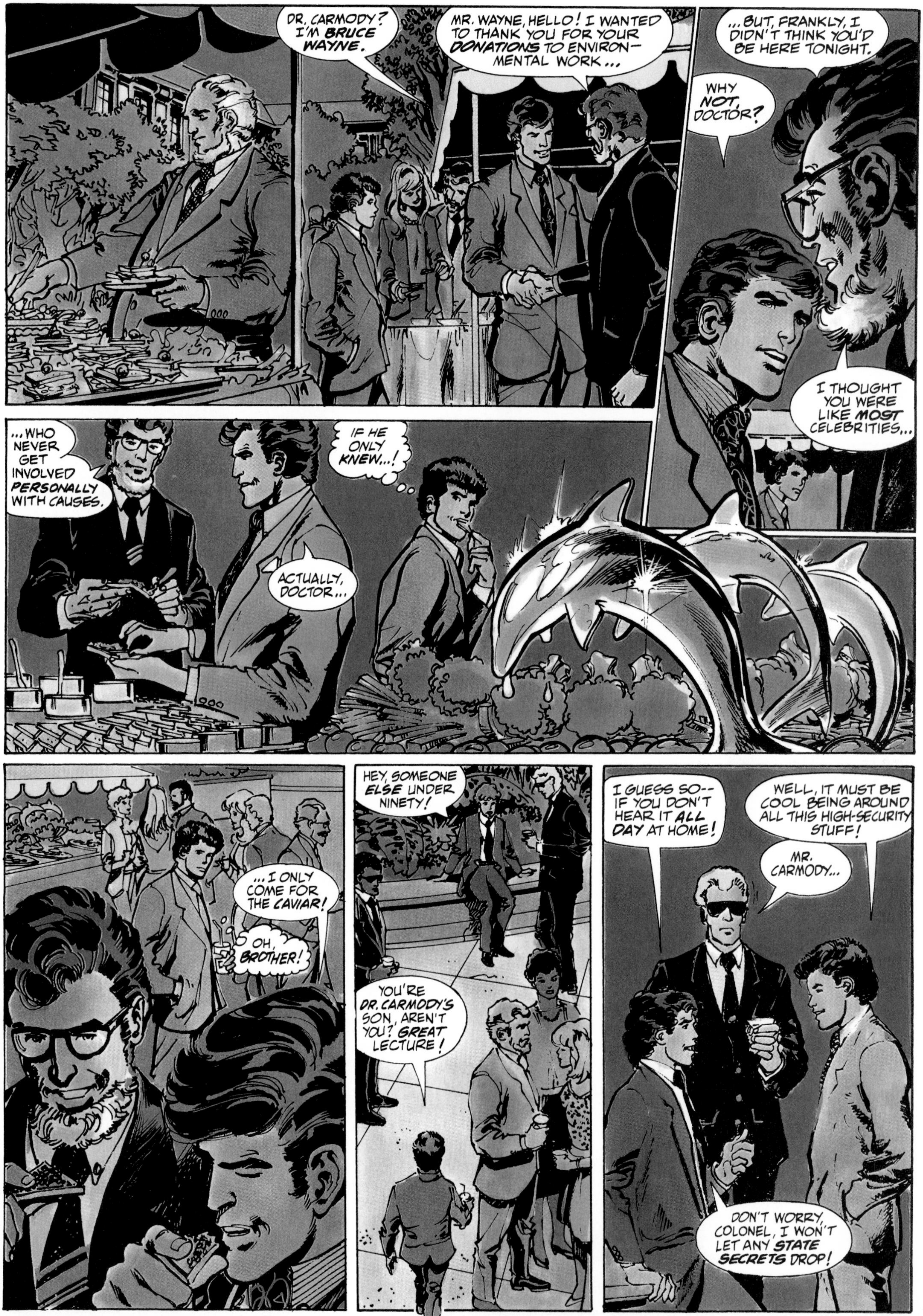
DR. CARMODY? I'M BRUCE WAYNE.
MR. WAYNE, HELLO! I WANTED TO THANK YOU FOR YOUR DONATIONS TO ENVIRONMENTAL WORK...
...BUT, FRANKLY, I DIDN'T THINK YOU'D BE HERE TONIGHT.
WHY NOT, DOCTOR?
I THOUGHT YOU WERE LIKE MOST CELEBRITIES...
...WHO NEVER GET INVOLVED PERSONALLY WITH CAUSES.
IF HE ONLY KNEW...!
ACTUALLY, DOCTOR...
...I ONLY COME FOR THE CAVIAR!
OH, BROTHER!
HEY, SOMEONE ELSE UNDER NINETY!
YOU'RE DR. CARMODY'S SON, AREN'T YOU? GREAT LECTURE!
WELL, IT MUST BE COOL BEING AROUND ALL THIS HIGH-SECURITY STUFF!
I GUESS SO-- IF YOU DON'T HEAR IT ALL DAY AT HOME!
MR. CARMODY...
DON'T WORRY, COLONEL, I WON'T LET ANY STATE SECRETS DROP!

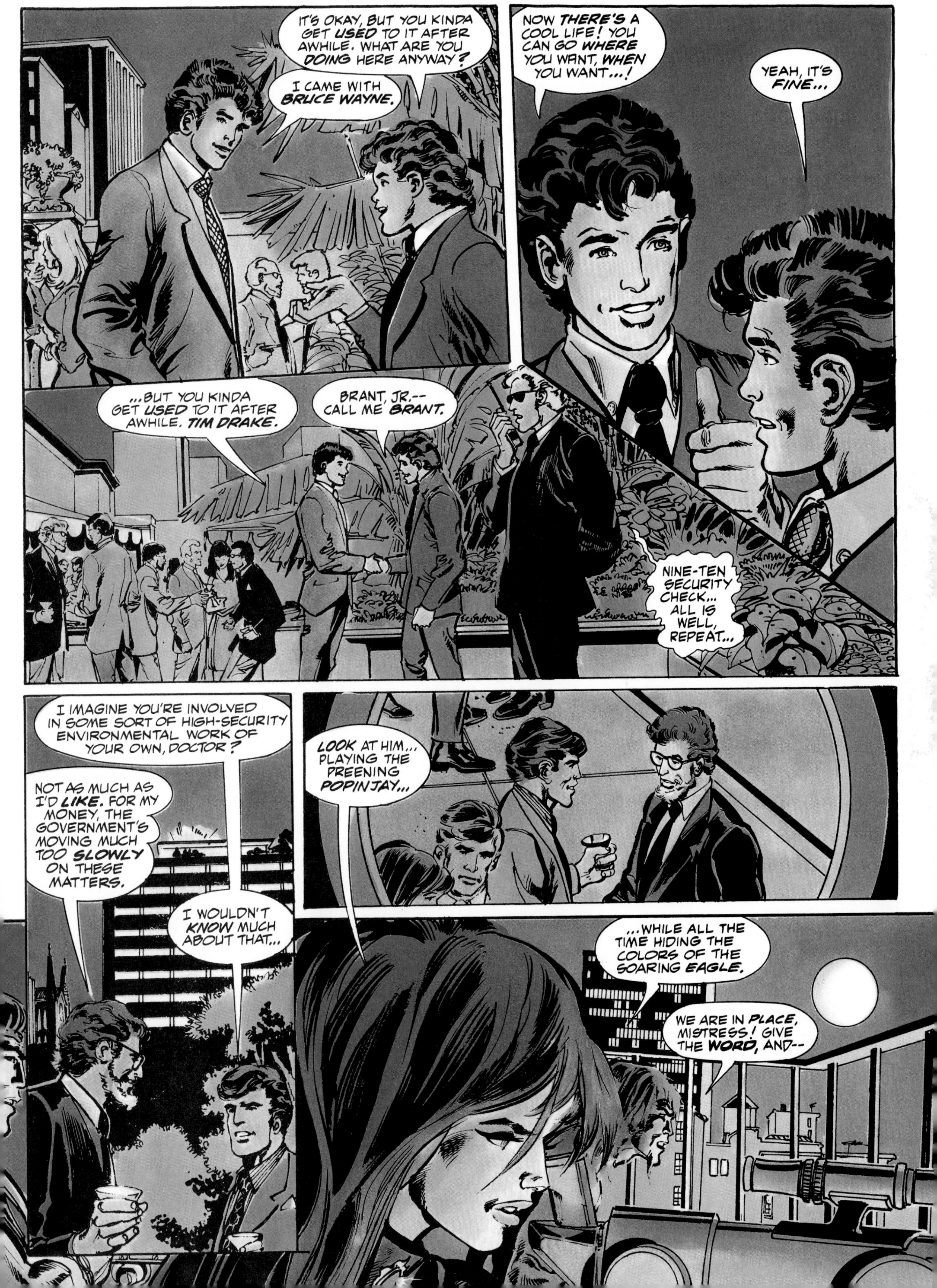
IT'S OKAY, BUT YOU KINDA GET USED TO IT AFTER AWHILE. WHAT ARE YOU DOING HERE ANYWAY?
I CAME WITH BRUCE WAYNE.
NOW THERE'S A COOL LIFE! YOU CAN GO WHERE YOU WANT, WHEN YOU WANT...!
YEAH, IT'S FINE...
...BUT YOU KINDA GET USED TO IT AFTER AWHILE. TIM DRAKE.
BRANT, JR.-- CALL ME BRANT.
NINE-TEN SECURITY CHECK... ALL IS WELL, REPEAT...
I IMAGINE YOU'RE INVOLVED IN SOME SORT OF HIGH-SECURITY ENVIRONMENTAL WORK OF YOUR OWN, DOCTOR?
NOT AS MUCH AS I'D LIKE. FOR MY MONEY, THE GOVERNMENT'S MOVING MUCH TOO SLOWLY ON THESE MATTERS.
I WOULDN'T KNOW MUCH ABOUT THAT...
LOOK AT HIM... PLAYING THE PREENING POPINJAY...
...WHILE ALL THE TIME HIDING THE COLORS OF THE SOARING EAGLE.
WE ARE IN PLACE, MISTRESS! GIVE THE WORD, AND--

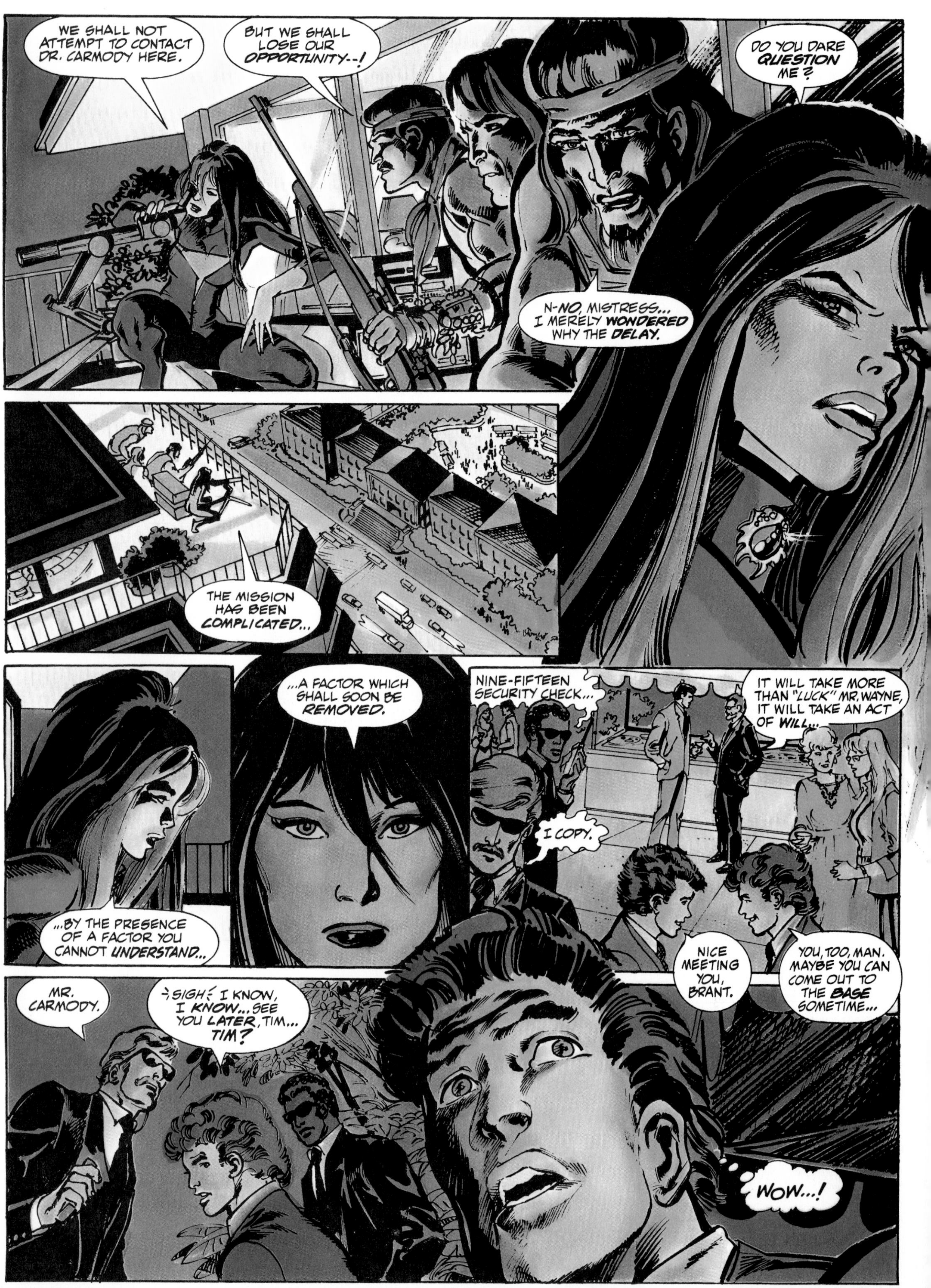
WE SHALL NOT ATTEMPT TO CONTACT DR. CARMODY HERE.
BUT WE SHALL LOSE OUR OPPORTUNITY--!
DO YOU DARE QUESTION ME?
N-NO, MISTRESS... I MERELY WONDERED WHY THE DELAY.
THE MISSION HAS BEEN COMPLICATED...
...BY THE PRESENCE OF A FACTOR YOU CANNOT UNDERSTAND...
...A FACTOR WHICH SHALL SOON BE REMOVED.
NINE-FIFTEEN SECURITY CHECK...
IT WILL TAKE MORE THAN "LUCK" MR. WAYNE, IT WILL TAKE AN ACT OF WILL...
I COPY.
NICE MEETING YOU, BRANT.
YOU, TOO, MAN. MAYBE YOU CAN COME OUT TO THE BASE SOMETIME...
MR. CARMODY.
SIGH I KNOW, I KNOW... SEE YOU LATER, TIM... TIM?
WOW...!

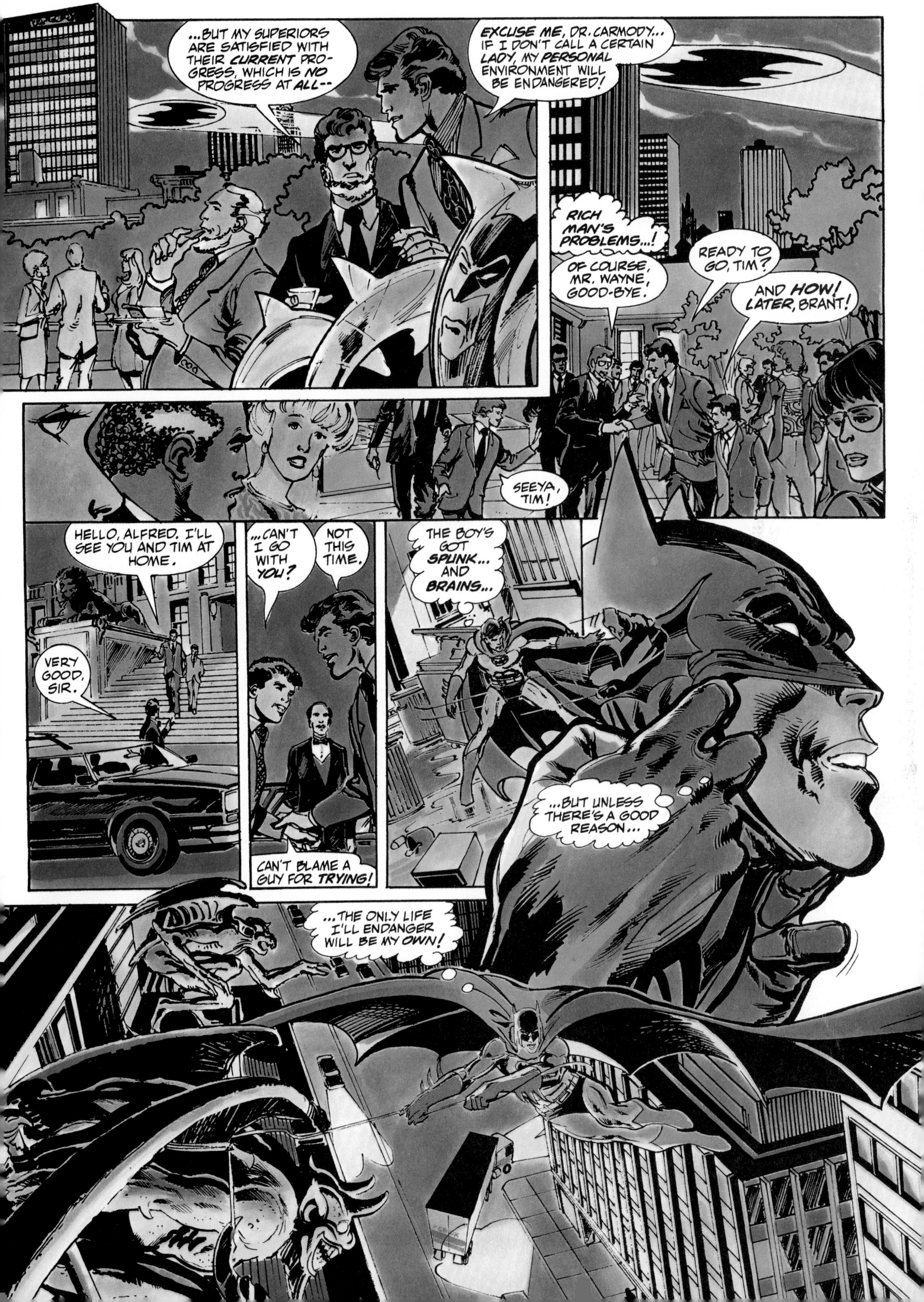
...BUT MY SUPERIORS ARE SATISFIED WITH THEIR CURRENT PROGRESS, WHICH IS NO PROGRESS AT ALL--
EXCUSE ME, DR. CARMODY... IF I DON'T CALL A CERTAIN LADY, MY PERSONAL ENVIRONMENT WILL BE ENDANGERED!
RICH MAN'S PROBLEMS...!
OF COURSE, MR. WAYNE, GOOD-BYE.
READY TO GO, TIM?
AND HOW! LATER, BRANT!
SEEYA, TIM!
HELLO, ALFRED. I'LL SEE YOU AND TIM AT HOME.
VERY GOOD, SIR.
...CAN'T I GO WITH YOU?
NOT THIS TIME.
CAN'T BLAME A GUY FOR TRYING!
THE BOY'S GOT SPUNK... AND BRAINS...
...BUT UNLESS THERE'S A GOOD REASON...
...THE ONLY LIFE I'LL ENDANGER WILL BE MY OWN!

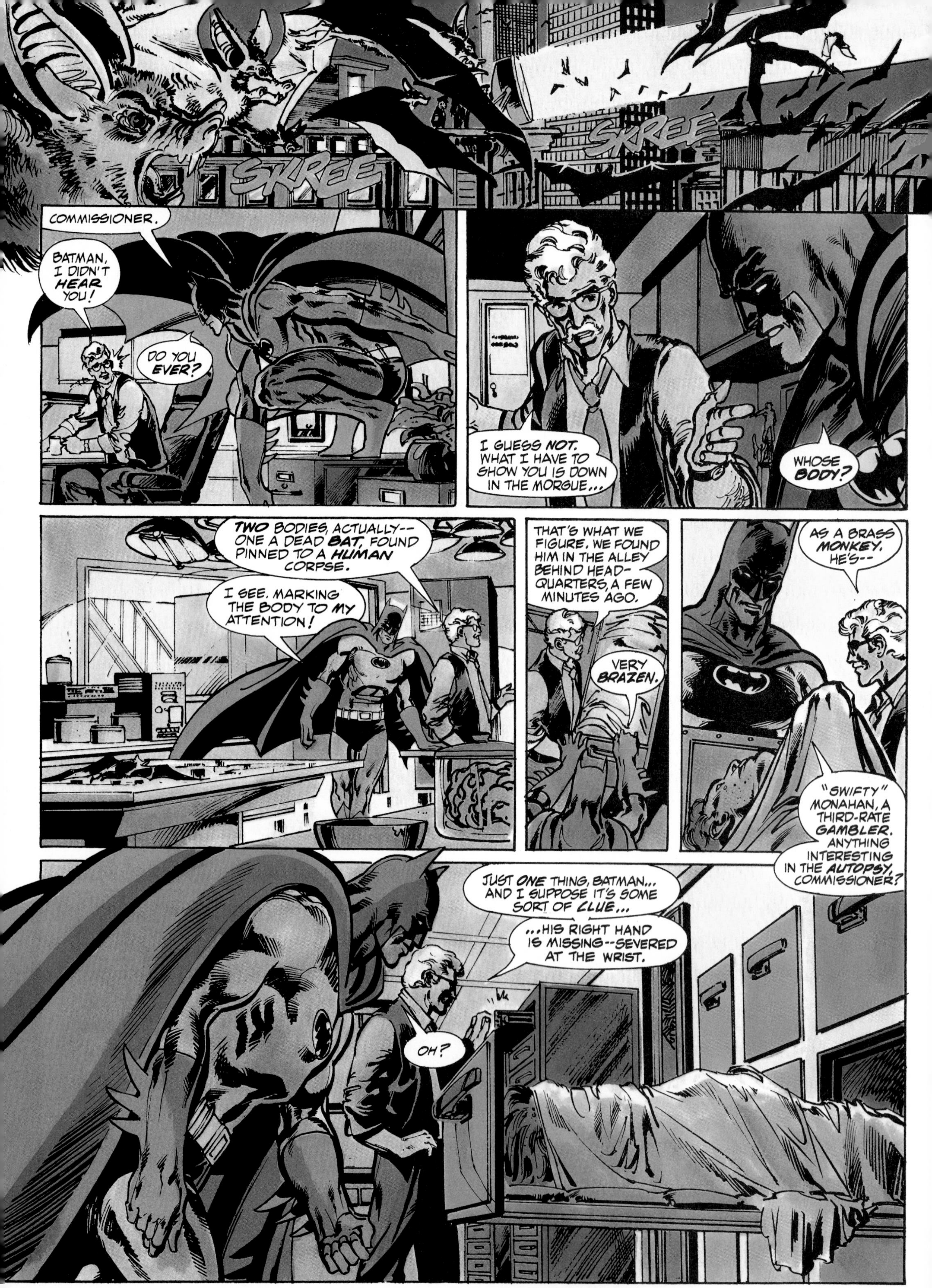
SKREE
SKREE
COMMISSIONER.
BATMAN, I DIDN'T HEAR YOU!
DO YOU EVER?
I GUESS NOT. WHAT I HAVE TO SHOW YOU IS DOWN IN THE MORGUE...
WHOSE BODY?
TWO BODIES, ACTUALLY-- ONE A DEAD BAT, FOUND PINNED TO A HUMAN CORPSE.
I SEE. MARKING THE BODY TO MY ATTENTION!
THAT'S WHAT WE FIGURE. WE FOUND HIM IN THE ALLEY BEHIND HEAD-QUARTERS, A FEW MINUTES AGO.
VERY BRAZEN.
AS A BRASS MONKEY. HE'S--
"SWIFTY" MONAHAN, A THIRD-RATE GAMBLER. ANYTHING INTERESTING IN THE AUTOPSY, COMMISSIONER?
JUST ONE THING, BATMAN... AND I SUPPOSE IT'S SOME SORT OF CLUE...
...HIS RIGHT HAND IS MISSING--SEVERED AT THE WRIST.
OH?

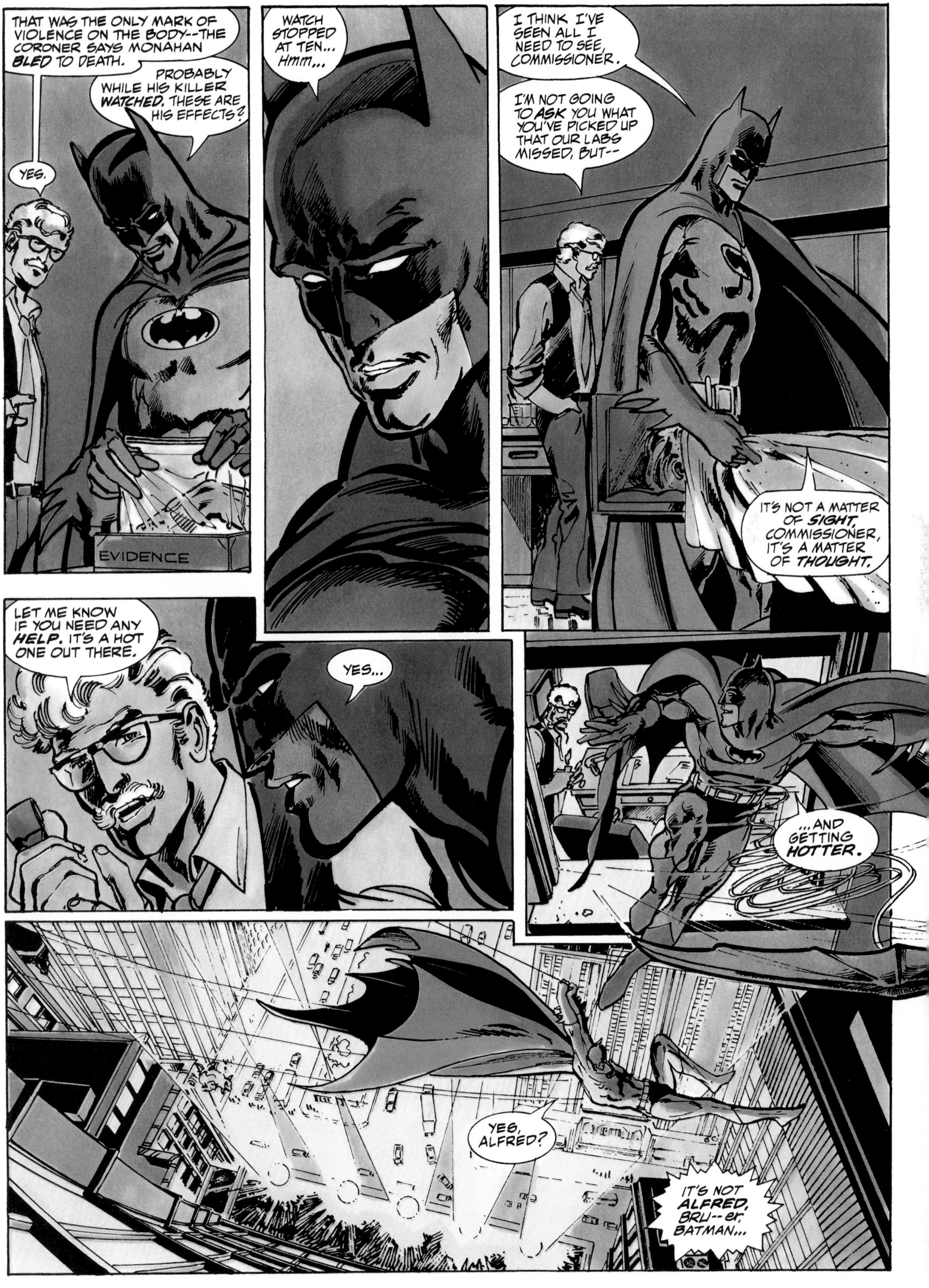
THAT WAS THE ONLY MARK OF VIOLENCE ON THE BODY--THE CORONER SAYS MONAHAN BLED TO DEATH.
PROBABLY WHILE HIS KILLER WATCHED. THESE ARE HIS EFFECTS?
YES.
EVIDENCE
WATCH STOPPED AT TEN... Hmm...
I THINK I'VE SEEN ALL I NEED TO SEE, COMMISSIONER.
I'M NOT GOING TO ASK YOU WHAT YOU'VE PICKED UP THAT OUR LABS MISSED, BUT--
IT'S NOT A MATTER OF SIGHT, COMMISSIONER, IT'S A MATTER OF THOUGHT.
LET ME KNOW IF YOU NEED ANY HELP. IT'S A HOT ONE OUT THERE.
YES...
...AND GETTING HOTTER.
YES, ALFRED?
IT'S NOT ALFRED, BRU--er, BATMAN...

IT'S ME. YOU KNOW. TIM?
WHAT DO YOU WANT?
I WAS JUST, YOU KNOW, WONDERING IF YOU NEEDED ANY HELP!
MASTER TIM...!
IT'S ALL RIGHT, ALFRED. TRY YOUR WITS ON THIS ONE:
A GAMBLER IS FOUND, MURDERED, ONE HAND SEVERED, HIS WATCH STOPPED AT TEN O'CLOCK. WHERE DOES THE KILLER WANT ME TO GO?
OR... I DON'T KNOW... SOME KIND OF ORGAN BANK, OR--
USE A LITTLE THOUGHT, AND YOU'LL REALIZE...
GOOD GUESS BUT THAT'S ALL IT IS.
...THE KILLER WANTS ME AT TEN AT THE ACES CLUB, ON EIGHT STREET.
HUH?
A

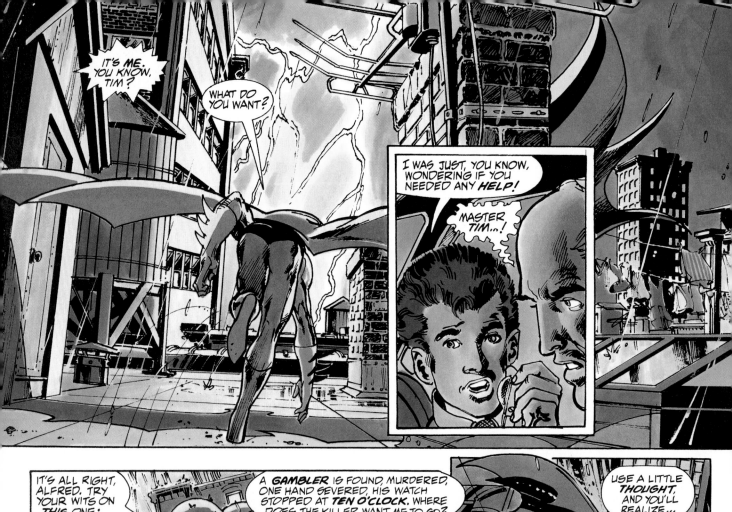

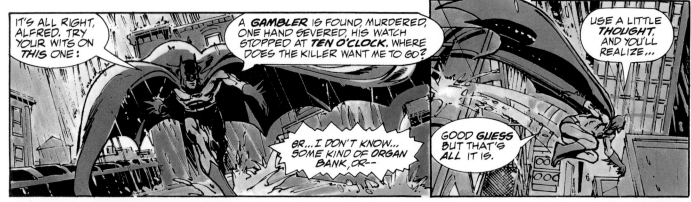

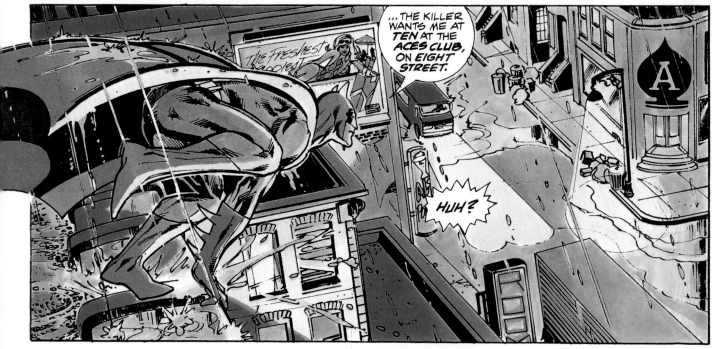

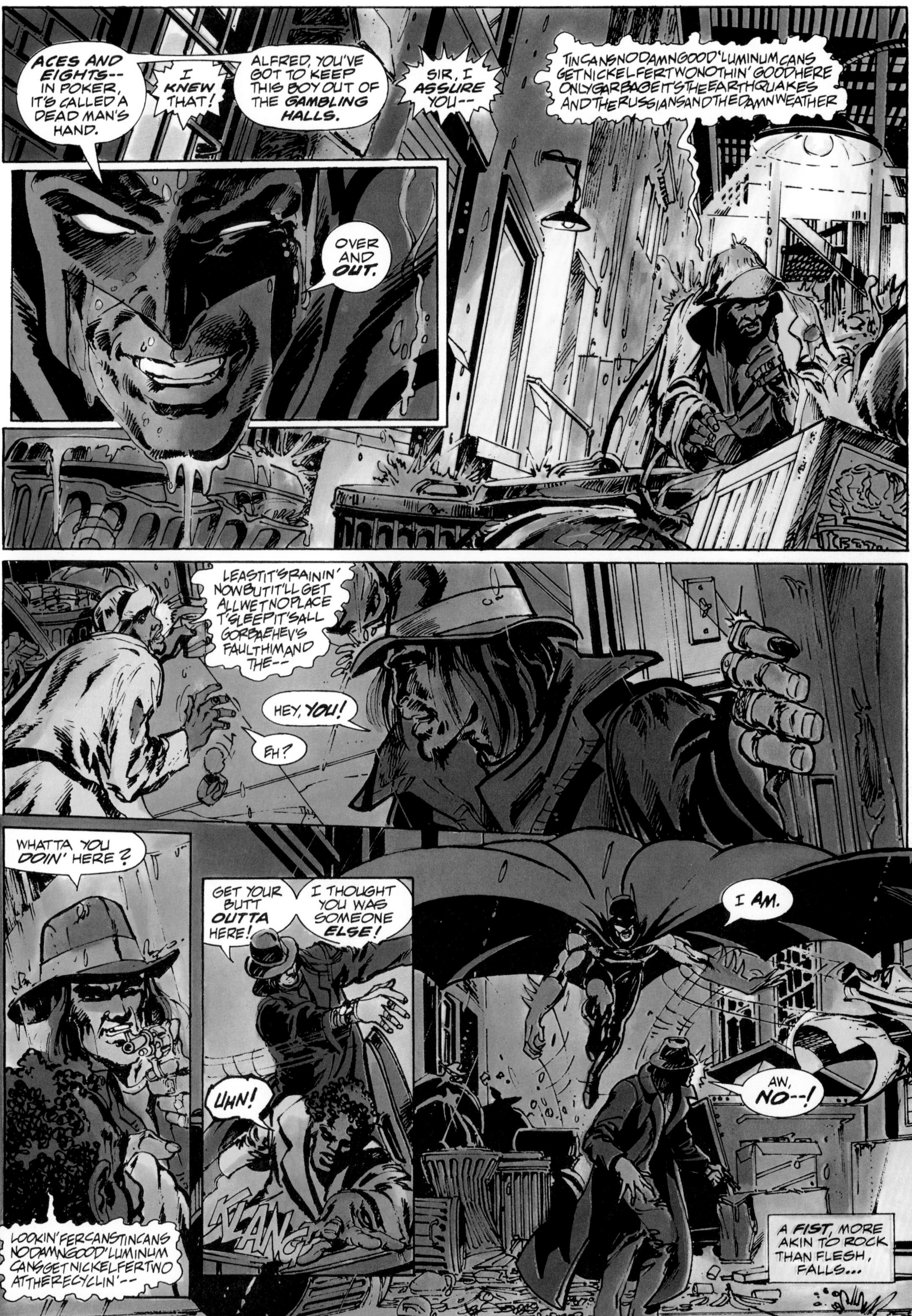
ACES AND EIGHTS-- IN POKER, IT'S CALLED A DEAD MAN'S HAND.
I KNEW THAT!
ALFRED, YOU'VE GOT TO KEEP THIS BOY OUT OF THE GAMBLING HALLS.
SIR, I ASSURE YOU--
OVER AND OUT.
TINCANSNODAMNGOOD'LUMINUMCANS GETNICKELFERTWONOTHIN'GOODHERE ONLYGARBAGEIT'STHEEARTHQUAKES ANDTHERUSSIANSANDTHEDAMNWEATHER
LEASTIT'SRAININ' NOWBUTIT'LLGET ALLWETNOPLACE T'SLEEPIT'SALL GORBAEHEV'S FAULTHIMAND THE--
HEY, YOU!
EH?
WHATTA YOU DOIN' HERE?
LOOKIN'FERCANSTINCANS NODAMNGOOD'LUMINUM CANSGETNICKELFERTWO ATTHERECYCLIN'--
GET YOUR BUTT OUTTA HERE!
I THOUGHT YOU WAS SOMEONE ELSE!
UHN!
KLANG
I AM.
AW, NO--!
A FIST, MORE AKIN TO ROCK THAN FLESH, FALLS...

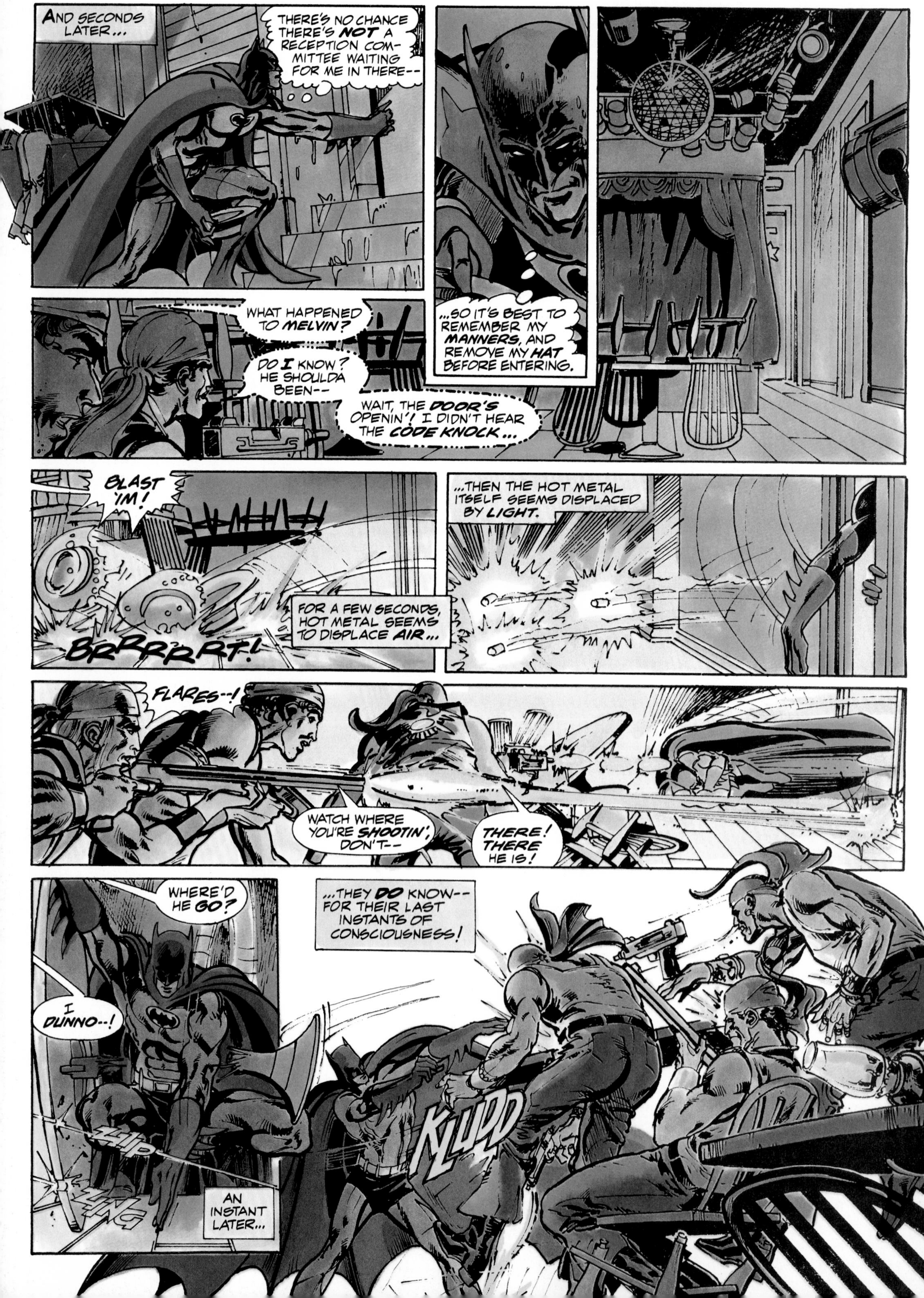
AND SECONDS LATER...
THERE'S NO CHANCE THERE'S NOT A RECEPTION COMMITTEE WAITING FOR ME IN THERE--
...SO IT'S BEST TO REMEMBER MY MANNERS, AND REMOVE MY HAT BEFORE ENTERING.
WHAT HAPPENED TO MELVIN?
DO I KNOW? HE SHOULDA BEEN--
WAIT, THE DOOR'S OPENIN'! I DIDN'T HEAR THE CODE KNOCK...
BLAST 'IM!
BRRRRRT!
FOR A FEW SECONDS, HOT METAL SEEMS TO DISPLACE AIR...
...THEN THE HOT METAL ITSELF SEEMS DISPLACED BY LIGHT.
FLARES--!
WATCH WHERE YOU'RE SHOOTIN', DON'T--
THERE! THERE HE IS!
WHERE'D HE GO?
I DUNNO--!
AN INSTANT LATER...
...THEY DO KNOW--FOR THEIR LAST INSTANTS OF CONSCIOUSNESS!
KLUDD

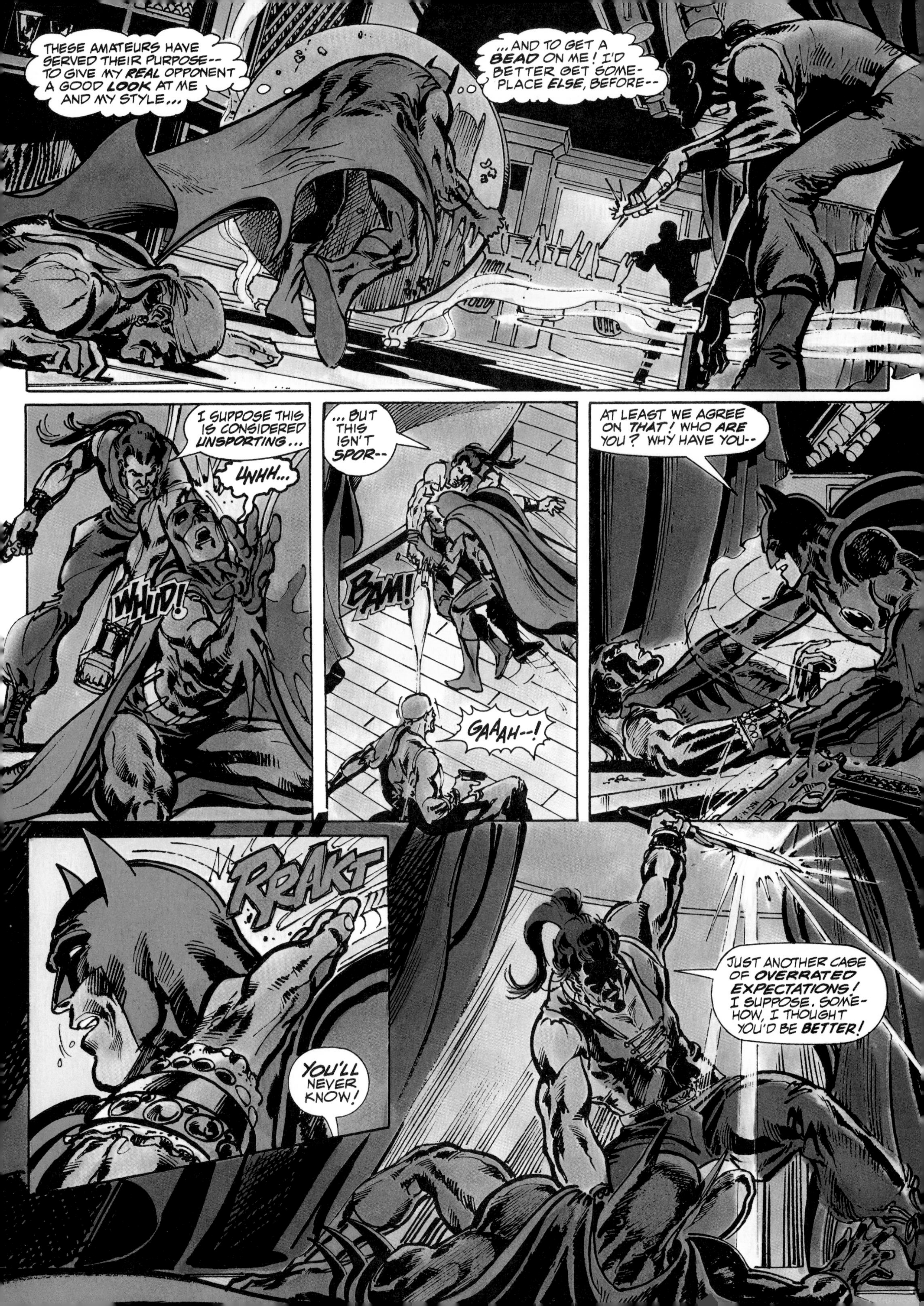
THESE AMATEURS HAVE SERVED THEIR PURPOSE-- TO GIVE MY REAL OPPONENT A GOOD LOOK AT ME AND MY STYLE...
...AND TO GET A BEAD ON ME! I'D BETTER GET SOME-PLACE ELSE, BEFORE--
I SUPPOSE THIS IS CONSIDERED UNSPORTING...
UNHH...
WHUD!
...BUT THIS ISN'T SPOR--
BAM!
GAAAH--!
AT LEAST WE AGREE ON THAT! WHO ARE YOU? WHY HAVE YOU--
RRAKT
YOU'LL NEVER KNOW!
JUST ANOTHER CASE OF OVERRATED EXPECTATIONS! I SUPPOSE. SOME-HOW, I THOUGHT YOU'D BE BETTER!

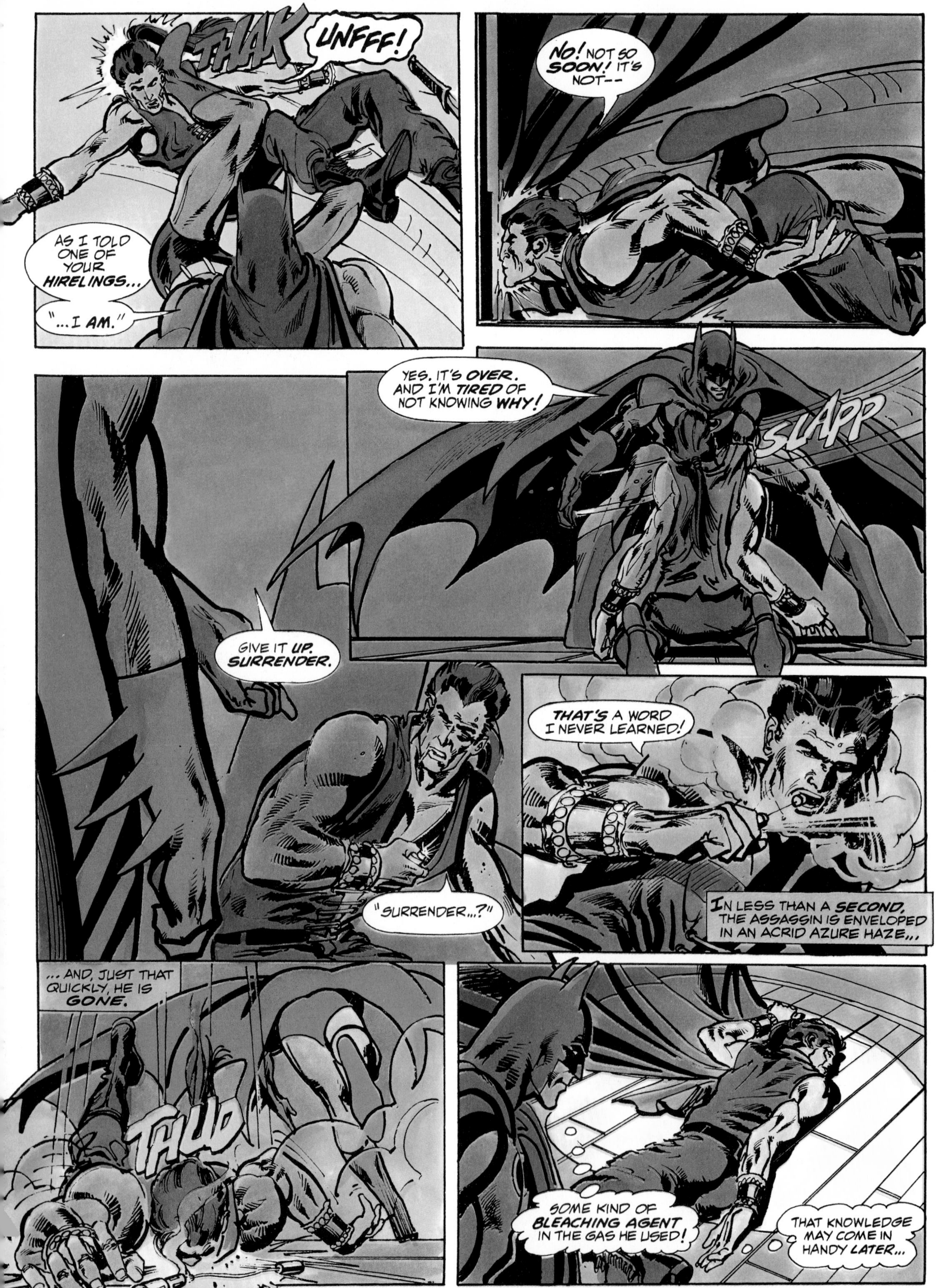
THAK
UNFFF!
AS I TOLD ONE OF YOUR HIRELINGS...
"...I AM."
NO! NOT SO SOON! IT'S NOT--
YES. IT'S OVER. AND I'M TIRED OF NOT KNOWING WHY!
SLAPP
GIVE IT UP. SURRENDER.
"SURRENDER...?"
THAT'S A WORD I NEVER LEARNED!
IN LESS THAN A SECOND, THE ASSASSIN IS ENVELOPED IN AN ACRID AZURE HAZE...
... AND, JUST THAT QUICKLY, HE IS GONE.
THUD
SOME KIND OF BLEACHING AGENT IN THE GAS HE USED!
THAT KNOWLEDGE MAY COME IN HANDY LATER...

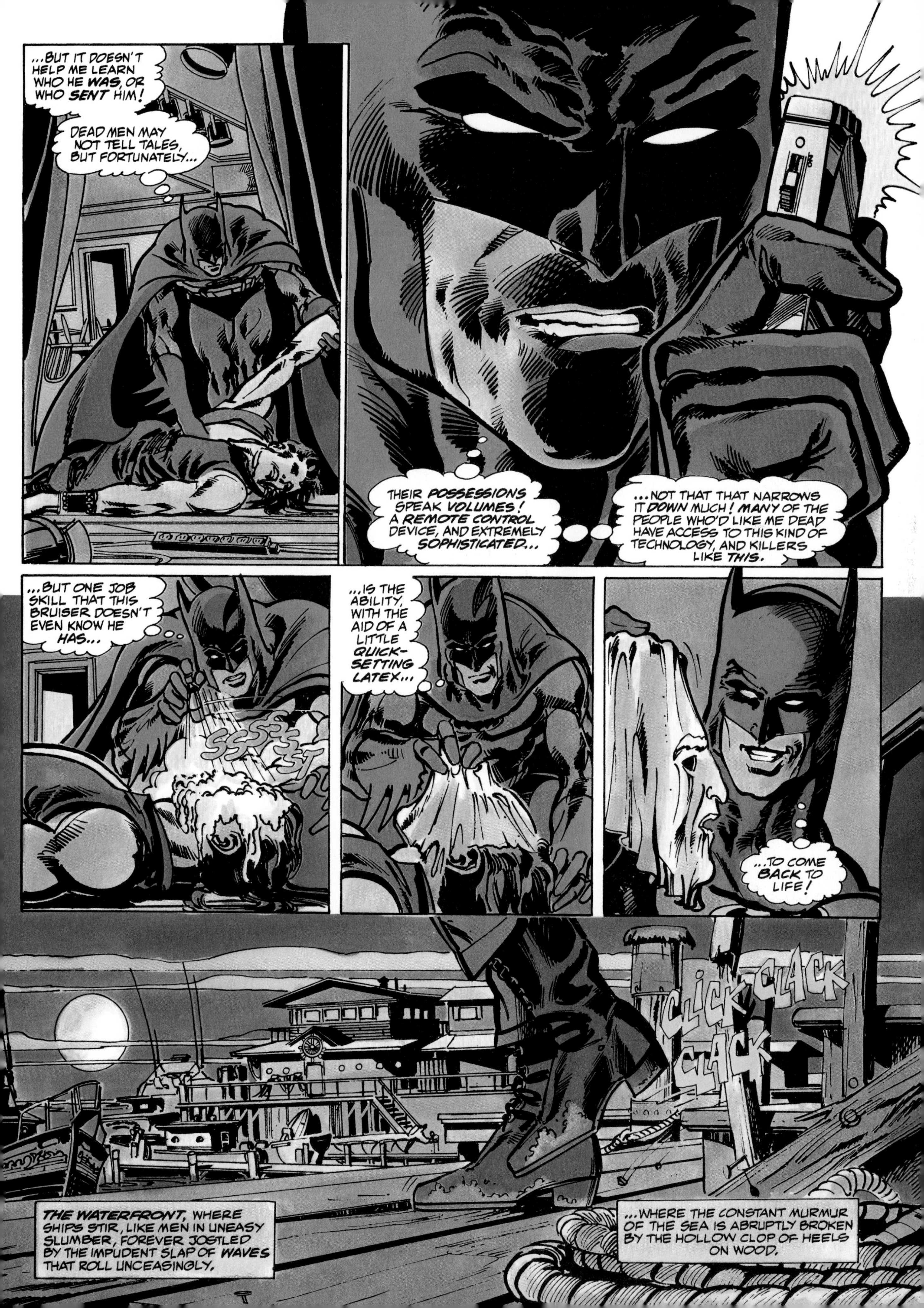
...BUT IT DOESN'T HELP ME LEARN WHO HE WAS, OR WHO SENT HIM!
DEAD MEN MAY NOT TELL TALES, BUT FORTUNATELY...
THEIR POSSESSIONS SPEAK VOLUMES! A REMOTE CONTROL DEVICE, AND EXTREMELY SOPHISTICATED...
...NOT THAT THAT NARROWS IT DOWN MUCH! MANY OF THE PEOPLE WHO'D LIKE ME DEAD HAVE ACCESS TO THIS KIND OF TECHNOLOGY, AND KILLERS LIKE THIS.
...BUT ONE JOB SKILL THAT THIS BRUISER DOESN'T EVEN KNOW HE HAS...
SSSSSSST
...IS THE ABILITY, WITH THE AID OF A LITTLE QUICK-SETTING LATEX...
...TO COME BACK TO LIFE!
CLICK CLACK
CLACK
THE WATERFRONT, WHERE SHIPS STIR, LIKE MEN IN UNEASY SLUMBER, FOREVER JOSTLED BY THE IMPUDENT SLAP OF WAVES THAT ROLL UNCEASINGLY.
...WHERE THE CONSTANT MURMUR OF THE SEA IS ABRUPTLY BROKEN BY THE HOLLOW CLOP OF HEELS ON WOOD.

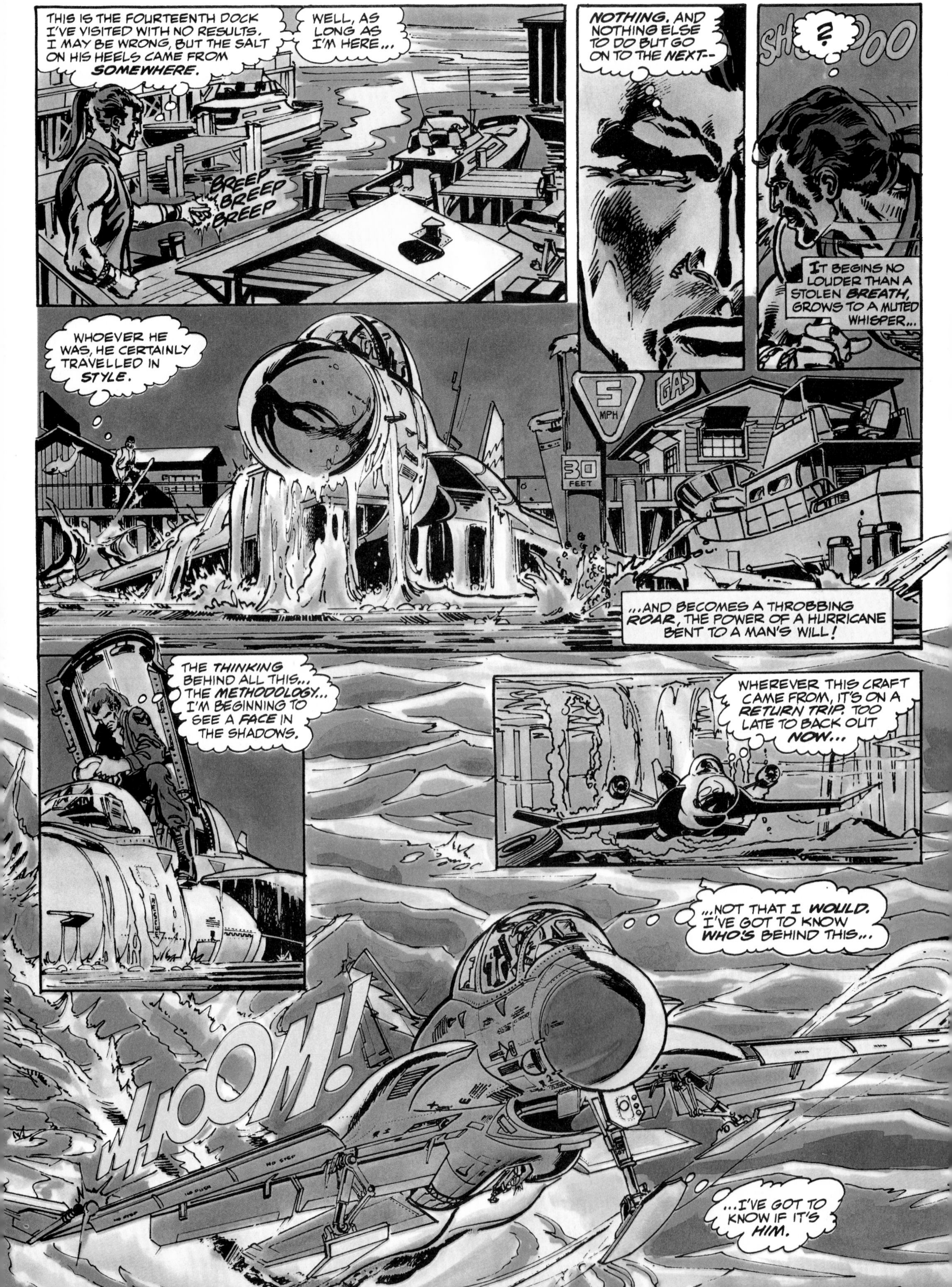

THIS IS THE FOURTEENTH DOCK I'VE VISITED WITH NO RESULTS. I MAY BE WRONG, BUT THE SALT ON HIS HEELS CAME FROM SOMEWHERE.
WELL, AS LONG AS I'M HERE...
BREEP BREEP BREEP
NOTHING. AND NOTHING ELSE TO DO BUT GO ON TO THE NEXT--
SHOOOOO
?
IT BEGINS NO LOUDER THAN A STOLEN BREATH, GROWS TO A MUTED WHISPER...
WHOEVER HE WAS, HE CERTAINLY TRAVELLED IN STYLE.
5 MPH
GAS
30 FEET
...AND BECOMES A THROBBING ROAR, THE POWER OF A HURRICANE BENT TO A MAN'S WILL!
THE THINKING BEHIND ALL THIS... THE METHODOLOGY... I'M BEGINNING TO SEE A FACE IN THE SHADOWS.
WHEREVER THIS CRAFT CAME FROM, IT'S ON A RETURN TRIP. TOO LATE TO BACK OUT NOW...
...NOT THAT I WOULD. I'VE GOT TO KNOW WHO'S BEHIND THIS...
WHOOM!
...I'VE GOT TO KNOW IF IT'S HIM.

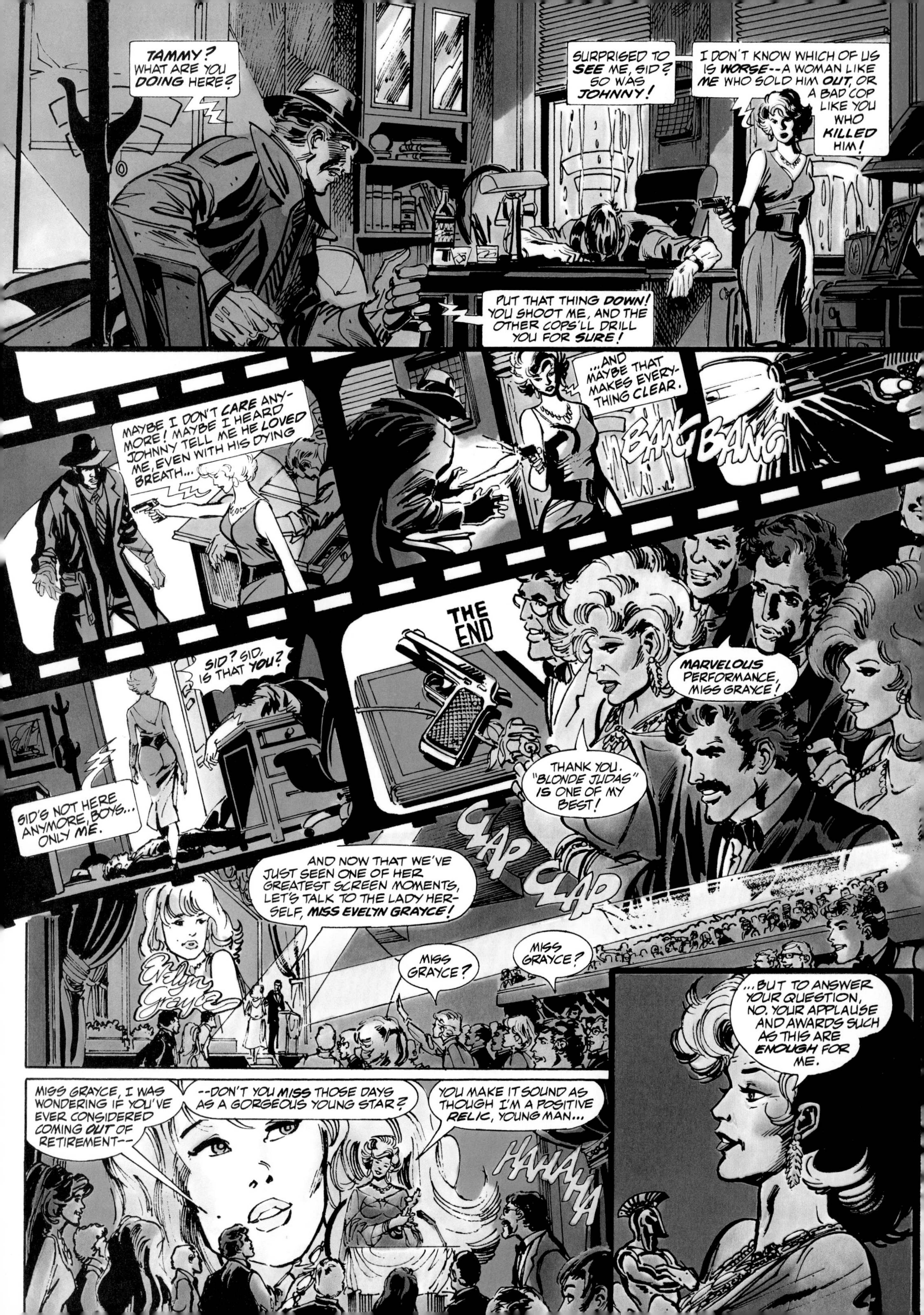

TAMMY? WHAT ARE YOU DOING HERE?
SURPRISED TO SEE ME, SID? SO WAS JOHNNY!
I DON'T KNOW WHICH OF US IS WORSE--A WOMAN LIKE ME WHO SOLD HIM OUT, OR A BAD COP LIKE YOU WHO KILLED HIM!
PUT THAT THING DOWN! YOU SHOOT ME, AND THE OTHER COPS'LL DRILL YOU FOR SURE!
MAYBE I DON'T CARE ANYMORE! MAYBE I HEARD JOHNNY TELL ME HE LOVED ME, EVEN WITH HIS DYING BREATH...
...AND MAYBE THAT MAKES EVERYTHING CLEAR.
BANG BANG
SID? SID, IS THAT YOU?
SID'S NOT HERE ANYMORE, BOYS... ONLY ME.
THE END
MARVELOUS PERFORMANCE, MISS GRAYCE!
THANK YOU. "BLONDE JUDAS" IS ONE OF MY BEST!
CLAP CLAP CLAP
AND NOW THAT WE'VE JUST SEEN ONE OF HER GREATEST SCREEN MOMENTS, LET'S TALK TO THE LADY HERSELF, MISS EVELYN GRAYCE!
Evelyn Grayce
MISS GRAYCE?
MISS GRAYCE?
MISS GRAYCE, I WAS WONDERING IF YOU'VE EVER CONSIDERED COMING OUT OF RETIREMENT--
--DON'T YOU MISS THOSE DAYS AS A GORGEOUS YOUNG STAR?
YOU MAKE IT SOUND AS THOUGH I'M A POSITIVE RELIC, YOUNG MAN...
HAHAHAHA
...BUT TO ANSWER YOUR QUESTION, NO. YOUR APPLAUSE AND AWARDS SUCH AS THIS ARE ENOUGH FOR ME.

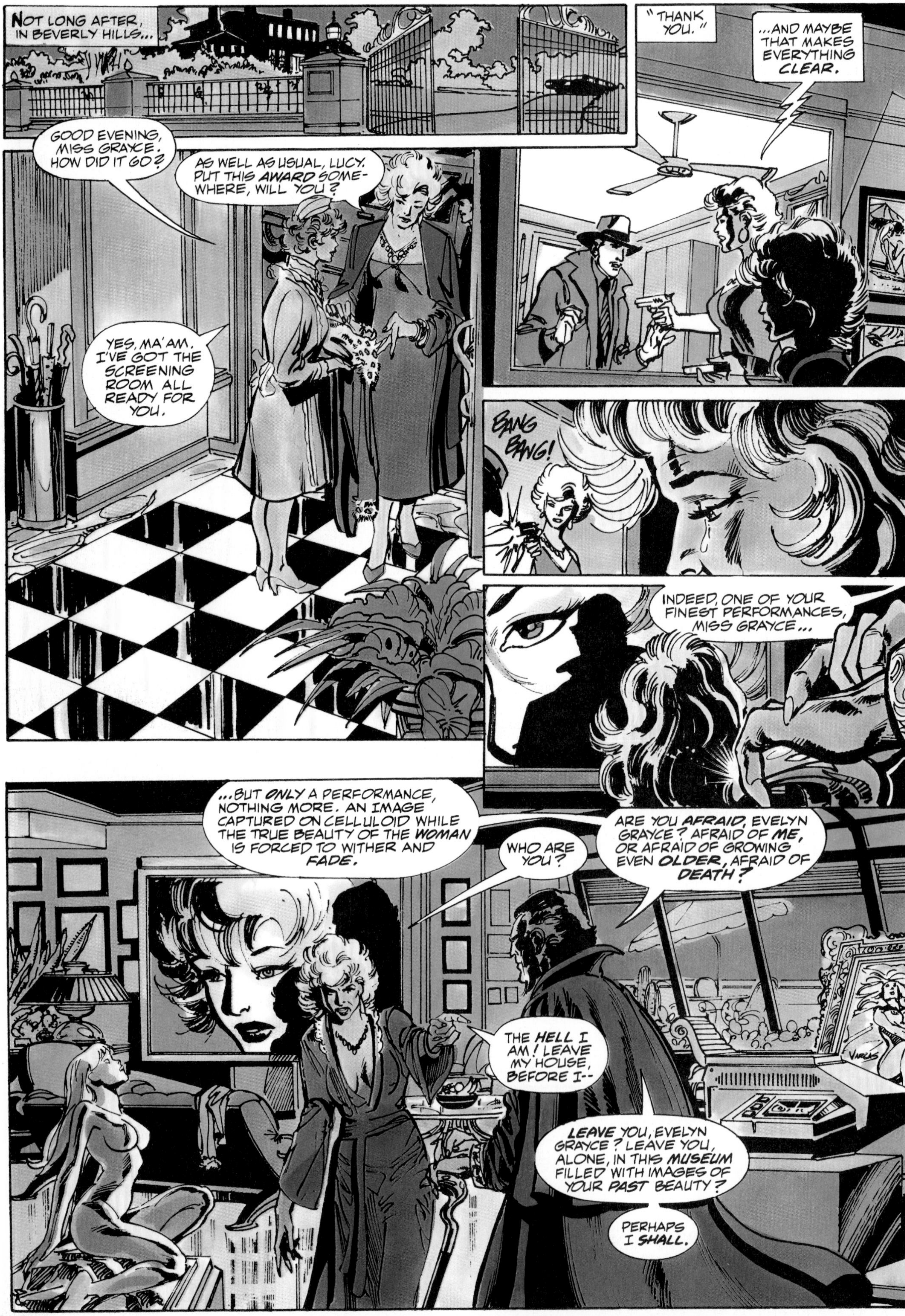
NOT LONG AFTER, IN BEVERLY HILLS...
"THANK YOU."
...AND MAYBE THAT MAKES EVERYTHING CLEAR.
GOOD EVENING, MISS GRAYCE. HOW DID IT GO?
AS WELL AS USUAL, LUCY. PUT THIS AWARD SOMEWHERE, WILL YOU?
YES, MA'AM. I'VE GOT THE SCREENING ROOM ALL READY FOR YOU.
BANG BANG!
INDEED, ONE OF YOUR FINEST PERFORMANCES, MISS GRAYCE...
...BUT ONLY A PERFORMANCE, NOTHING MORE. AN IMAGE CAPTURED ON CELLULOID WHILE THE TRUE BEAUTY OF THE WOMAN IS FORCED TO WITHER AND FADE.
WHO ARE YOU?
ARE YOU AFRAID, EVELYN GRAYCE? AFRAID OF ME, OR AFRAID OF GROWING EVEN OLDER, AFRAID OF DEATH?
THE HELL I AM! LEAVE MY HOUSE, BEFORE I--
LEAVE YOU, EVELYN GRAYCE? LEAVE YOU, ALONE, IN THIS MUSEUM FILLED WITH IMAGES OF YOUR PAST BEAUTY?
PERHAPS I SHALL.
VARGAS

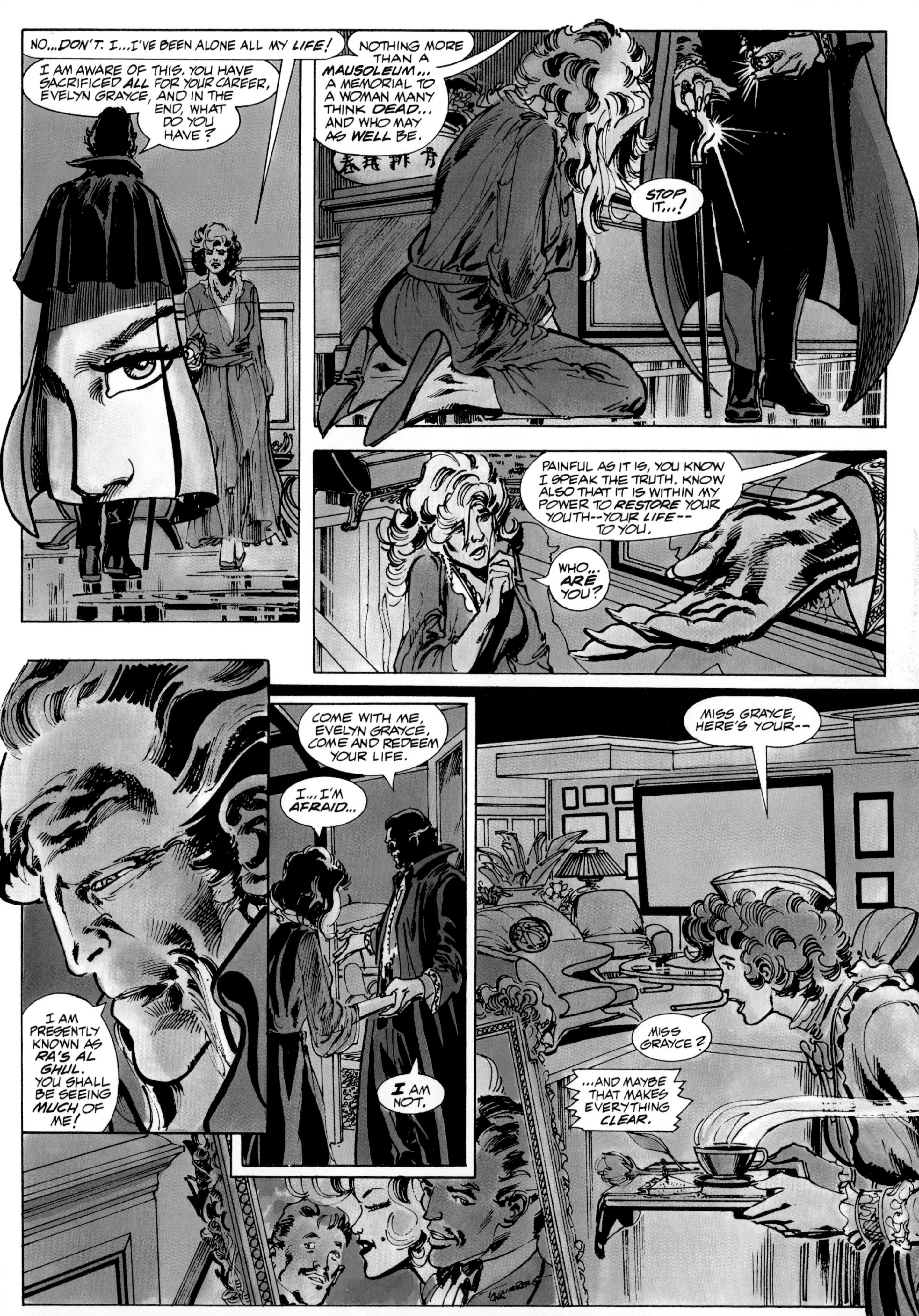
NO...DON'T. I...I'VE BEEN ALONE ALL MY LIFE!
I AM AWARE OF THIS. YOU HAVE SACRIFICED ALL FOR YOUR CAREER, EVELYN GRAYCE, AND IN THE END, WHAT DO YOU HAVE?
NOTHING MORE THAN A MAUSOLEUM... A MEMORIAL TO A WOMAN MANY THINK DEAD... AND WHO MAY AS WELL BE.
STOP IT...!
PAINFUL AS IT IS, YOU KNOW I SPEAK THE TRUTH. KNOW ALSO THAT IT IS WITHIN MY POWER TO RESTORE YOUR YOUTH--YOUR LIFE--TO YOU.
WHO... ARE YOU?
I AM PRESENTLY KNOWN AS RA'S AL GHUL. YOU SHALL BE SEEING MUCH OF ME!
COME WITH ME, EVELYN GRAYCE, COME AND REDEEM YOUR LIFE.
I...I'M AFRAID...
I AM NOT.
MISS GRAYCE, HERE'S YOUR--
MISS GRAYCE?
...AND MAYBE THAT MAKES EVERYTHING CLEAR.

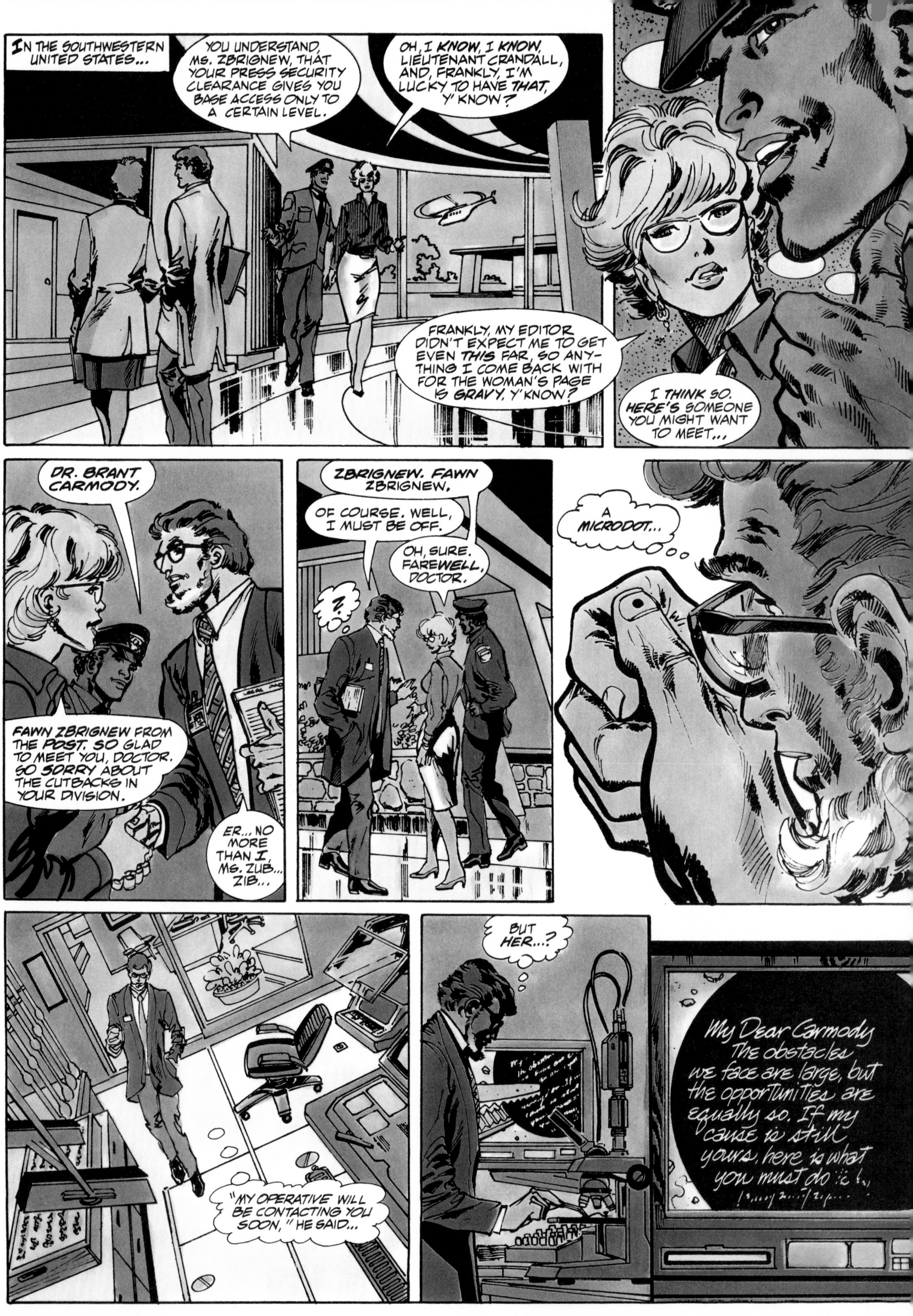

IN THE SOUTHWESTERN UNITED STATES...
YOU UNDERSTAND, MS. ZBRIGNEW, THAT YOUR PRESS SECURITY CLEARANCE GIVES YOU BASE ACCESS ONLY TO A CERTAIN LEVEL.
OH, I KNOW, I KNOW, LIEUTENANT CRANDALL, AND, FRANKLY, I'M LUCKY TO HAVE THAT, Y' KNOW?
FRANKLY, MY EDITOR DIDN'T EXPECT ME TO GET EVEN THIS FAR, SO ANYTHING I COME BACK WITH FOR THE WOMAN'S PAGE IS GRAVY, Y' KNOW?
I THINK SO. HERE'S SOMEONE YOU MIGHT WANT TO MEET...
DR. BRANT CARMODY.
FAWN ZBRIGNEW FROM THE POST. SO GLAD TO MEET YOU, DOCTOR. SO SORRY ABOUT THE CUTBACKS IN YOUR DIVISION.
ER... NO MORE THAN I, MS. ZUB... ZIB...
ZBRIGNEW. FAWN ZBRIGNEW.
OF COURSE. WELL, I MUST BE OFF.
OH, SURE. FAREWELL, DOCTOR.
?
A MICRODOT...
"MY OPERATIVE WILL BE CONTACTING YOU SOON," HE SAID...
BUT HER...?
My Dear Carmody
The obstacles
we face are large, but
the opportunities are
equally so. If my
cause is still
yours, here is what
you must do:

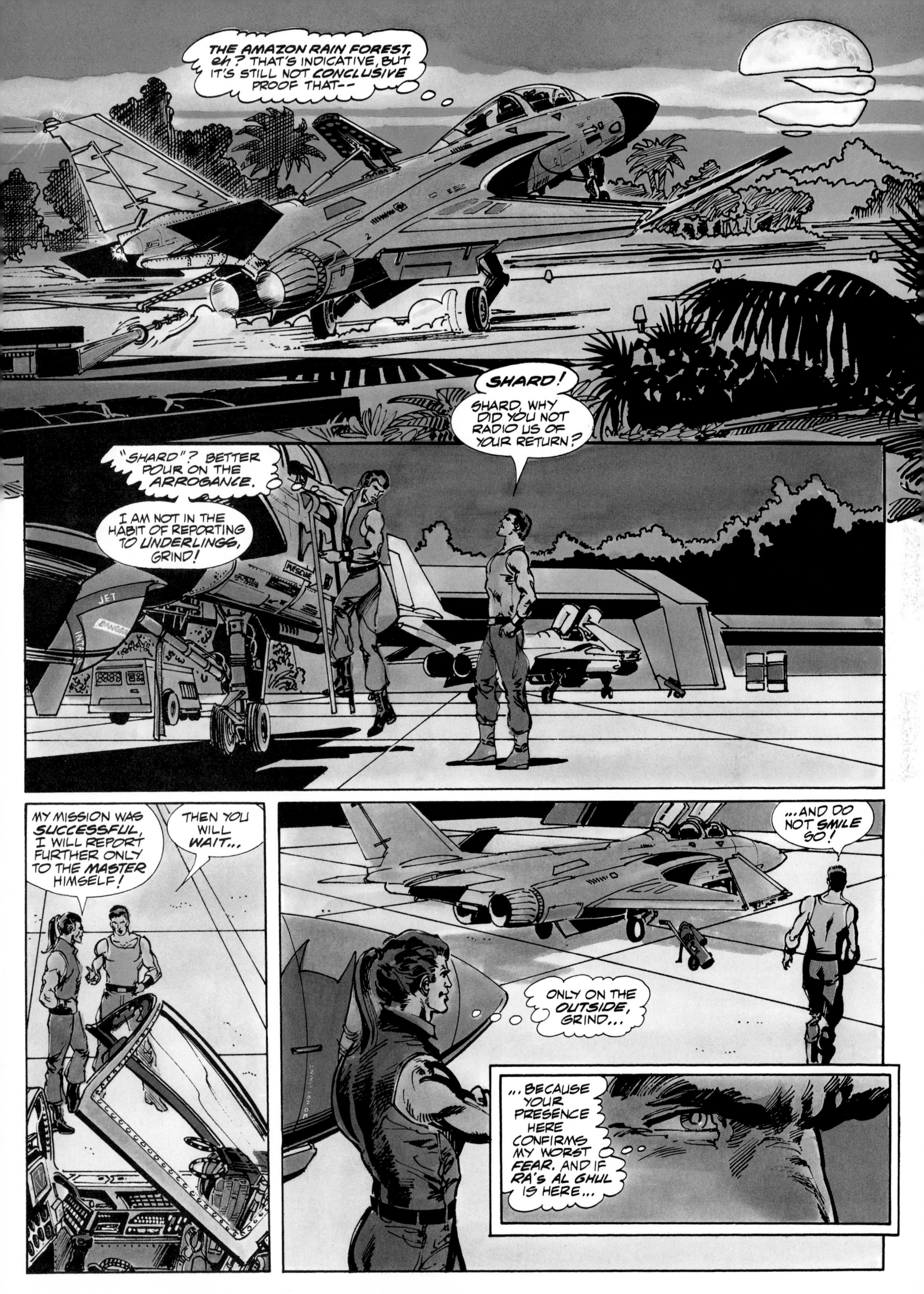

THE AMAZON RAIN FOREST, eh? THAT'S INDICATIVE, BUT IT'S STILL NOT CONCLUSIVE PROOF THAT--
SHARD!
SHARD, WHY DID YOU NOT RADIO US OF YOUR RETURN?
"SHARD"? BETTER POUR ON THE ARROGANCE.
I AM NOT IN THE HABIT OF REPORTING TO UNDERLINGS, GRIND!
MY MISSION WAS SUCCESSFUL, I WILL REPORT FURTHER ONLY TO THE MASTER HIMSELF!
THEN YOU WILL WAIT...
...AND DO NOT SMILE SO!
ONLY ON THE OUTSIDE, GRIND...
...BECAUSE YOUR PRESENCE HERE CONFIRMS MY WORST FEAR. AND IF RA'S AL GHUL IS HERE...

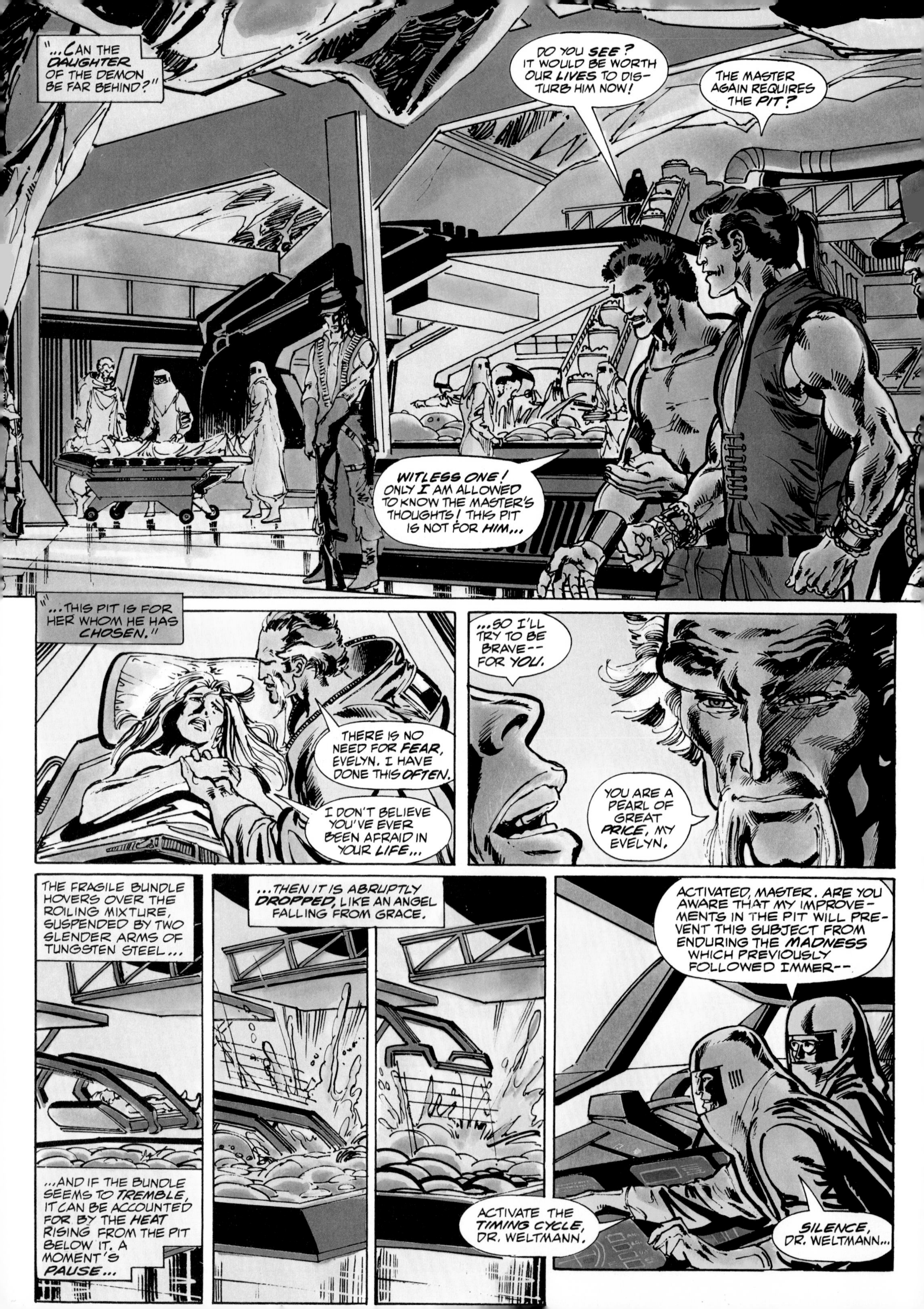
"...CAN THE DAUGHTER OF THE DEMON BE FAR BEHIND?"
DO YOU SEE? IT WOULD BE WORTH OUR LIVES TO DISTURB HIM NOW!
THE MASTER AGAIN REQUIRES THE PIT?
WITLESS ONE! ONLY I AM ALLOWED TO KNOW THE MASTER'S THOUGHTS! THIS PIT IS NOT FOR HIM...
"...THIS PIT IS FOR HER WHOM HE HAS CHOSEN."
THERE IS NO NEED FOR FEAR, EVELYN. I HAVE DONE THIS OFTEN.
I DON'T BELIEVE YOU'VE EVER BEEN AFRAID IN YOUR LIFE...
...SO I'LL TRY TO BE BRAVE-- FOR YOU.
YOU ARE A PEARL OF GREAT PRICE, MY EVELYN.
THE FRAGILE BUNDLE HOVERS OVER THE ROILING MIXTURE, SUSPENDED BY TWO SLENDER ARMS OF TUNGSTEN STEEL...
...AND IF THE BUNDLE SEEMS TO TREMBLE, IT CAN BE ACCOUNTED FOR BY THE HEAT RISING FROM THE PIT BELOW IT. A MOMENT'S PAUSE...
...THEN IT IS ABRUPTLY DROPPED, LIKE AN ANGEL FALLING FROM GRACE.
ACTIVATE THE TIMING CYCLE, DR. WELTMANN.
ACTIVATED, MASTER. ARE YOU AWARE THAT MY IMPROVEMENTS IN THE PIT WILL PREVENT THIS SUBJECT FROM ENDURING THE MADNESS WHICH PREVIOUSLY FOLLOWED IMMER--
SILENCE, DR. WELTMANN...

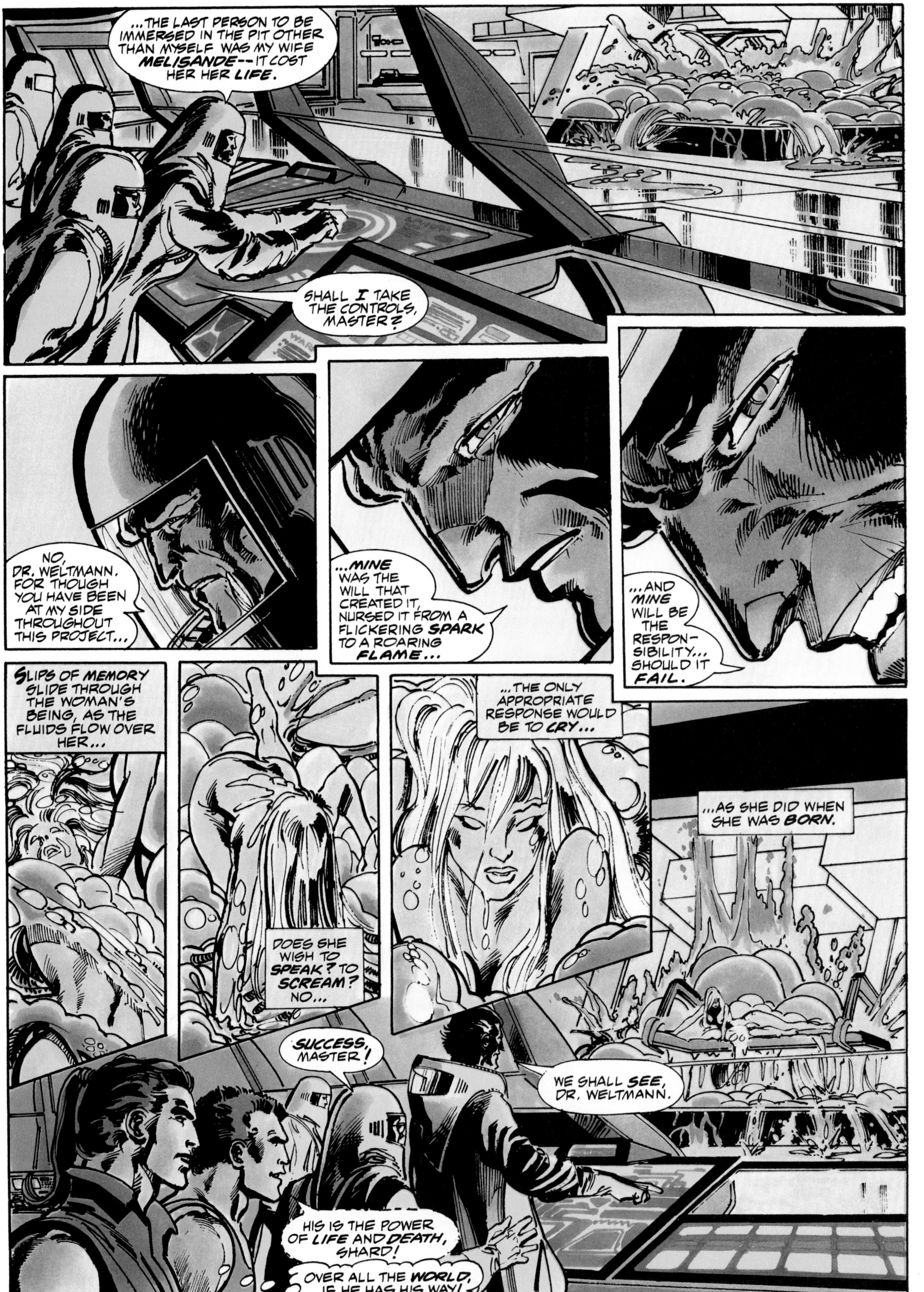
...THE LAST PERSON TO BE IMMERSED IN THE PIT OTHER THAN MYSELF WAS MY WIFE MELISANDE--IT COST HER HER LIFE.
SHALL I TAKE THE CONTROLS, MASTER?
NO, DR. WELTMANN. FOR THOUGH YOU HAVE BEEN AT MY SIDE THROUGHOUT THIS PROJECT...
...MINE WAS THE WILL THAT CREATED IT, NURSED IT FROM A FLICKERING SPARK TO A ROARING FLAME...
...AND MINE WILL BE THE RESPON-SIBILITY... SHOULD IT FAIL.
SLIPS OF MEMORY SLIDE THROUGH THE WOMAN'S BEING, AS THE FLUIDS FLOW OVER HER...
DOES SHE WISH TO SPEAK? TO SCREAM? NO...
...THE ONLY APPROPRIATE RESPONSE WOULD BE TO CRY...
...AS SHE DID WHEN SHE WAS BORN.
SUCCESS, MASTER!
WE SHALL SEE, DR. WELTMANN.
HIS IS THE POWER OF LIFE AND DEATH, SHARD!
OVER ALL THE WORLD, IF HE HAS HIS WAY!

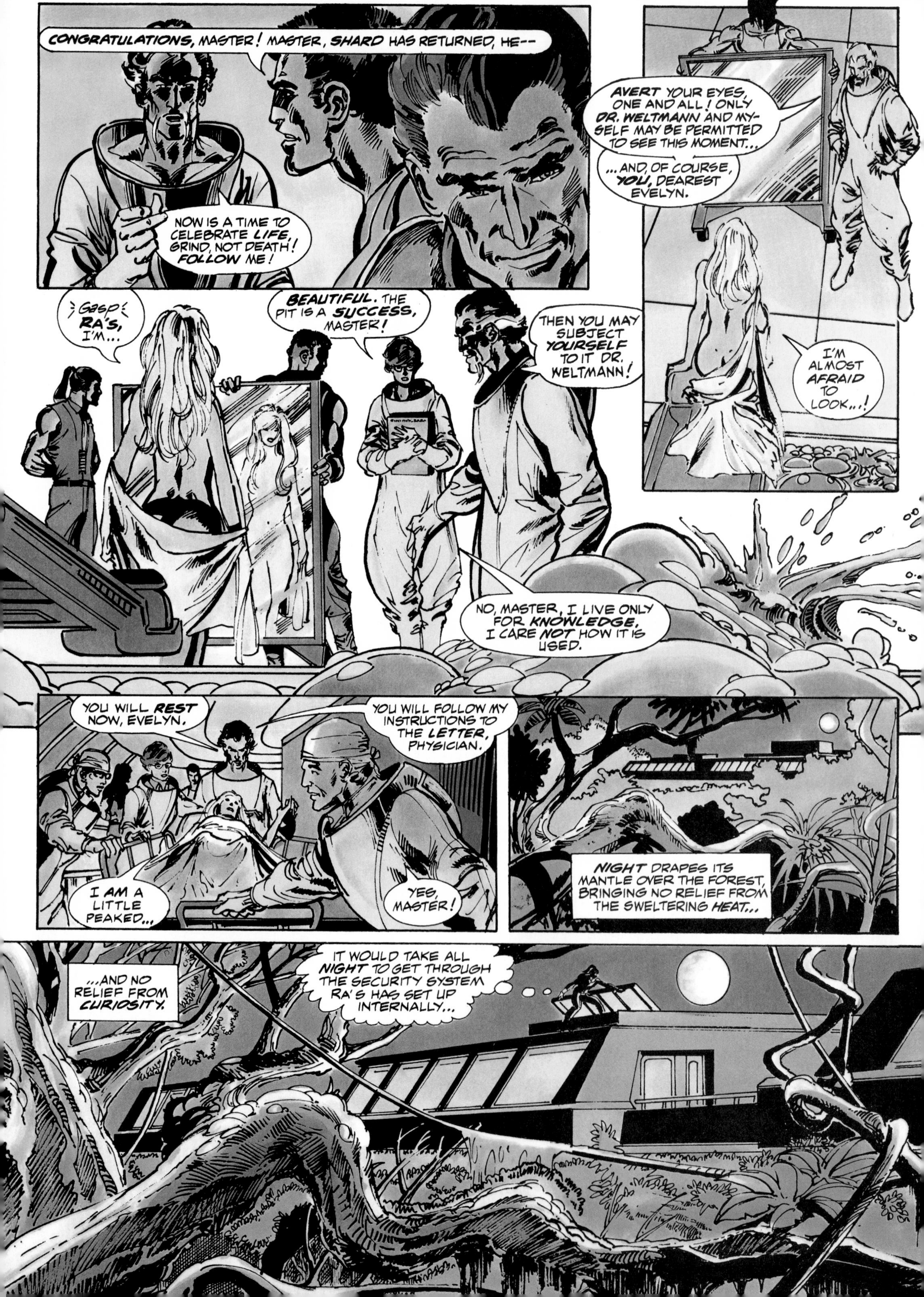
CONGRATULATIONS, MASTER! MASTER, SHARD HAS RETURNED, HE--
NOW IS A TIME TO CELEBRATE LIFE, GRIND, NOT DEATH! FOLLOW ME!
AVERT YOUR EYES, ONE AND ALL! ONLY DR. WELTMANN AND MY-SELF MAY BE PERMITTED TO SEE THIS MOMENT...
...AND, OF COURSE, YOU, DEAREST EVELYN.
I'M ALMOST AFRAID TO LOOK...!
Gasp RA'S, I'M...
BEAUTIFUL. THE PIT IS A SUCCESS, MASTER!
THEN YOU MAY SUBJECT YOURSELF TO IT DR. WELTMANN!
NO, MASTER, I LIVE ONLY FOR KNOWLEDGE, I CARE NOT HOW IT IS USED.
YOU WILL REST NOW, EVELYN.
YOU WILL FOLLOW MY INSTRUCTIONS TO THE LETTER, PHYSICIAN.
I AM A LITTLE PEAKED...
YES, MASTER!
NIGHT DRAPES ITS MANTLE OVER THE FOREST, BRINGING NO RELIEF FROM THE SWELTERING HEAT...
...AND NO RELIEF FROM CURIOSITY.
IT WOULD TAKE ALL NIGHT TO GET THROUGH THE SECURITY SYSTEM RA'S HAS SET UP INTERNALLY...

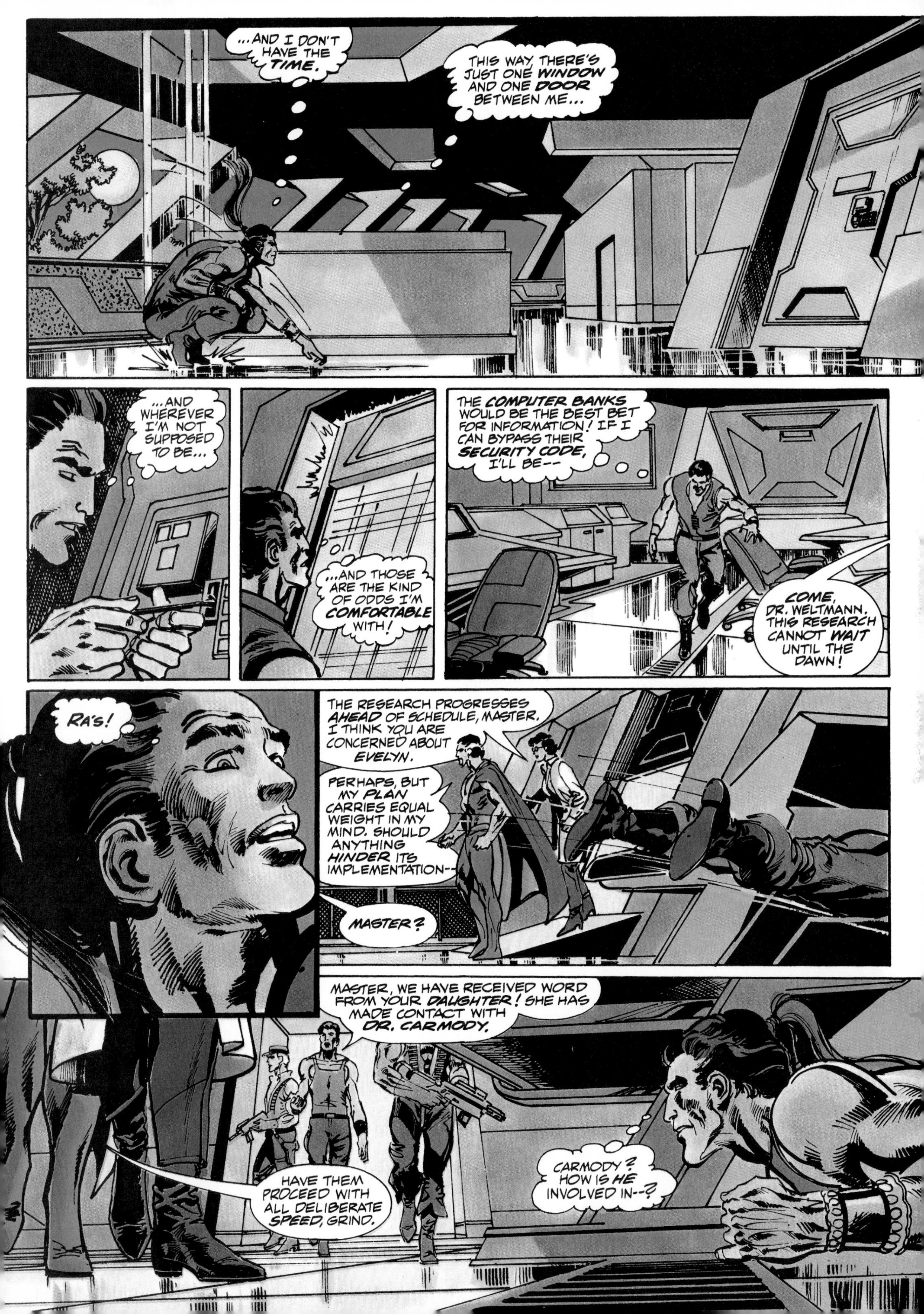
...AND I DON'T HAVE THE TIME.
THIS WAY, THERE'S JUST ONE WINDOW AND ONE DOOR BETWEEN ME...
...AND WHEREVER I'M NOT SUPPOSED TO BE...
...AND THOSE ARE THE KIND OF ODDS I'M COMFORTABLE WITH!
THE COMPUTER BANKS WOULD BE THE BEST BET FOR INFORMATION! IF I CAN BYPASS THEIR SECURITY CODE, I'LL BE--
COME, DR. WELTMANN. THIS RESEARCH CANNOT WAIT UNTIL THE DAWN!
RA'S!
THE RESEARCH PROGRESSES AHEAD OF SCHEDULE, MASTER. I THINK YOU ARE CONCERNED ABOUT EVELYN.
PERHAPS, BUT MY PLAN CARRIES EQUAL WEIGHT IN MY MIND. SHOULD ANYTHING HINDER ITS IMPLEMENTATION--
MASTER?
MASTER, WE HAVE RECEIVED WORD FROM YOUR DAUGHTER! SHE HAS MADE CONTACT WITH DR. CARMODY.
HAVE THEM PROCEED WITH ALL DELIBERATE SPEED, GRIND.
CARMODY? HOW IS HE INVOLVED IN--?

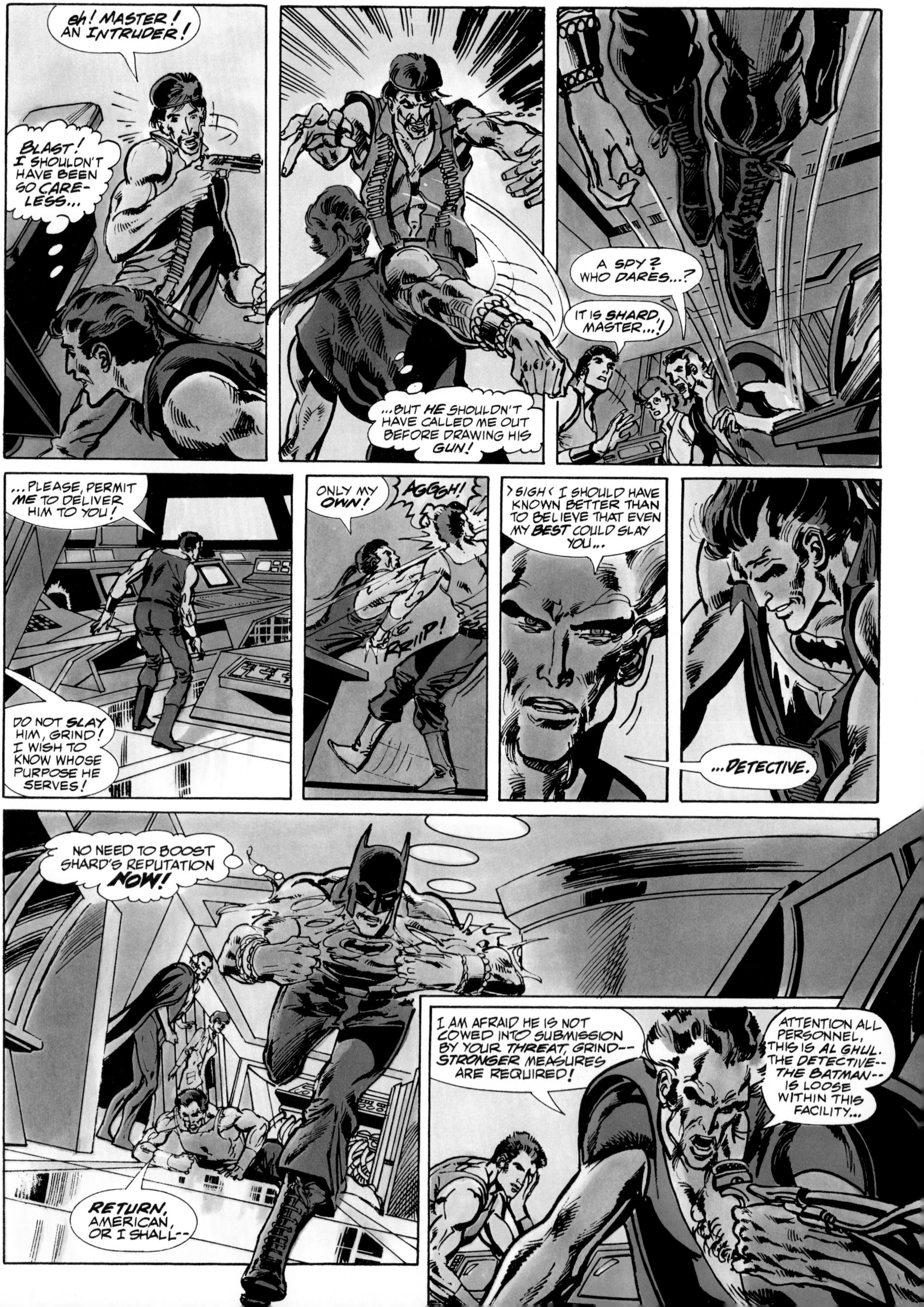

eh! MASTER! AN INTRUDER!
BLAST! I SHOULDN'T HAVE BEEN SO CARE-LESS...
...BUT HE SHOULDN'T HAVE CALLED ME OUT BEFORE DRAWING HIS GUN!
A SPY? WHO DARES...?
IT IS SHARD, MASTER...!
...PLEASE, PERMIT ME TO DELIVER HIM TO YOU!
DO NOT SLAY HIM, GRIND! I WISH TO KNOW WHOSE PURPOSE HE SERVES!
ONLY MY OWN!
AGGGH!
RRIIP!
>SIGH< I SHOULD HAVE KNOWN BETTER THAN TO BELIEVE THAT EVEN MY BEST COULD SLAY YOU...
...DETECTIVE.
NO NEED TO BOOST SHARD'S REPUTATION NOW!
RETURN, AMERICAN, OR I SHALL--
I AM AFRAID HE IS NOT COWED INTO SUBMISSION BY YOUR THREAT, GRIND-- STRONGER MEASURES ARE REQUIRED!
ATTENTION ALL PERSONNEL, THIS IS AL GHUL. THE DETECTIVE-- THE BATMAN-- IS LOOSE WITHIN THIS FACILITY...

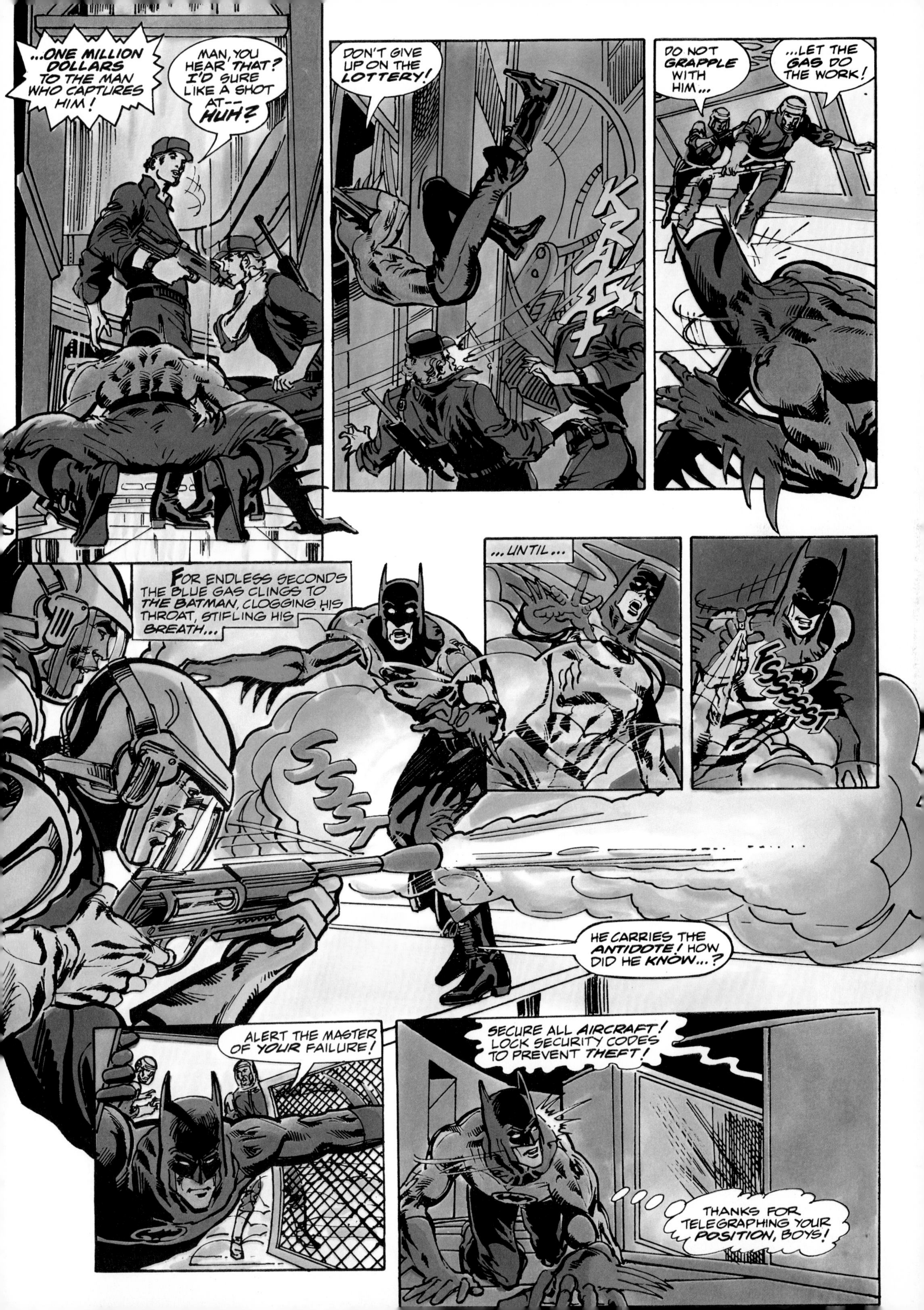

...ONE MILLION DOLLARS TO THE MAN WHO CAPTURES HIM!
MAN, YOU HEAR THAT? I'D SURE LIKE A SHOT AT-- HUH?
DON'T GIVE UP ON THE LOTTERY!
KRAK
DO NOT GRAPPLE WITH HIM...
...LET THE GAS DO THE WORK!
FOR ENDLESS SECONDS THE BLUE GAS CLINGS TO THE BATMAN, CLOGGING HIS THROAT, STIFLING HIS BREATH...
SSSST
...UNTIL...
FSSSSSST
HE CARRIES THE ANTIDOTE! HOW DID HE KNOW...?
ALERT THE MASTER OF YOUR FAILURE!
SECURE ALL AIRCRAFT! LOCK SECURITY CODES TO PREVENT THEFT!
THANKS FOR TELEGRAPHING YOUR POSITION, BOYS!

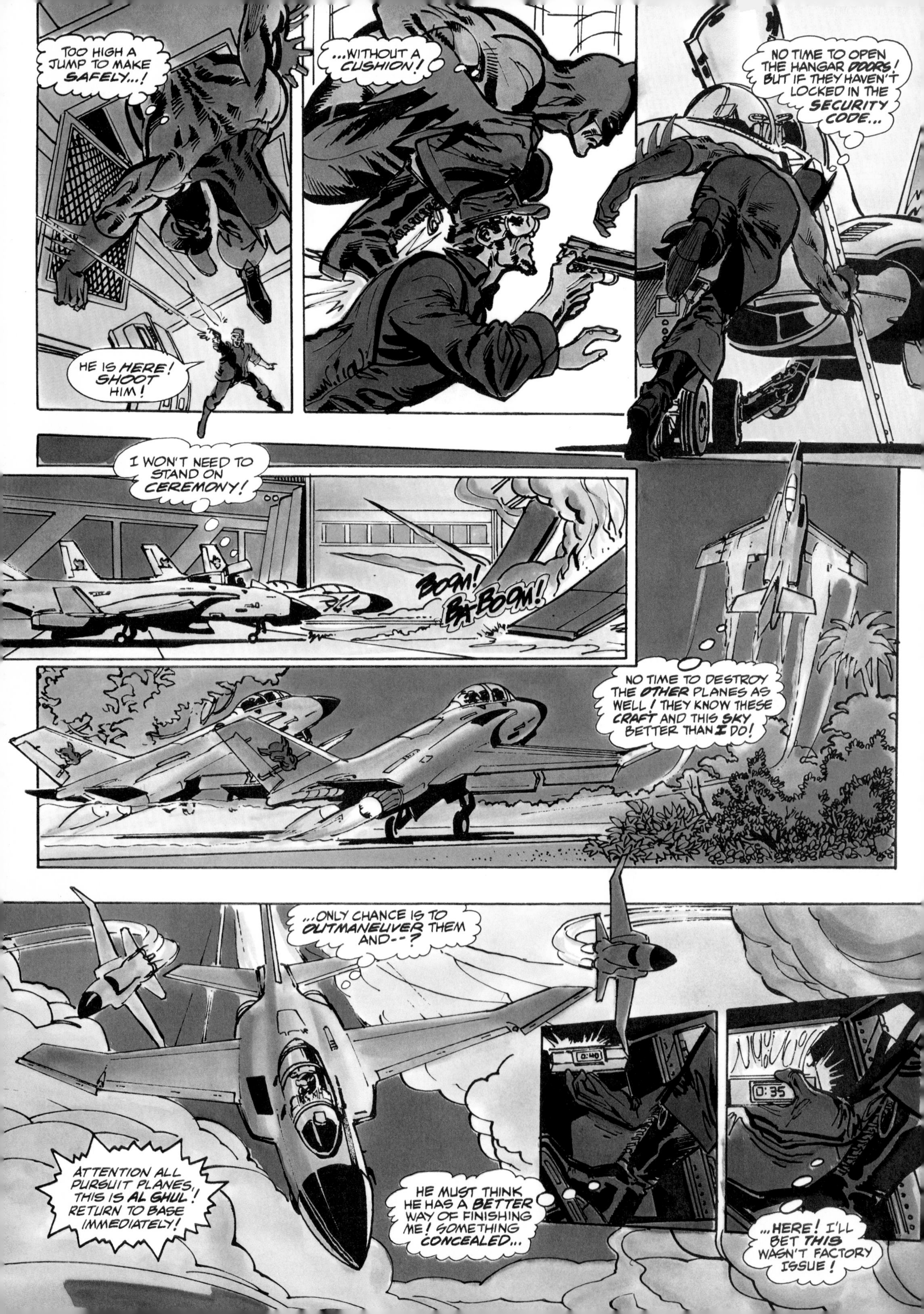

TOO HIGH A JUMP TO MAKE SAFELY...!
HE IS HERE! SHOOT HIM!
...WITHOUT A CUSHION!
NO TIME TO OPEN THE HANGAR DOORS! BUT IF THEY HAVEN'T LOCKED IN THE SECURITY CODE...
I WON'T NEED TO STAND ON CEREMONY!
BOOM! BA-BOOM!
NO TIME TO DESTROY THE OTHER PLANES AS WELL! THEY KNOW THESE CRAFT AND THIS SKY BETTER THAN I DO!
...ONLY CHANCE IS TO OUTMANEUVER THEM AND--?
ATTENTION ALL PURSUIT PLANES, THIS IS AL GHUL! RETURN TO BASE IMMEDIATELY!
HE MUST THINK HE HAS A BETTER WAY OF FINISHING ME! SOMETHING CONCEALED...
0:40
0:35
...HERE! I'LL BET THIS WASN'T FACTORY ISSUE!

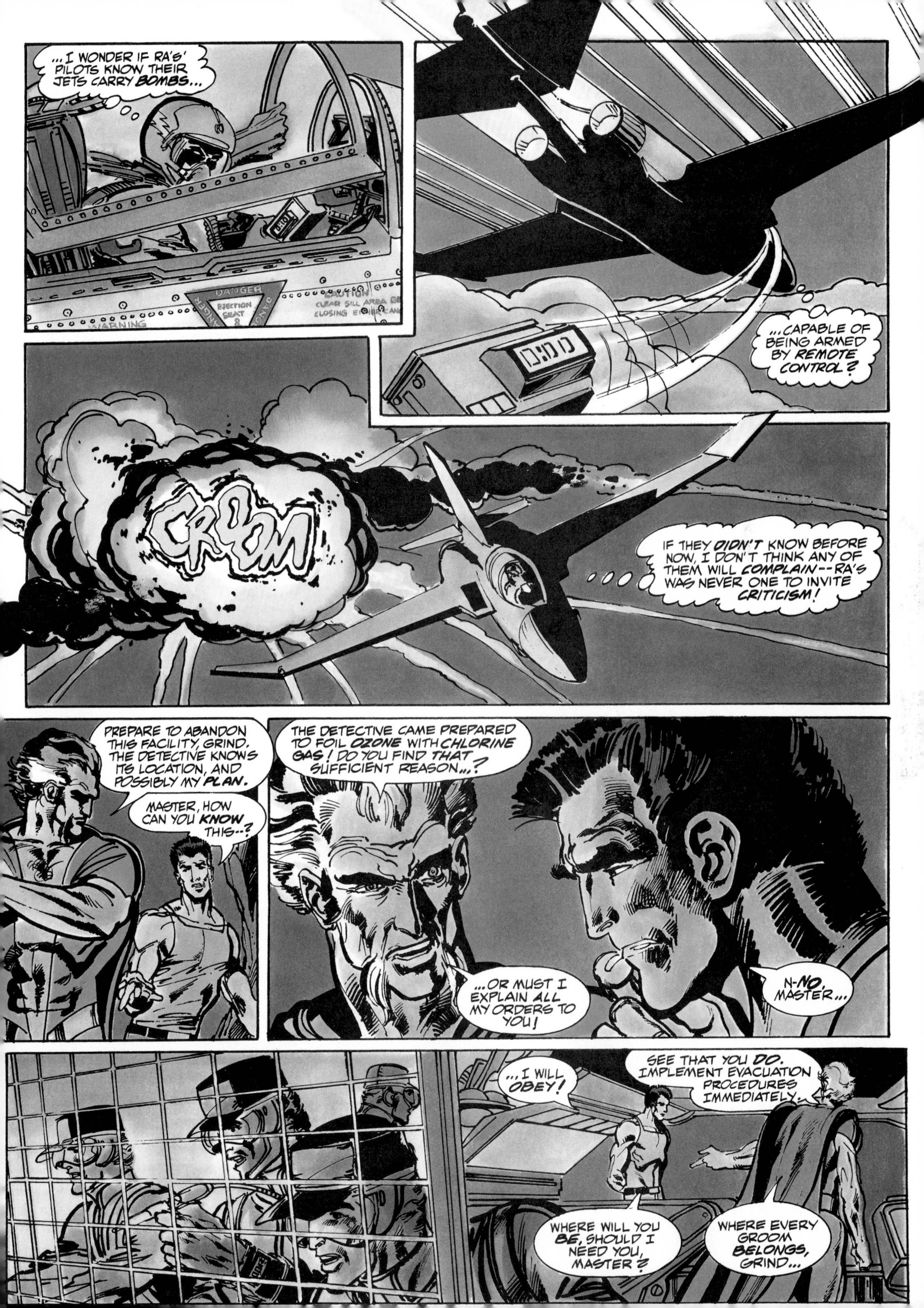
...I WONDER IF RA'S' PILOTS KNOW THEIR JETS CARRY BOMBS...
DANGER
EJECTION SEAT
CAUTION
CLEAR SILL AREA BE
WARNING
...CAPABLE OF BEING ARMED BY REMOTE CONTROL?
CROOM
IF THEY DIDN'T KNOW BEFORE NOW, I DON'T THINK ANY OF THEM WILL COMPLAIN--RA'S WAS NEVER ONE TO INVITE CRITICISM!
PREPARE TO ABANDON THIS FACILITY, GRIND. THE DETECTIVE KNOWS ITS LOCATION, AND POSSIBLY MY PLAN.
MASTER, HOW CAN YOU KNOW THIS--?
THE DETECTIVE CAME PREPARED TO FOIL OZONE WITH CHLORINE GAS! DO YOU FIND THAT SUFFICIENT REASON...?
...OR MUST I EXPLAIN ALL MY ORDERS TO YOU!
N-NO, MASTER...
...I WILL OBEY!
SEE THAT YOU DO. IMPLEMENT EVACUATION PROCEDURES IMMEDIATELY.
WHERE WILL YOU BE, SHOULD I NEED YOU, MASTER?
WHERE EVERY GROOM BELONGS, GRIND...

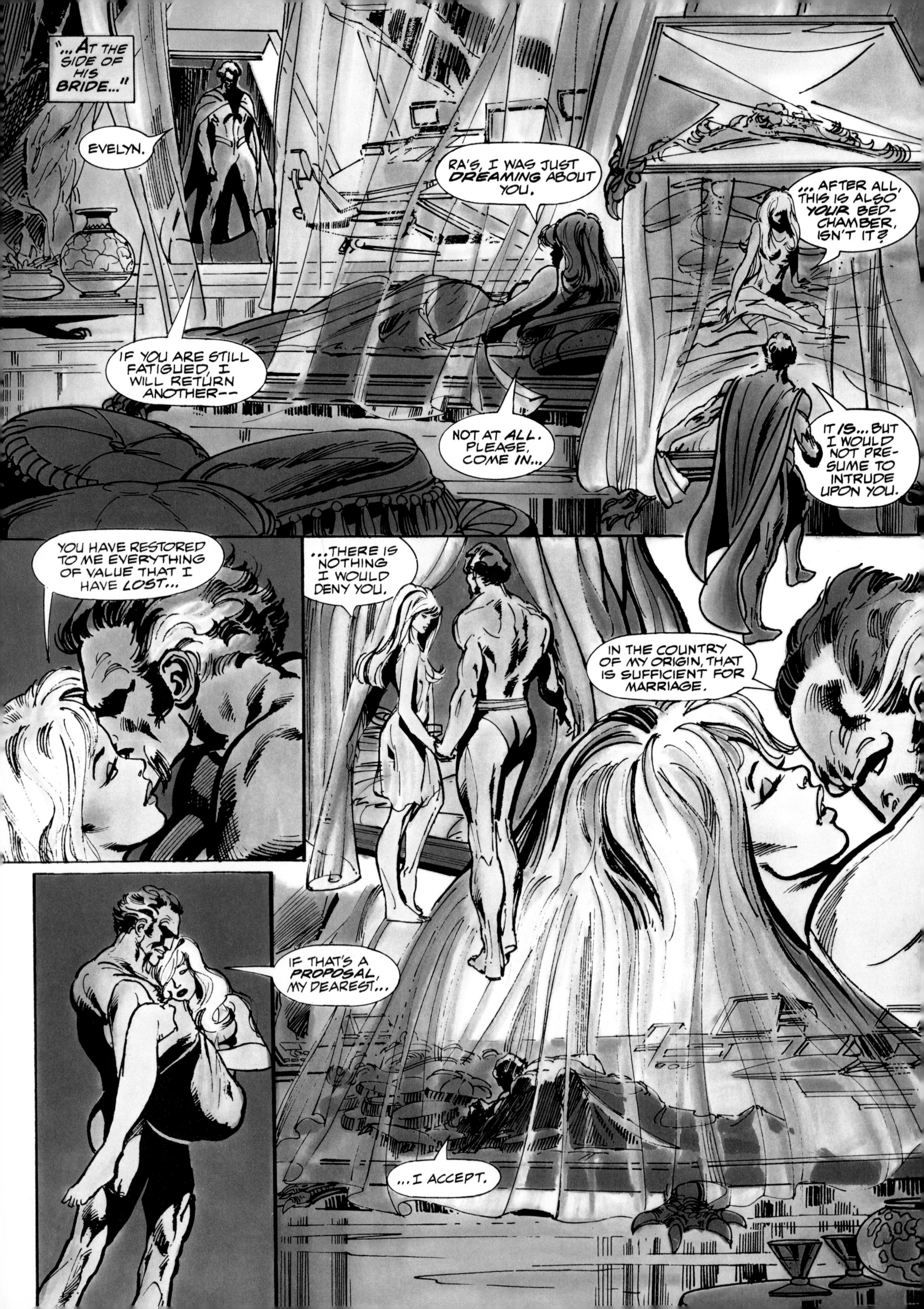
"...AT THE SIDE OF HIS BRIDE..."
EVELYN.
RA'S, I WAS JUST DREAMING ABOUT YOU.
IF YOU ARE STILL FATIGUED, I WILL RETURN ANOTHER--
NOT AT ALL. PLEASE, COME IN...
...AFTER ALL, THIS IS ALSO YOUR BED-CHAMBER, ISN'T IT?
IT IS... BUT I WOULD NOT PRE-SUME TO INTRUDE UPON YOU.
YOU HAVE RESTORED TO ME EVERYTHING OF VALUE THAT I HAVE LOST...
...THERE IS NOTHING I WOULD DENY YOU.
IN THE COUNTRY OF MY ORIGIN, THAT IS SUFFICIENT FOR MARRIAGE.
IF THAT'S A PROPOSAL, MY DEAREST...
...I ACCEPT.

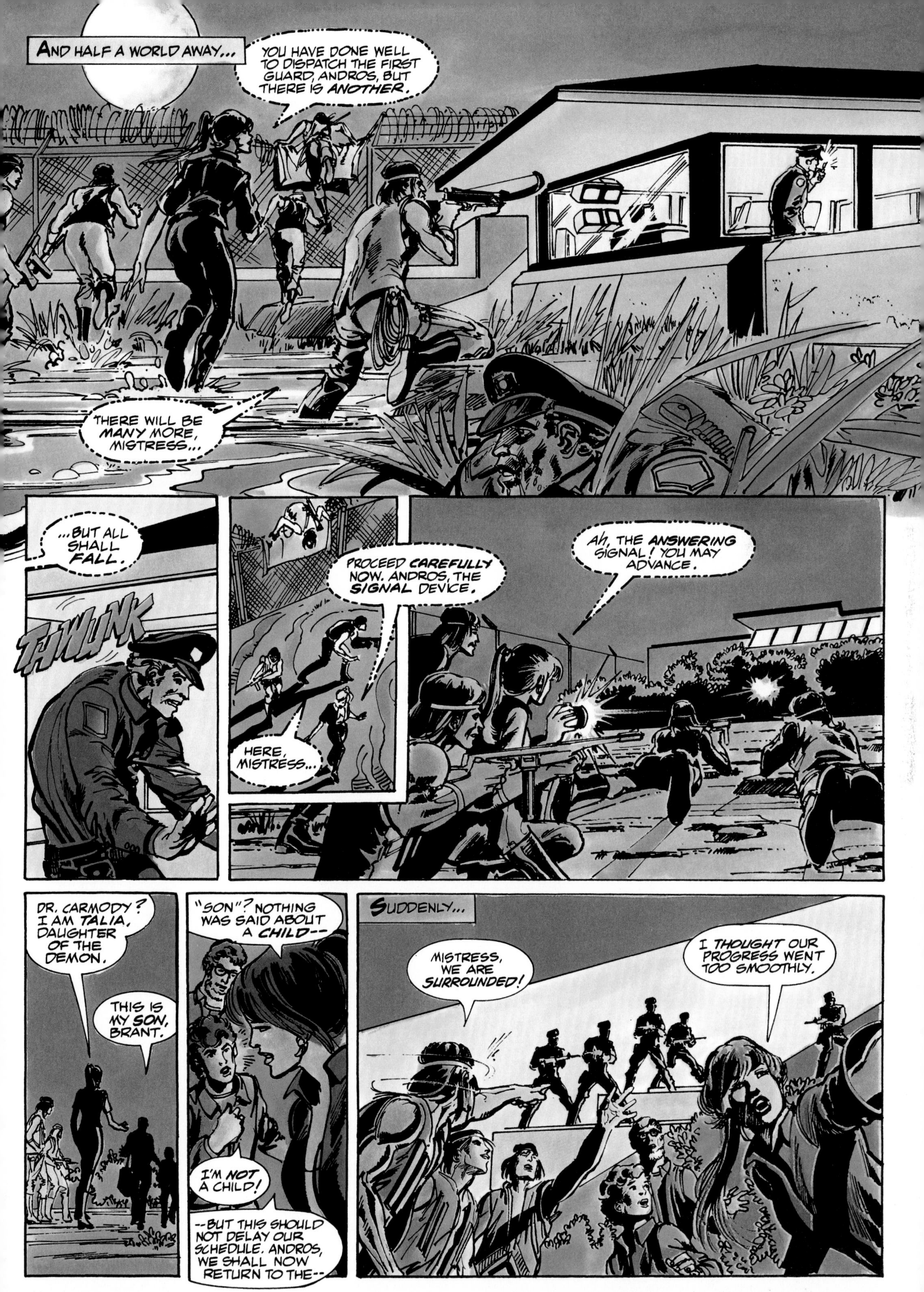

AND HALF A WORLD AWAY...
YOU HAVE DONE WELL TO DISPATCH THE FIRST GUARD, ANDROS, BUT THERE IS ANOTHER.
THERE WILL BE MANY MORE, MISTRESS...
...BUT ALL SHALL FALL.
THWUNK
PROCEED CAREFULLY NOW. ANDROS, THE SIGNAL DEVICE.
HERE, MISTRESS...
AH, THE ANSWERING SIGNAL! YOU MAY ADVANCE.
DR. CARMODY? I AM TALIA, DAUGHTER OF THE DEMON.
THIS IS MY SON, BRANT.
"SON"? NOTHING WAS SAID ABOUT A CHILD--
I'M NOT A CHILD!
--BUT THIS SHOULD NOT DELAY OUR SCHEDULE. ANDROS, WE SHALL NOW RETURN TO THE--
SUDDENLY...
MISTRESS, WE ARE SURROUNDED!
I THOUGHT OUR PROGRESS WENT TOO SMOOTHLY.

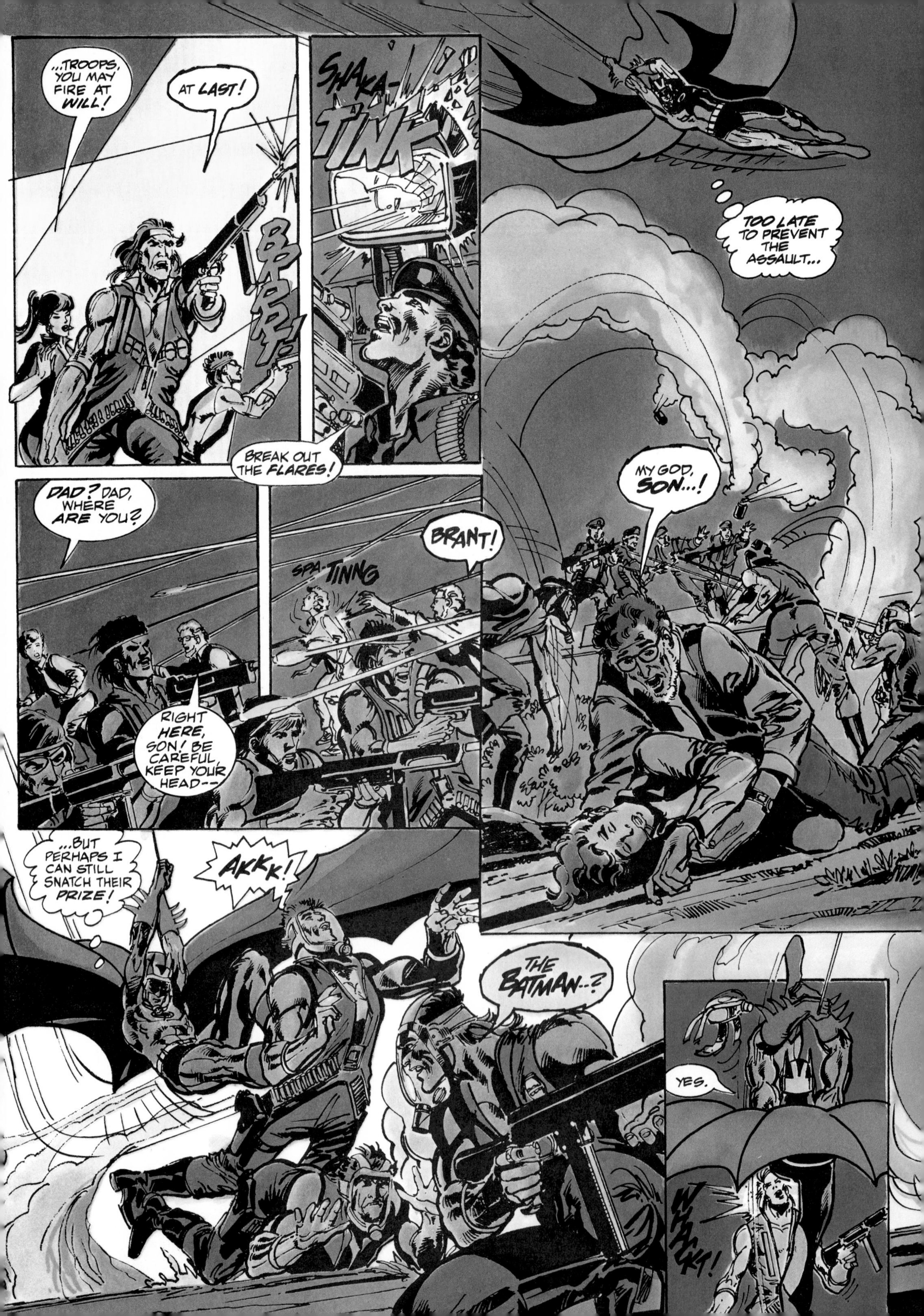
...TROOPS, YOU MAY FIRE AT WILL!
AT LAST!
SHAKA-TINK
BRRRT!
BREAK OUT THE FLARES!
TOO LATE TO PREVENT THE ASSAULT...
DAD? DAD, WHERE ARE YOU?
SPA-TINNG
BRANT!
RIGHT HERE, SON! BE CAREFUL KEEP YOUR HEAD--
MY GOD, SON...!
...BUT PERHAPS I CAN STILL SNATCH THEIR PRIZE!
AKKK!
THE BATMAN..?
YES.
WHACK!

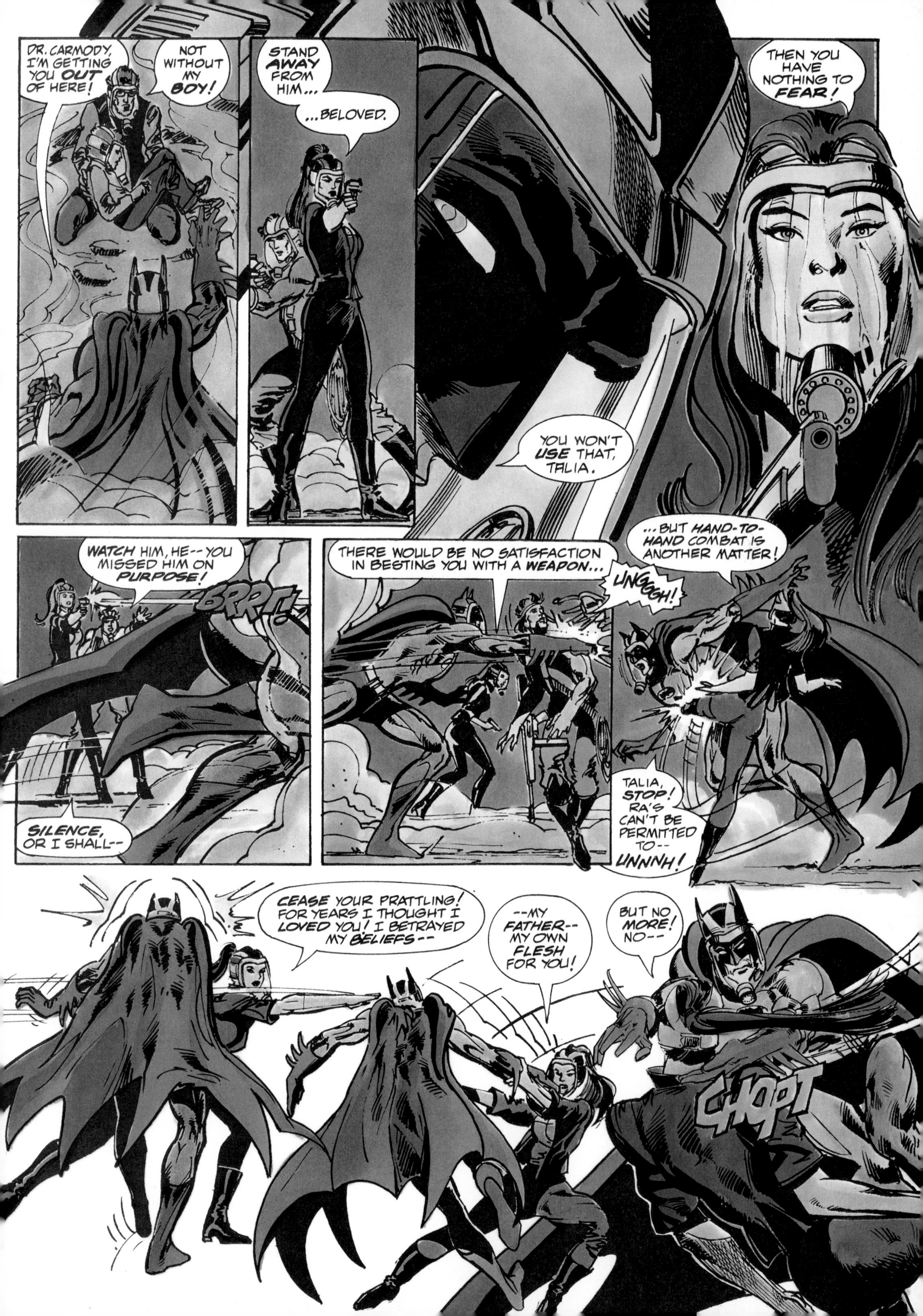
DR. CARMODY, I'M GETTING YOU OUT OF HERE!
NOT WITHOUT MY BOY!
STAND AWAY FROM HIM...
...BELOVED.
THEN YOU HAVE NOTHING TO FEAR!
YOU WON'T USE THAT, TALIA.
WATCH HIM, HE-- YOU MISSED HIM ON PURPOSE!
BRRT!
SILENCE, OR I SHALL--
THERE WOULD BE NO SATISFACTION IN BESTING YOU WITH A WEAPON...
...BUT HAND-TO-HAND COMBAT IS ANOTHER MATTER!
UNGGGH!
TALIA, STOP! RA'S CAN'T BE PERMITTED TO-- UNNNH!
CEASE YOUR PRATTLING! FOR YEARS I THOUGHT I LOVED YOU! I BETRAYED MY BELIEFS--
--MY FATHER-- MY OWN FLESH FOR YOU!
BUT NO MORE! NO--
CHOPT

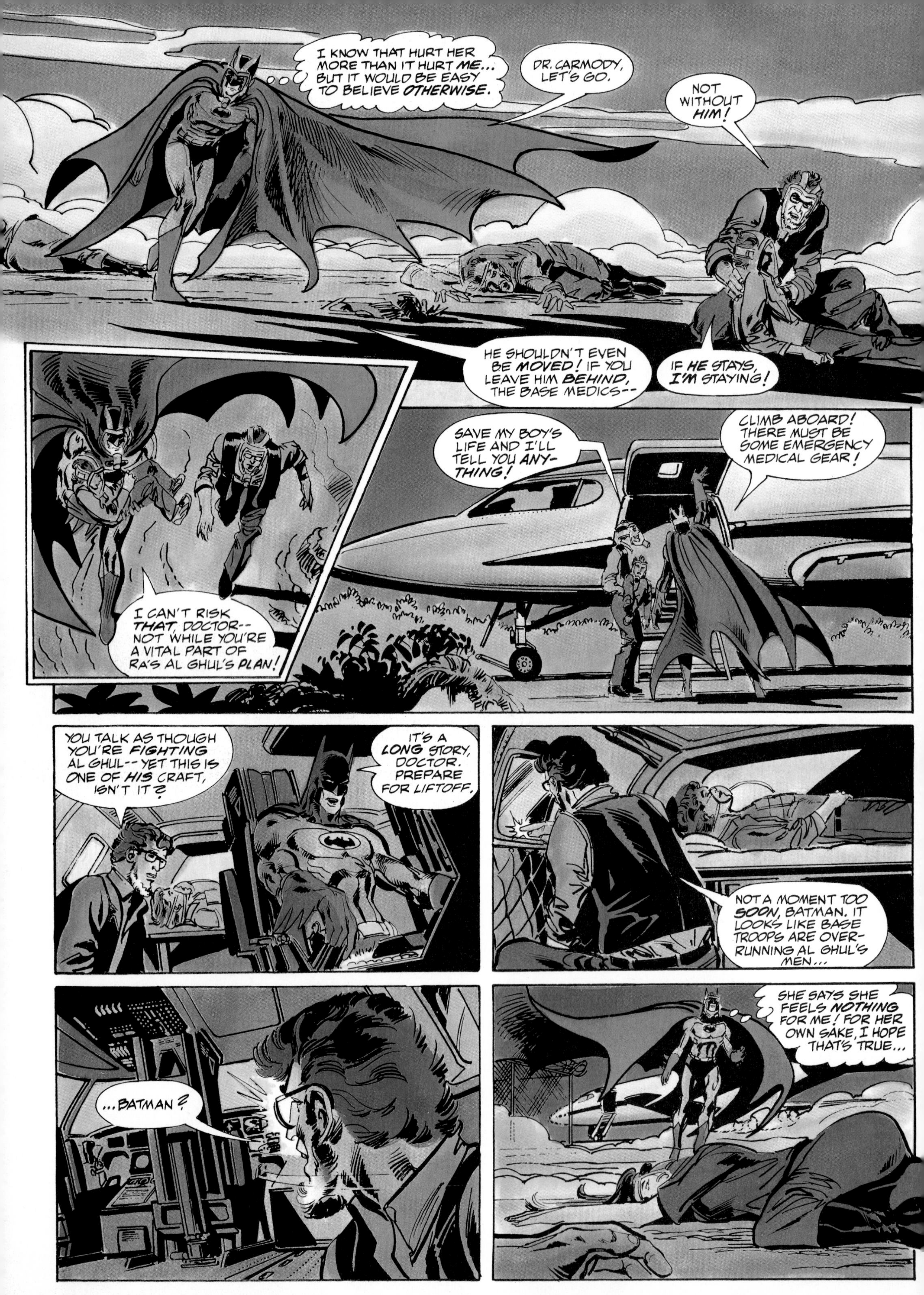
I KNOW THAT HURT HER MORE THAN IT HURT ME... BUT IT WOULD BE EASY TO BELIEVE OTHERWISE.
DR. CARMODY, LET'S GO.
NOT WITHOUT HIM!
HE SHOULDN'T EVEN BE MOVED! IF YOU LEAVE HIM BEHIND, THE BASE MEDICS--
IF HE STAYS, I'M STAYING!
I CAN'T RISK THAT, DOCTOR-- NOT WHILE YOU'RE A VITAL PART OF RA'S AL GHUL'S PLAN!
SAVE MY BOY'S LIFE AND I'LL TELL YOU ANY-THING!
CLIMB ABOARD! THERE MUST BE SOME EMERGENCY MEDICAL GEAR!
YOU TALK AS THOUGH YOU'RE FIGHTING AL GHUL-- YET THIS IS ONE OF HIS CRAFT, ISN'T IT?
IT'S A LONG STORY, DOCTOR. PREPARE FOR LIFTOFF.
NOT A MOMENT TOO SOON, BATMAN. IT LOOKS LIKE BASE TROOPS ARE OVER-RUNNING AL GHUL'S MEN...
...BATMAN?
SHE SAYS SHE FEELS NOTHING FOR ME! FOR HER OWN SAKE, I HOPE THAT'S TRUE...

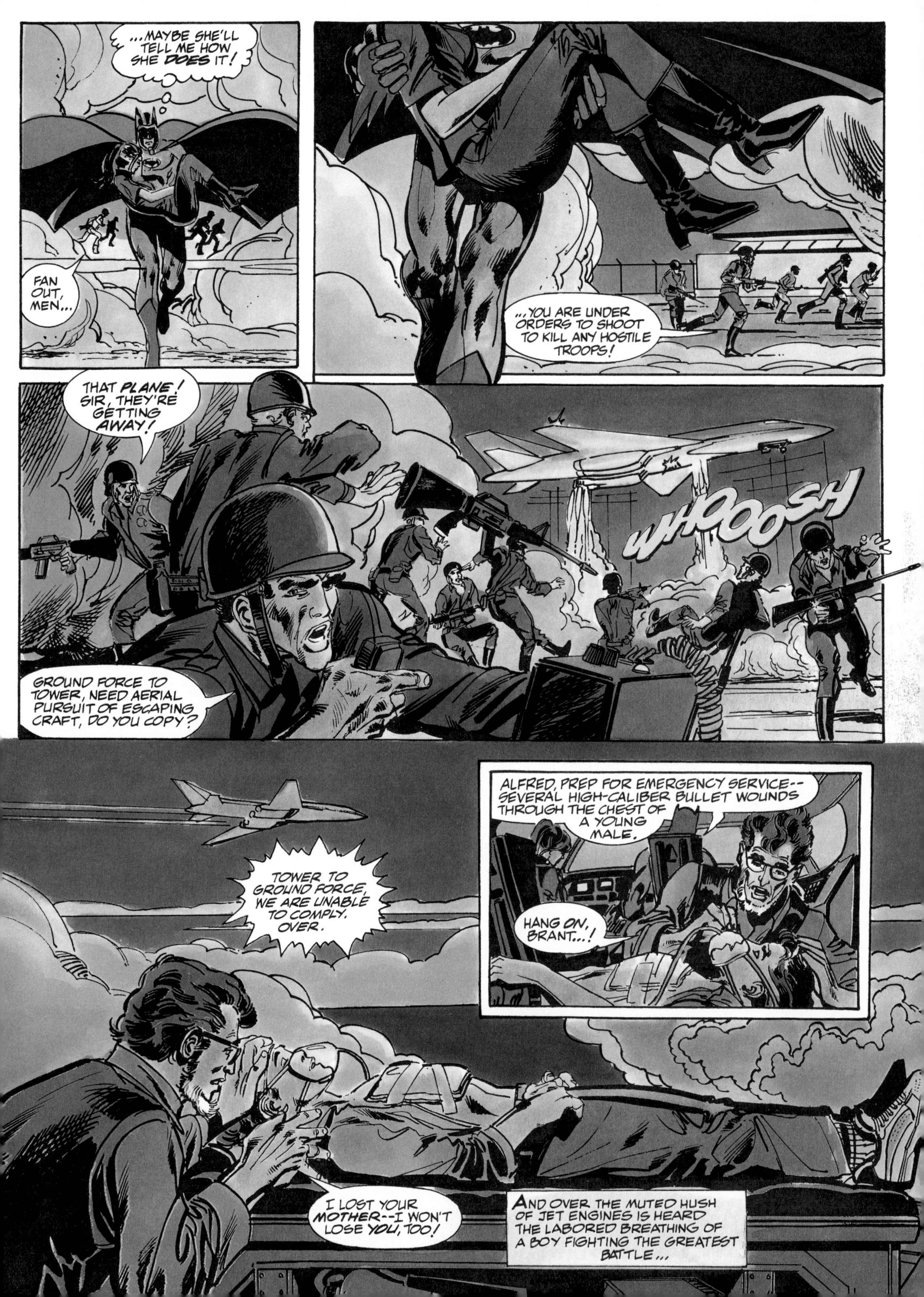

...MAYBE SHE'LL TELL ME HOW SHE DOES IT!
FAN OUT, MEN...
...YOU ARE UNDER ORDERS TO SHOOT TO KILL ANY HOSTILE TROOPS!
THAT PLANE! SIR, THEY'RE GETTING AWAY!
WHOOOOSH
GROUND FORCE TO TOWER, NEED AERIAL PURSUIT OF ESCAPING CRAFT, DO YOU COPY?
TOWER TO GROUND FORCE, WE ARE UNABLE TO COMPLY. OVER.
ALFRED, PREP FOR EMERGENCY SERVICE--SEVERAL HIGH-CALIBER BULLET WOUNDS THROUGH THE CHEST OF A YOUNG MALE.
HANG ON, BRANT...!
I LOST YOUR MOTHER--I WON'T LOSE YOU, TOO!
AND OVER THE MUTED HUSH OF JET ENGINES IS HEARD THE LABORED BREATHING OF A BOY FIGHTING THE GREATEST BATTLE...

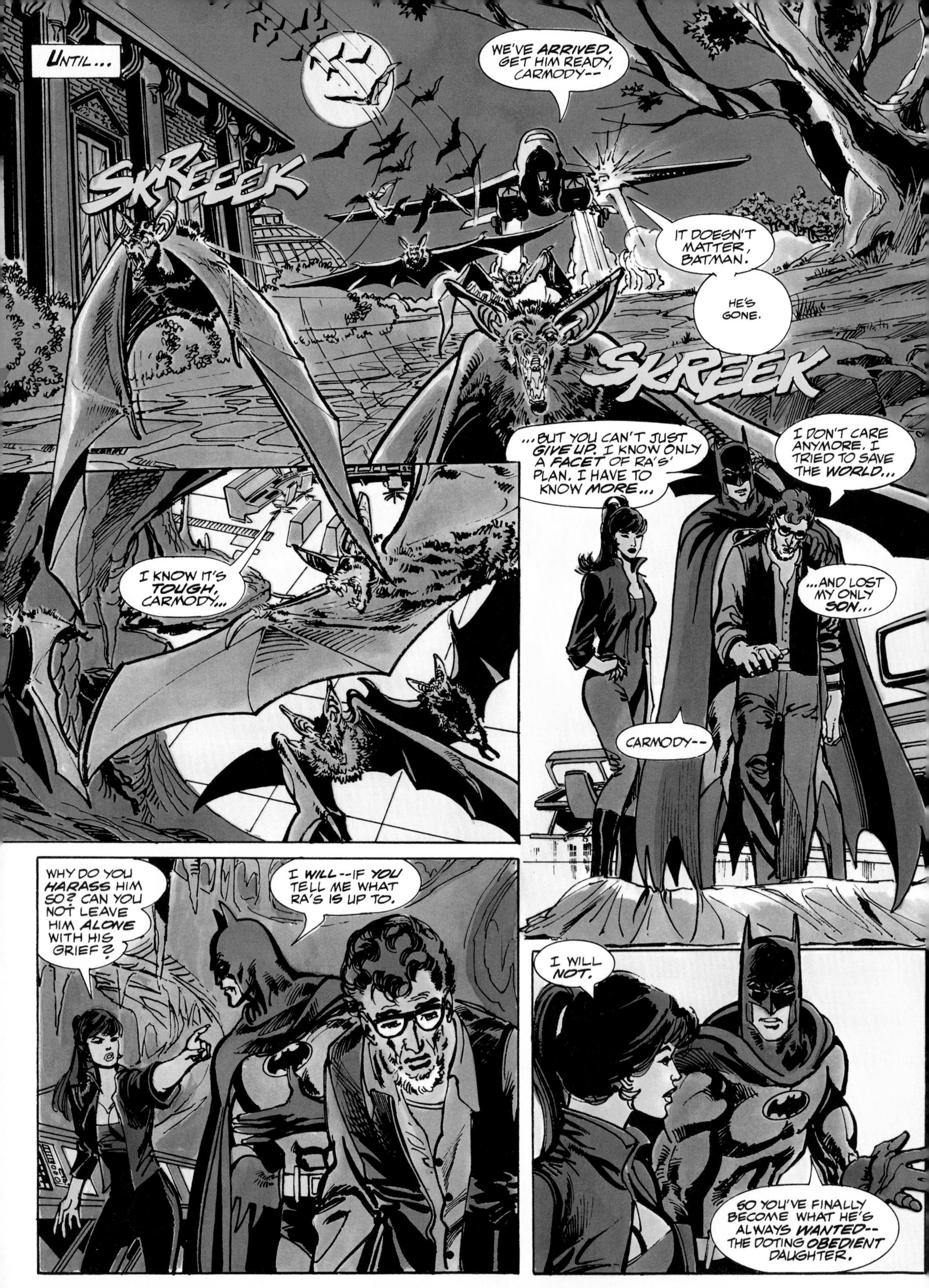
UNTIL...
WE'VE ARRIVED. GET HIM READY, CARMODY--
SKREEEK
IT DOESN'T MATTER, BATMAN.
HE'S GONE.
SKREEEK
I KNOW IT'S TOUGH, CARMODY...
...BUT YOU CAN'T JUST GIVE UP. I KNOW ONLY A FACET OF RA'S' PLAN. I HAVE TO KNOW MORE...
I DON'T CARE ANYMORE. I TRIED TO SAVE THE WORLD...
...AND LOST MY ONLY SON...
CARMODY--
WHY DO YOU HARASS HIM SO? CAN YOU NOT LEAVE HIM ALONE WITH HIS GRIEF?
I WILL--IF YOU TELL ME WHAT RA'S IS UP TO.
I WILL NOT.
SO YOU'VE FINALLY BECOME WHAT HE'S ALWAYS WANTED-- THE DOTING OBEDIENT DAUGHTER.

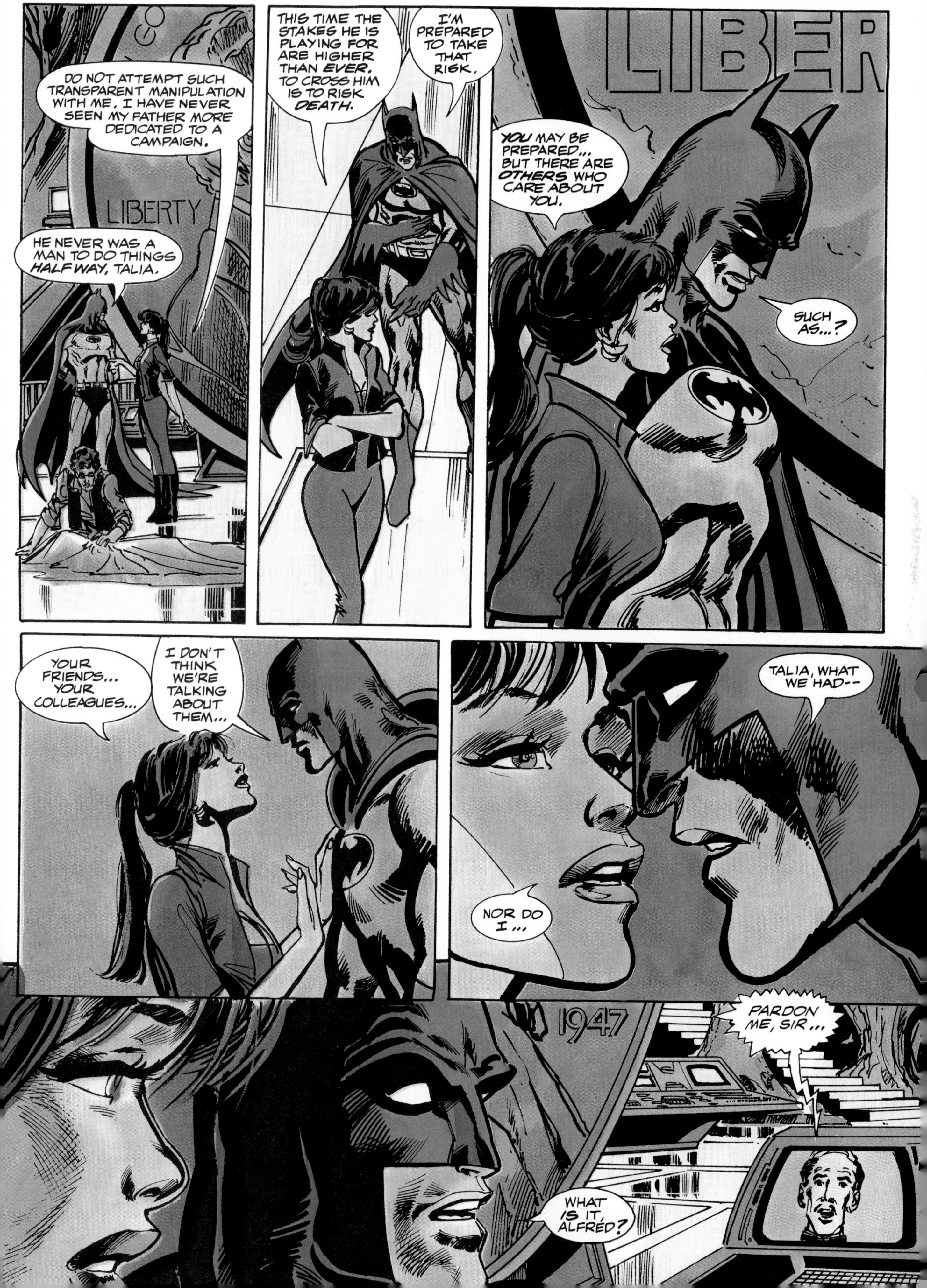
DO NOT ATTEMPT SUCH TRANSPARENT MANIPULATION WITH ME. I HAVE NEVER SEEN MY FATHER MORE DEDICATED TO A CAMPAIGN.
LIBERTY
HE NEVER WAS A MAN TO DO THINGS HALFWAY, TALIA.
THIS TIME THE STAKES HE IS PLAYING FOR ARE HIGHER THAN EVER. TO CROSS HIM IS TO RISK DEATH.
I'M PREPARED TO TAKE THAT RISK.
LIBER
YOU MAY BE PREPARED... BUT THERE ARE OTHERS WHO CARE ABOUT YOU.
SUCH AS...?
YOUR FRIENDS... YOUR COLLEAGUES...
I DON'T THINK WE'RE TALKING ABOUT THEM...
TALIA, WHAT WE HAD--
NOR DO I...
1947
PARDON ME, SIR...
WHAT IS IT, ALFRED?

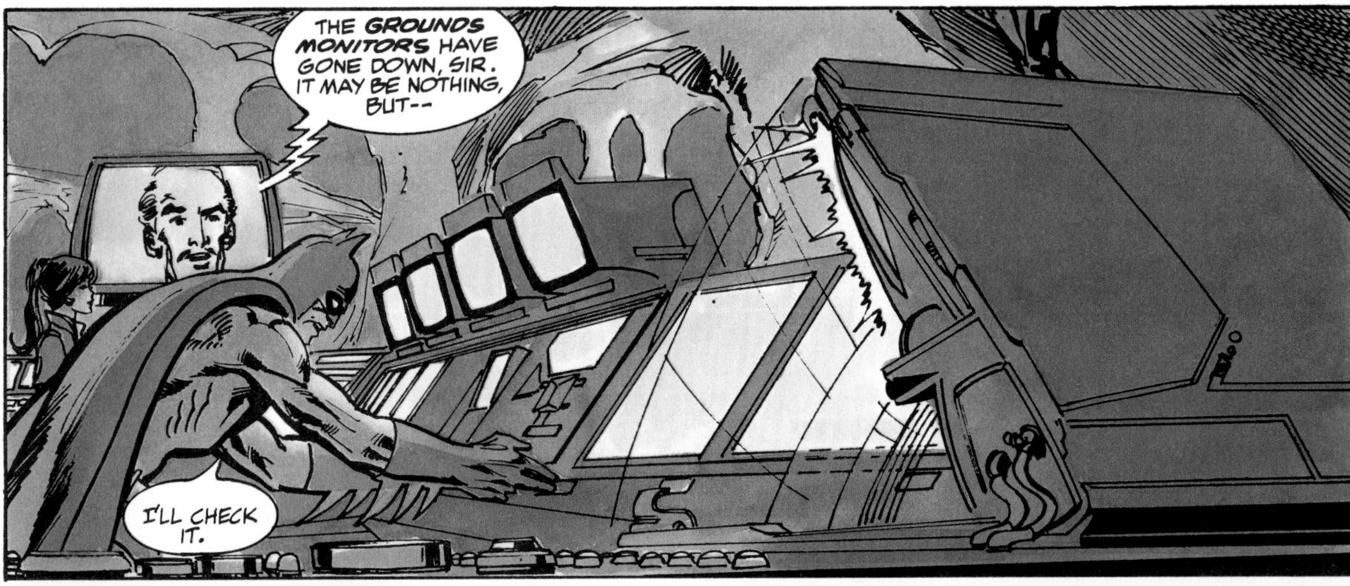
THE GROUNDS MONITORS HAVE GONE DOWN, SIR. IT MAY BE NOTHING, BUT--
I'LL CHECK IT.
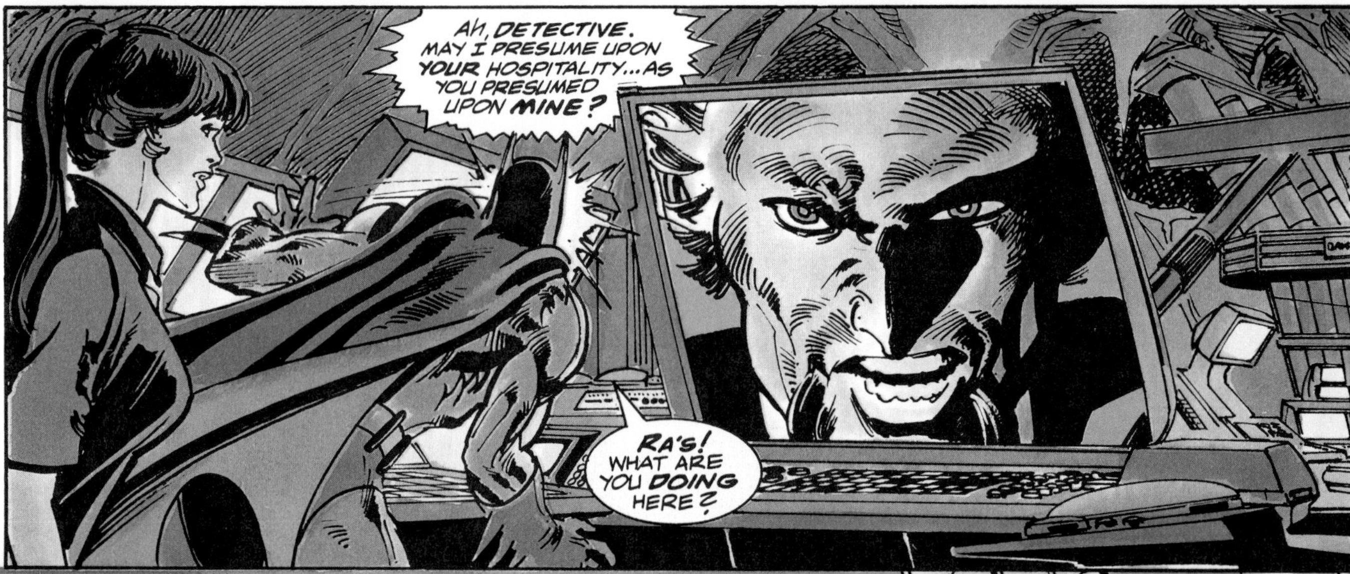
AH, DETECTIVE. MAY I PRESUME UPON YOUR HOSPITALITY... AS YOU PRESUMED UPON MINE?
RA'S! WHAT ARE YOU DOING HERE?
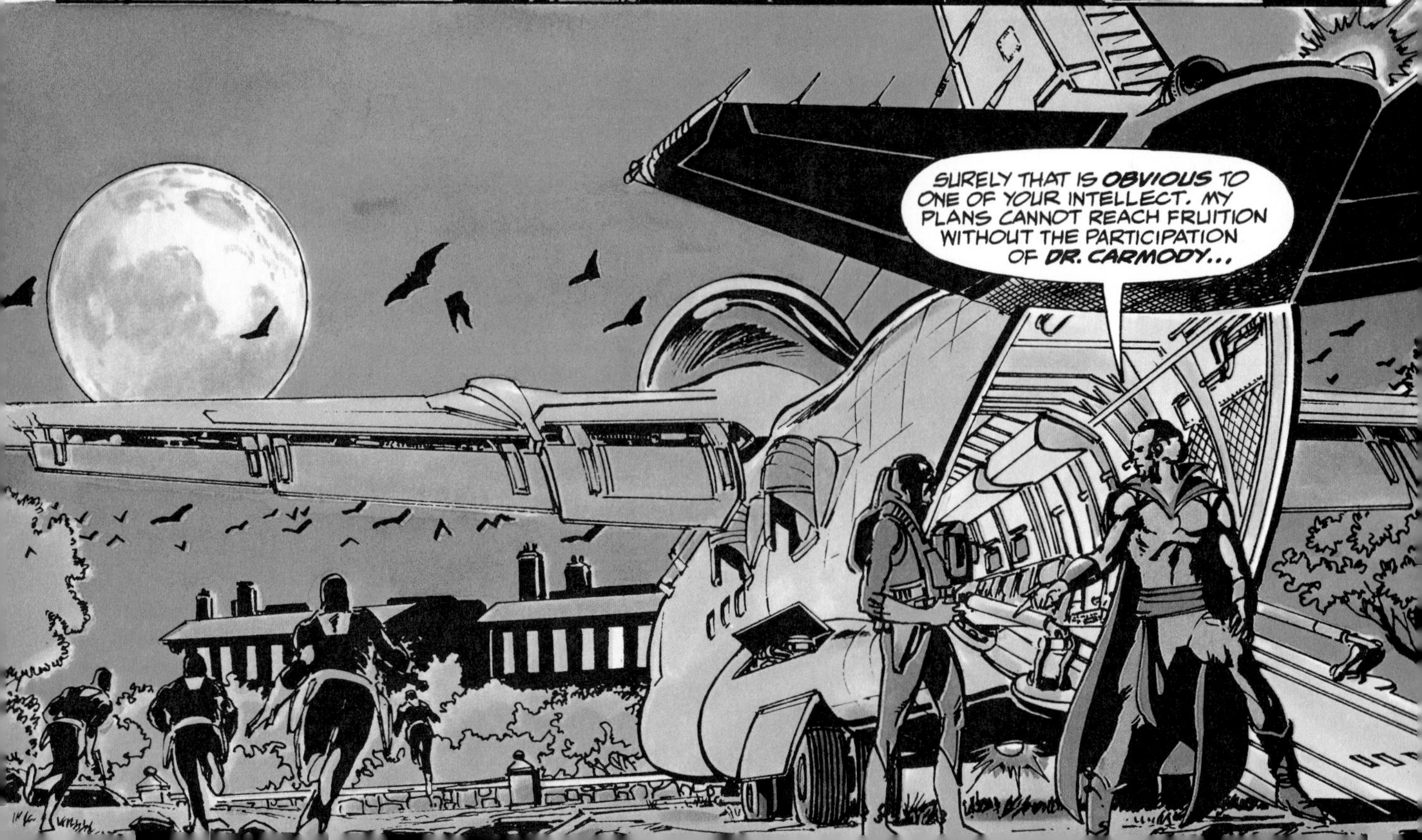
SURELY THAT IS OBVIOUS TO ONE OF YOUR INTELLECT. MY PLANS CANNOT REACH FRUITION WITHOUT THE PARTICIPATION OF DR. CARMODY...

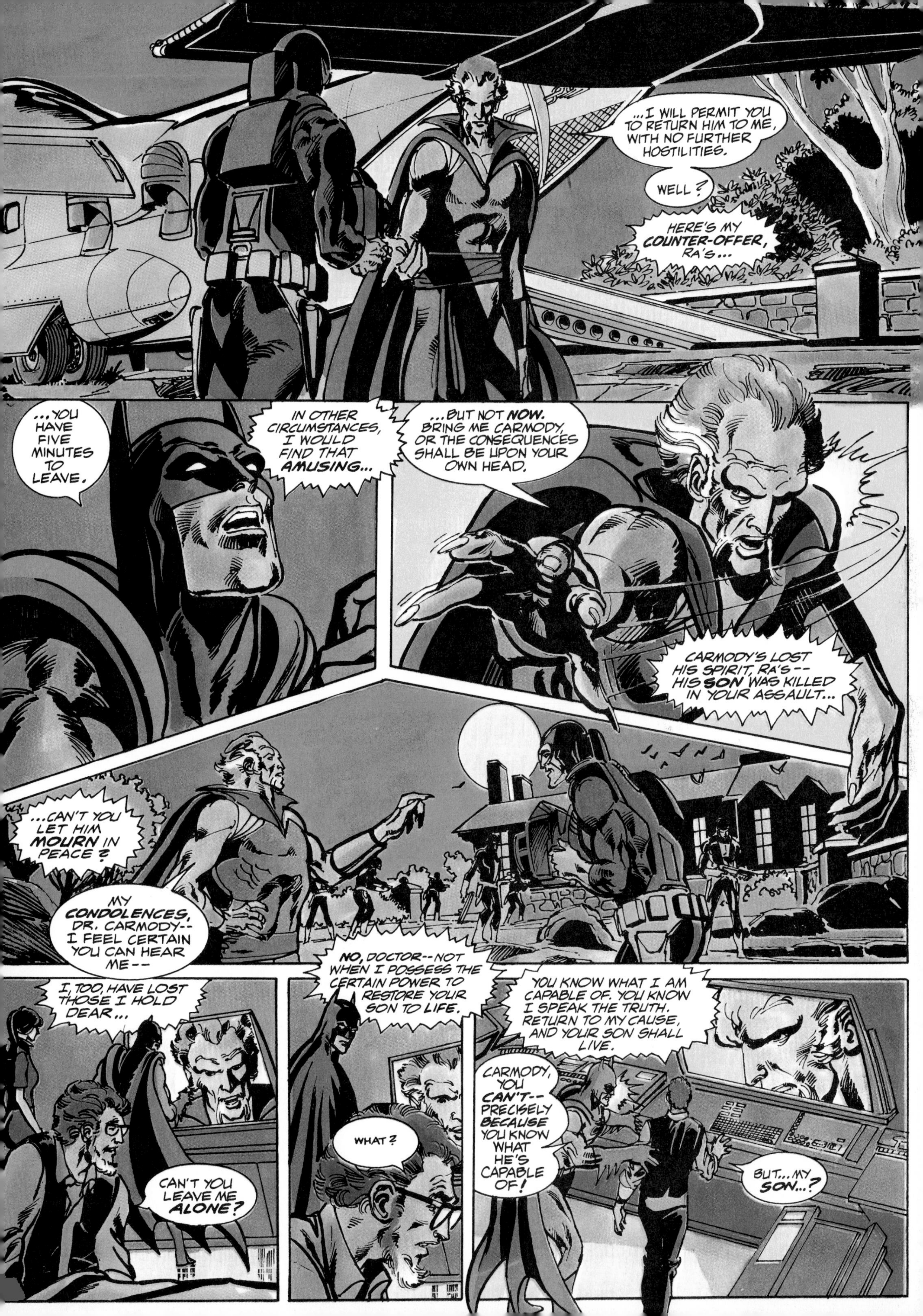
...I WILL PERMIT YOU TO RETURN HIM TO ME, WITH NO FURTHER HOSTILITIES.
WELL?
HERE'S MY COUNTER-OFFER, RA'S...
...YOU HAVE FIVE MINUTES TO LEAVE.
IN OTHER CIRCUMSTANCES, I WOULD FIND THAT AMUSING...
...BUT NOT NOW. BRING ME CARMODY, OR THE CONSEQUENCES SHALL BE UPON YOUR OWN HEAD.
CARMODY'S LOST HIS SPIRIT, RA'S-- HIS SON WAS KILLED IN YOUR ASSAULT...
...CAN'T YOU LET HIM MOURN IN PEACE?
MY CONDOLENCES, DR. CARMODY-- I FEEL CERTAIN YOU CAN HEAR ME--
I, TOO, HAVE LOST THOSE I HOLD DEAR...
CAN'T YOU LEAVE ME ALONE?
NO, DOCTOR--NOT WHEN I POSSESS THE CERTAIN POWER TO RESTORE YOUR SON TO LIFE.
WHAT?
YOU KNOW WHAT I AM CAPABLE OF. YOU KNOW I SPEAK THE TRUTH. RETURN TO MY CAUSE, AND YOUR SON SHALL LIVE.
CARMODY, YOU CAN'T-- PRECISELY BECAUSE YOU KNOW WHAT HE'S CAPABLE OF!
BUT...MY SON...?

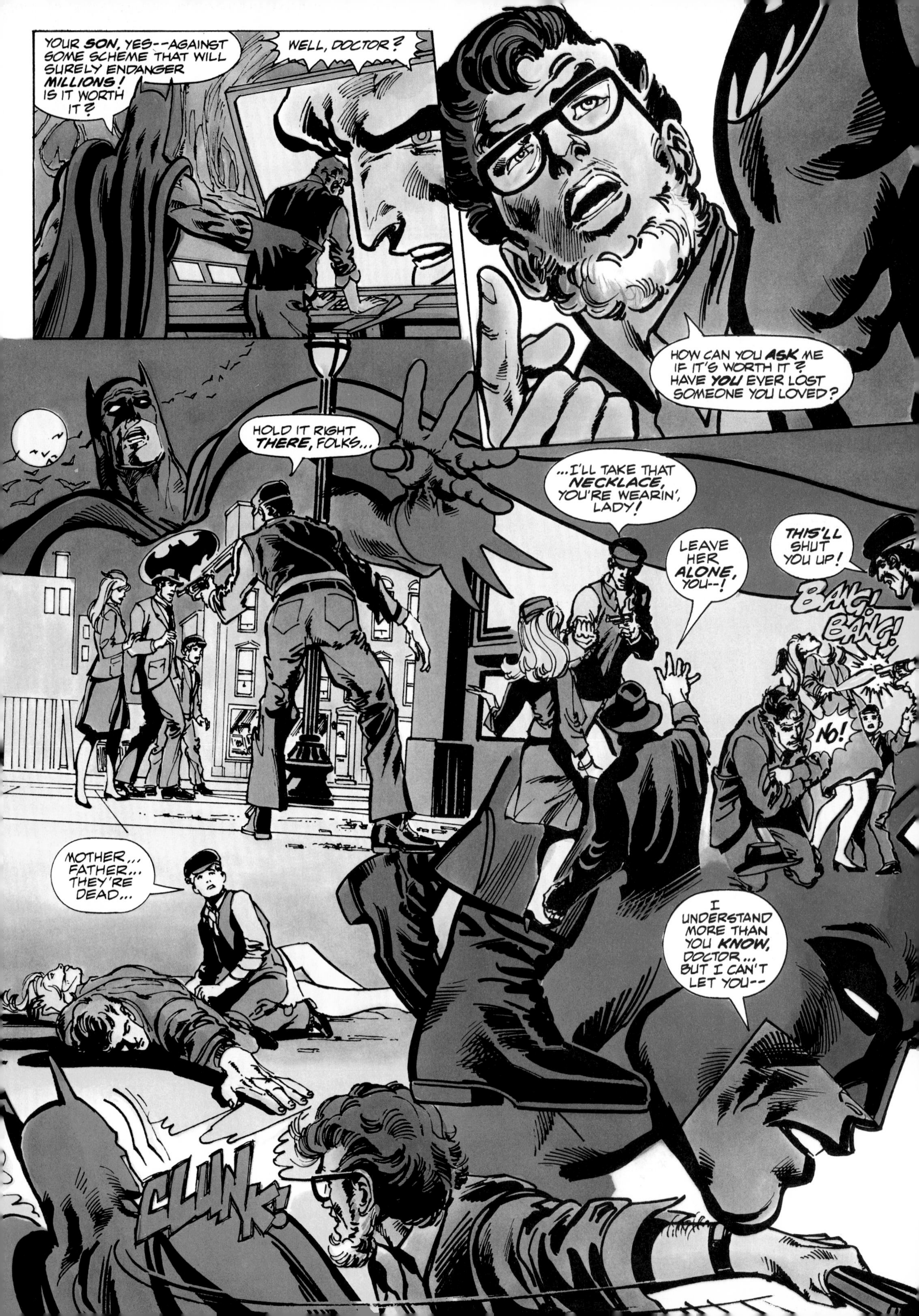
YOUR SON, YES--AGAINST SOME SCHEME THAT WILL SURELY ENDANGER MILLIONS! IS IT WORTH IT?
WELL, DOCTOR?
HOW CAN YOU ASK ME IF IT'S WORTH IT? HAVE YOU EVER LOST SOMEONE YOU LOVED?
HOLD IT RIGHT THERE, FOLKS...
...I'LL TAKE THAT NECKLACE, YOU'RE WEARIN', LADY!
LEAVE HER ALONE, YOU--!
THIS'LL SHUT YOU UP!
BANG! BANG!
NO!
MOTHER... FATHER... THEY'RE DEAD...
I UNDERSTAND MORE THAN YOU KNOW, DOCTOR... BUT I CAN'T LET YOU--
CLUNK!

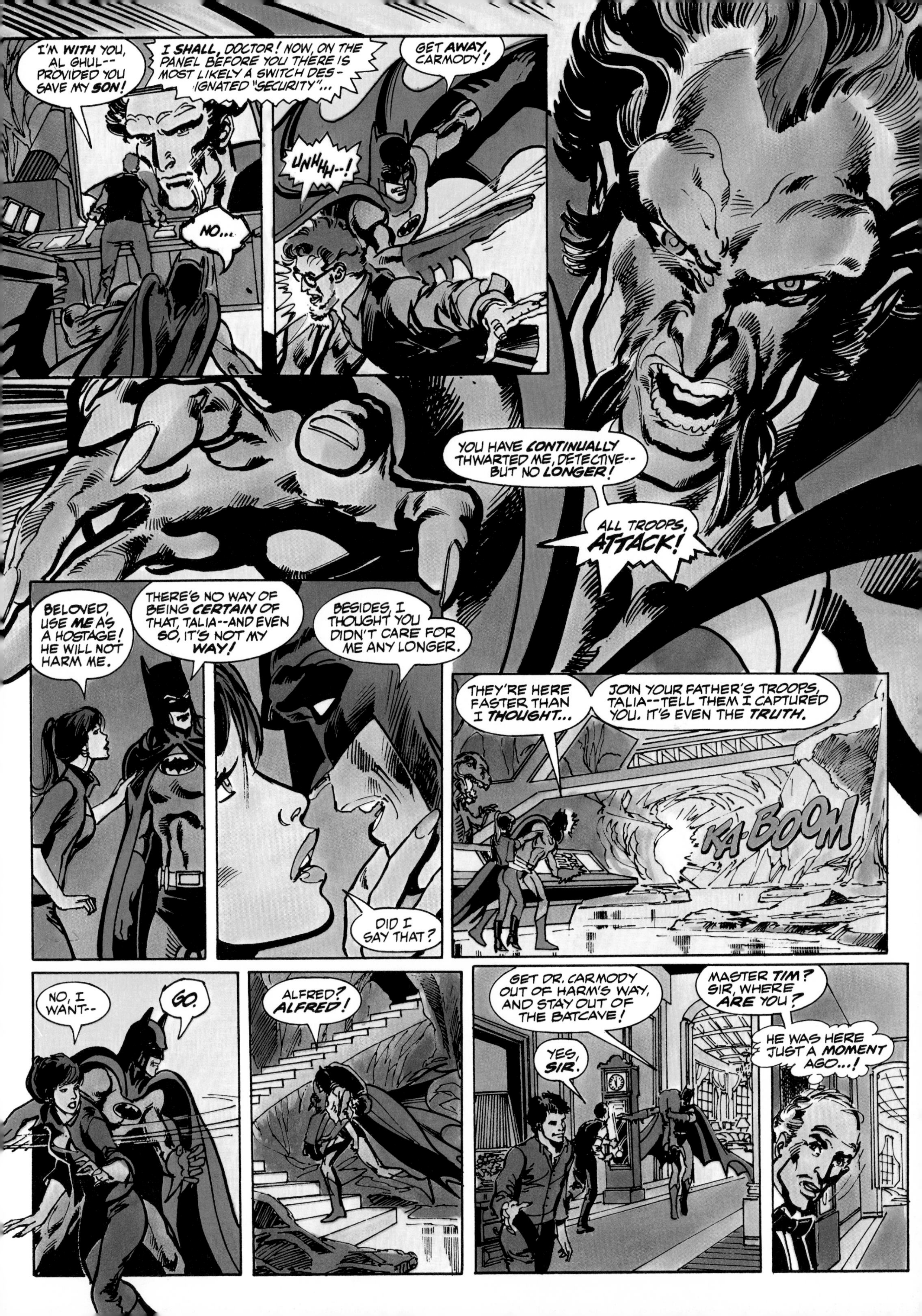
I'M WITH YOU, AL GHUL-- PROVIDED YOU SAVE MY SON!
I SHALL, DOCTOR! NOW, ON THE PANEL BEFORE YOU THERE IS MOST LIKELY A SWITCH DES-IGNATED "SECURITY"...
NO...
GET AWAY, CARMODY!
UNHHH--!
YOU HAVE CONTINUALLY THWARTED ME, DETECTIVE-- BUT NO LONGER!
ALL TROOPS, ATTACK!
BELOVED, USE ME AS A HOSTAGE! HE WILL NOT HARM ME.
THERE'S NO WAY OF BEING CERTAIN OF THAT, TALIA--AND EVEN SO, IT'S NOT MY WAY!
BESIDES, I THOUGHT YOU DIDN'T CARE FOR ME ANY LONGER.
DID I SAY THAT?
THEY'RE HERE FASTER THAN I THOUGHT...
JOIN YOUR FATHER'S TROOPS, TALIA--TELL THEM I CAPTURED YOU. IT'S EVEN THE TRUTH.
KA-BOOM
NO, I WANT--
GO.
ALFRED? ALFRED!
GET DR. CARMODY OUT OF HARM'S WAY, AND STAY OUT OF THE BATCAVE!
YES, SIR.
MASTER TIM? SIR, WHERE ARE YOU?
HE WAS HERE JUST A MOMENT AGO...!

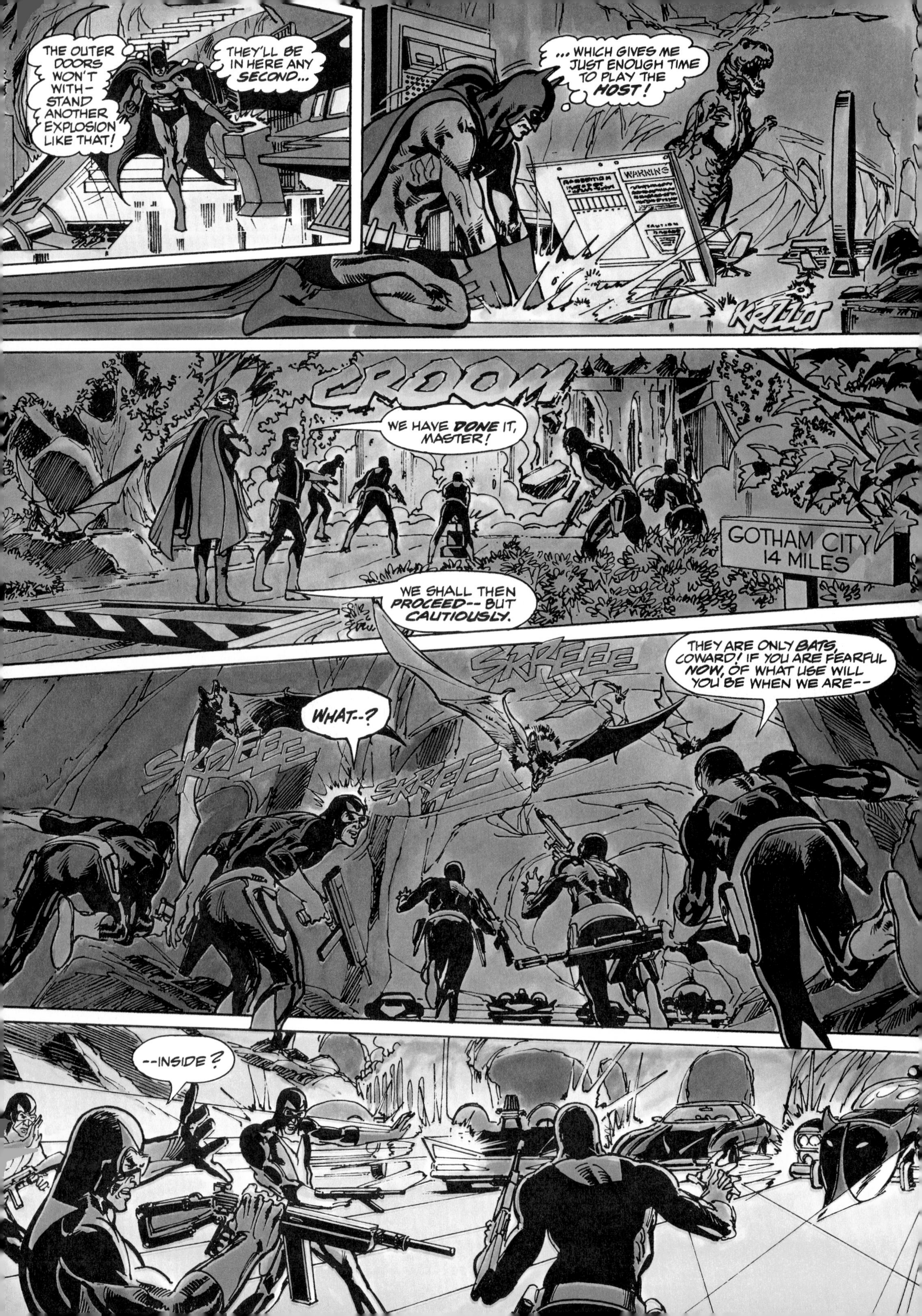
THE OUTER DOORS WON'T WITH-STAND ANOTHER EXPLOSION LIKE THAT!
THEY'LL BE IN HERE ANY SECOND...
...WHICH GIVES ME JUST ENOUGH TIME TO PLAY THE HOST!
WARNING
KRZZT
CROOM
WE HAVE DONE IT, MASTER!
GOTHAM CITY 14 MILES
WE SHALL THEN PROCEED-- BUT CAUTIOUSLY.
SKREEE
THEY ARE ONLY BATS, COWARD! IF YOU ARE FEARFUL NOW, OF WHAT USE WILL YOU BE WHEN WE ARE--
WHAT--?
SKREEE
SKREE
--INSIDE?

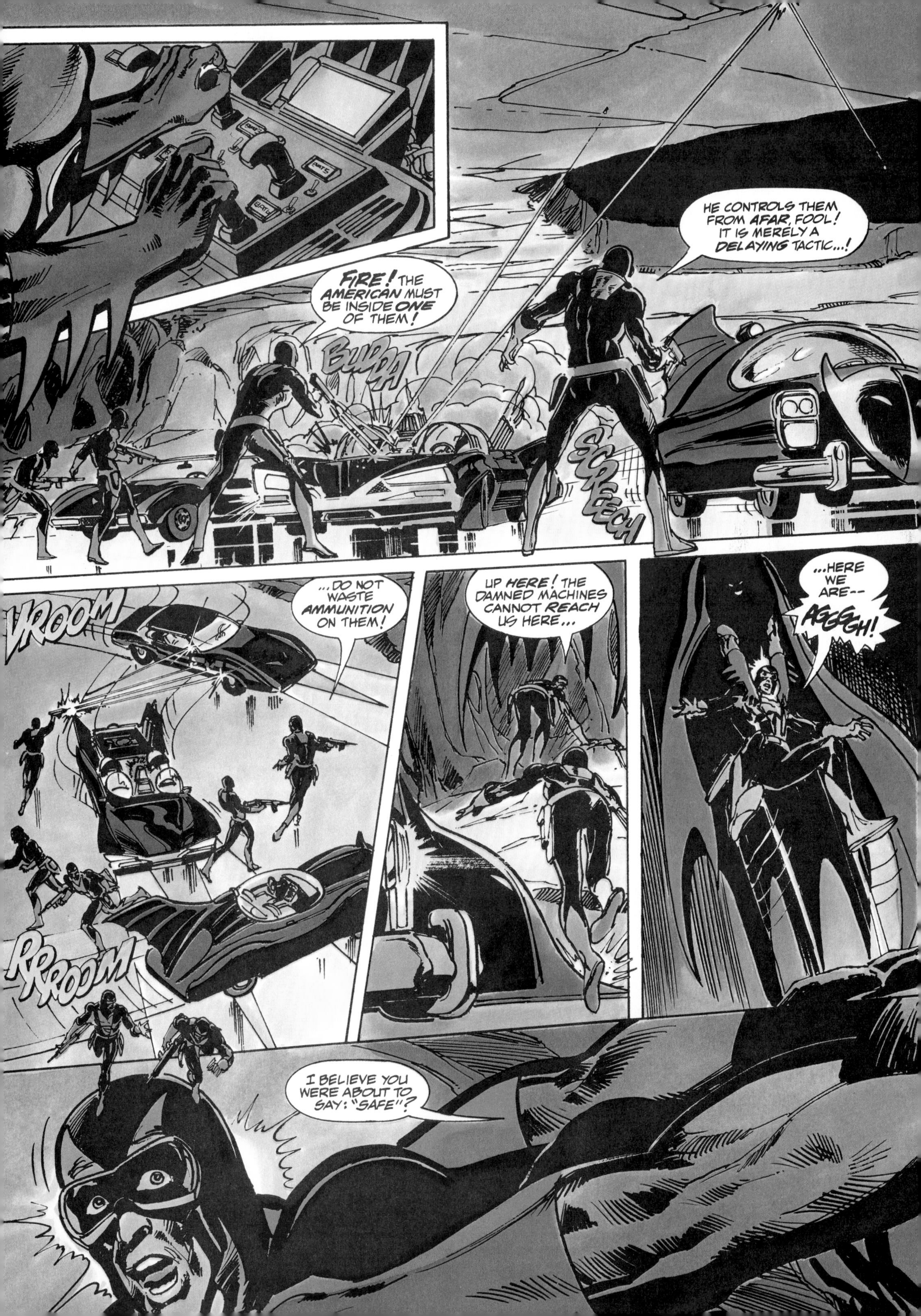
FIRE! THE AMERICAN MUST BE INSIDE ONE OF THEM!
BUDDA
HE CONTROLS THEM FROM AFAR, FOOL! IT IS MERELY A DELAYING TACTIC...!
SCREEECH
VROOOM
...DO NOT WASTE AMMUNITION ON THEM!
RRROOOM
UP HERE! THE DAMNED MACHINES CANNOT REACH US HERE...
...HERE WE ARE--
AGGGGH!
I BELIEVE YOU WERE ABOUT TO SAY: "SAFE"?

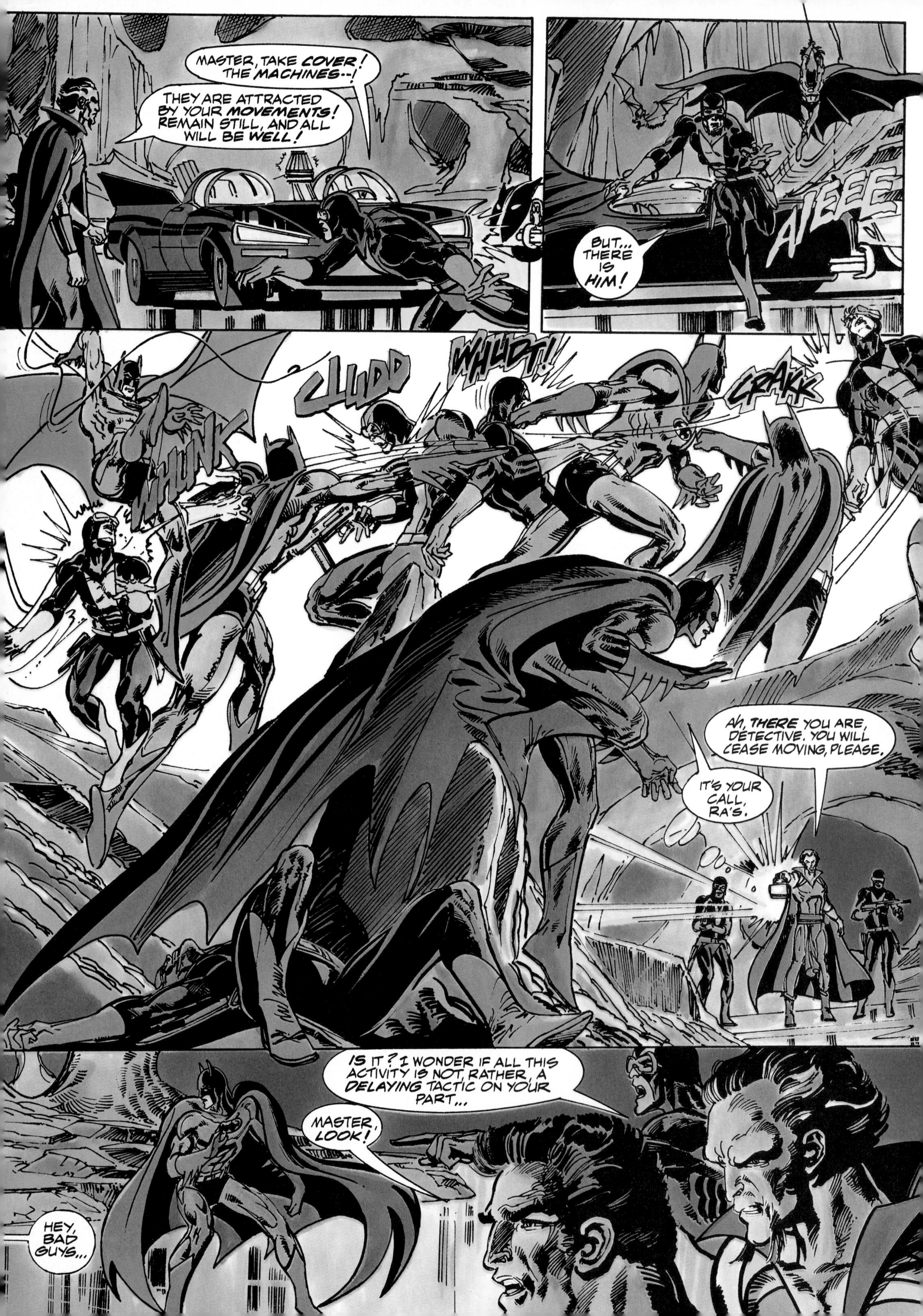
MASTER, TAKE COVER! THE MACHINES--!
THEY ARE ATTRACTED BY YOUR MOVEMENTS! REMAIN STILL, AND ALL WILL BE WELL!
BUT... THERE IS HIM!
AIEEE
CLUDD
WHUDT!!
CRAKK
WHUNK
AH, THERE YOU ARE, DETECTIVE. YOU WILL CEASE MOVING, PLEASE.
IT'S YOUR CALL, RA'S.
IS IT? I WONDER IF ALL THIS ACTIVITY IS NOT, RATHER, A DELAYING TACTIC ON YOUR PART...
MASTER, LOOK!
HEY, BAD GUYS...

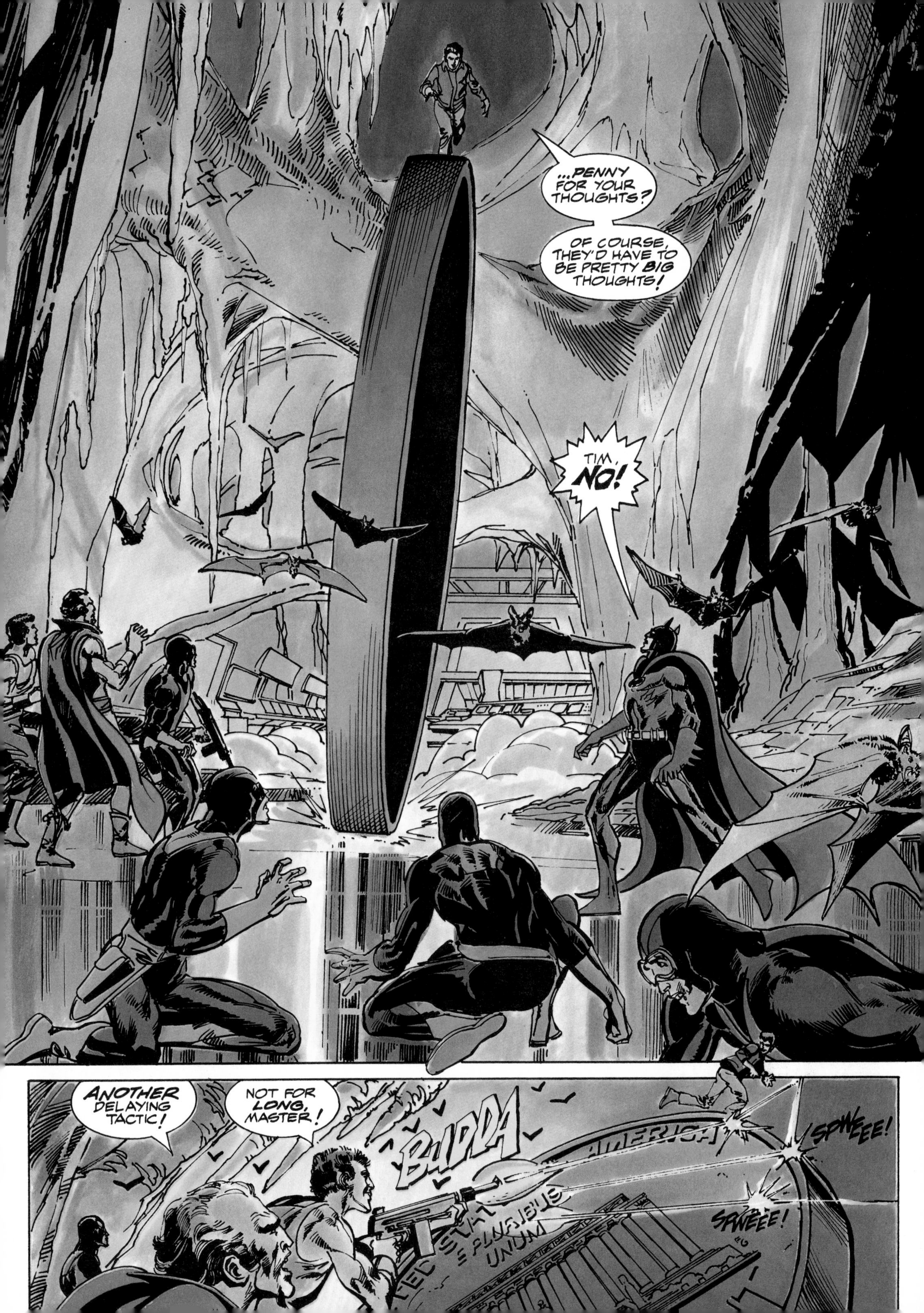
...PENNY FOR YOUR THOUGHTS?
OF COURSE, THEY'D HAVE TO BE PRETTY BIG THOUGHTS!
TIM, NO!
ANOTHER DELAYING TACTIC!
NOT FOR LONG, MASTER!
BUDDA
SPWEEE!
SPWEEE!

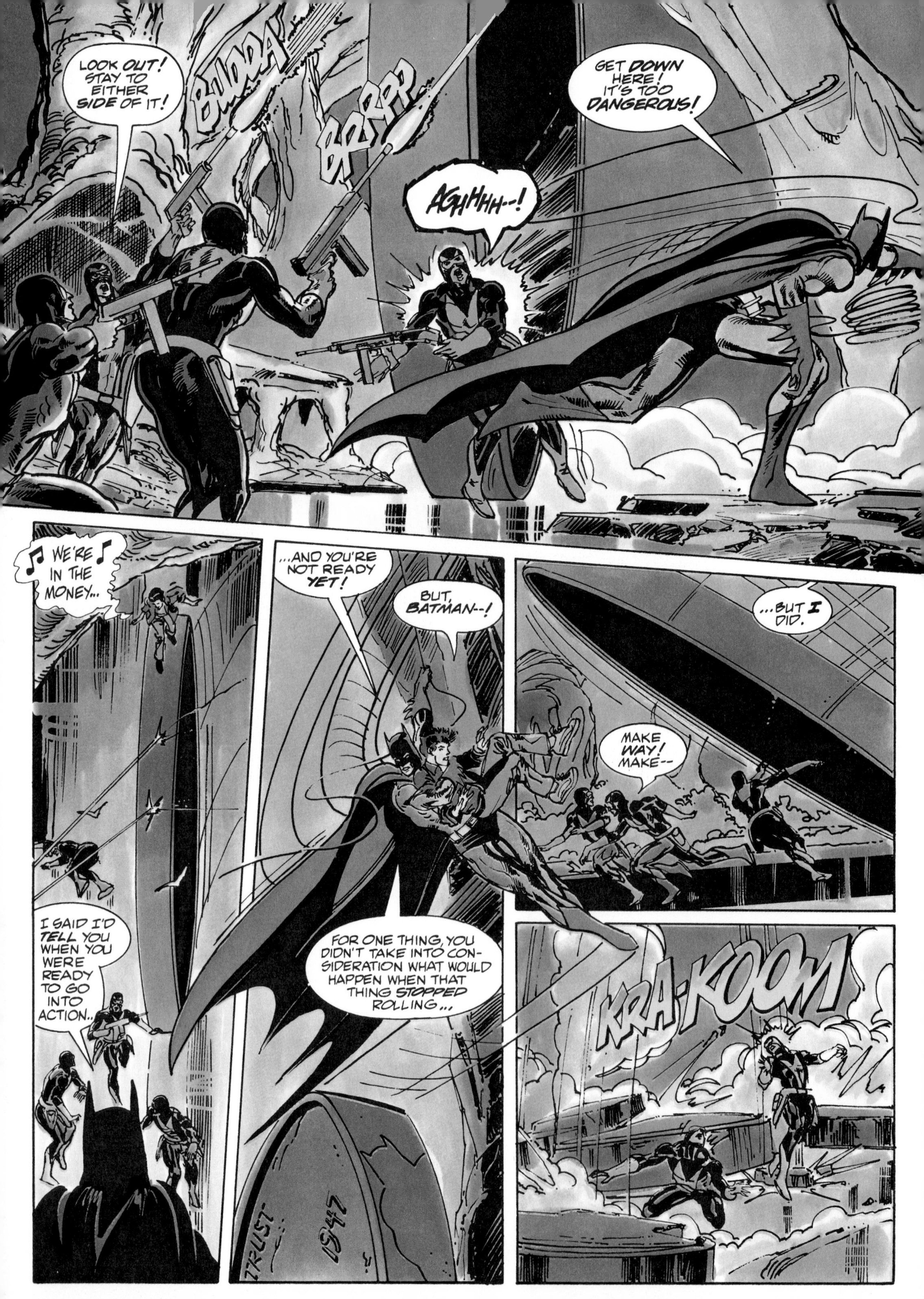

LOOK OUT! STAY TO EITHER SIDE OF IT!
BUDDA
BRRPP
GET DOWN HERE! IT'S TOO DANGEROUS!
AGHHHH--!
♫ WE'RE ♫ IN THE MONEY...
...AND YOU'RE NOT READY YET!
BUT, BATMAN--!
...BUT I DID.
MAKE WAY! MAKE--
I SAID I'D TELL YOU WHEN YOU WERE READY TO GO INTO ACTION...
FOR ONE THING, YOU DIDN'T TAKE INTO CONSIDERATION WHAT WOULD HAPPEN WHEN THAT THING STOPPED ROLLING...
KRA-KOOM
TRUST
1947

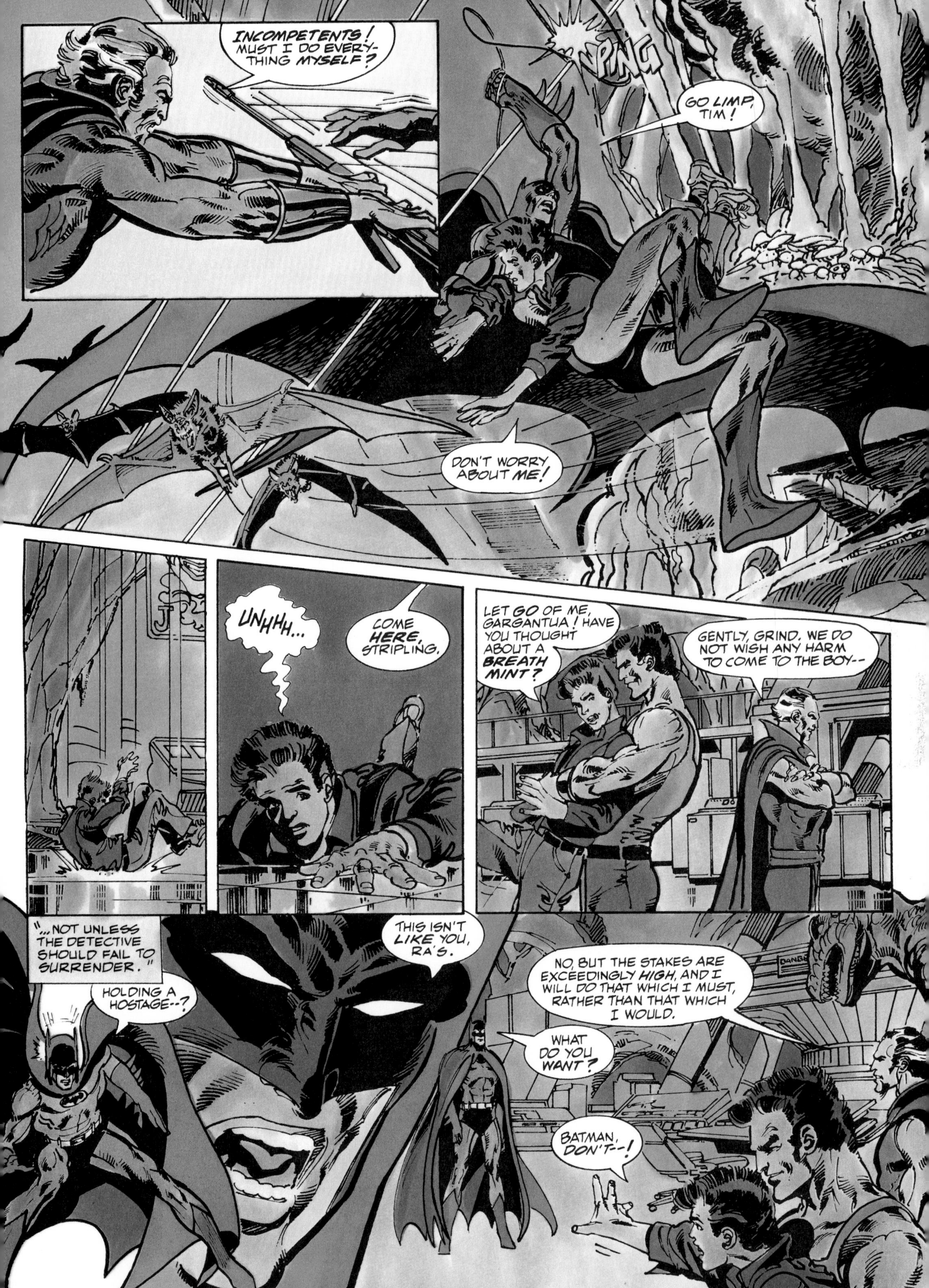
INCOMPETENTS! MUST I DO EVERYTHING MYSELF?
PING
GO LIMP, TIM!
DON'T WORRY ABOUT ME!
UNHHH...
COME HERE, STRIPLING.
LET GO OF ME, GARGANTUA! HAVE YOU THOUGHT ABOUT A BREATH MINT?
GENTLY, GRIND. WE DO NOT WISH ANY HARM TO COME TO THE BOY--
"...NOT UNLESS THE DETECTIVE SHOULD FAIL TO SURRENDER."
HOLDING A HOSTAGE--?
THIS ISN'T LIKE YOU, RA'S.
NO, BUT THE STAKES ARE EXCEEDINGLY HIGH, AND I WILL DO THAT WHICH I MUST, RATHER THAN THAT WHICH I WOULD.
WHAT DO YOU WANT?
BATMAN, DON'T--!

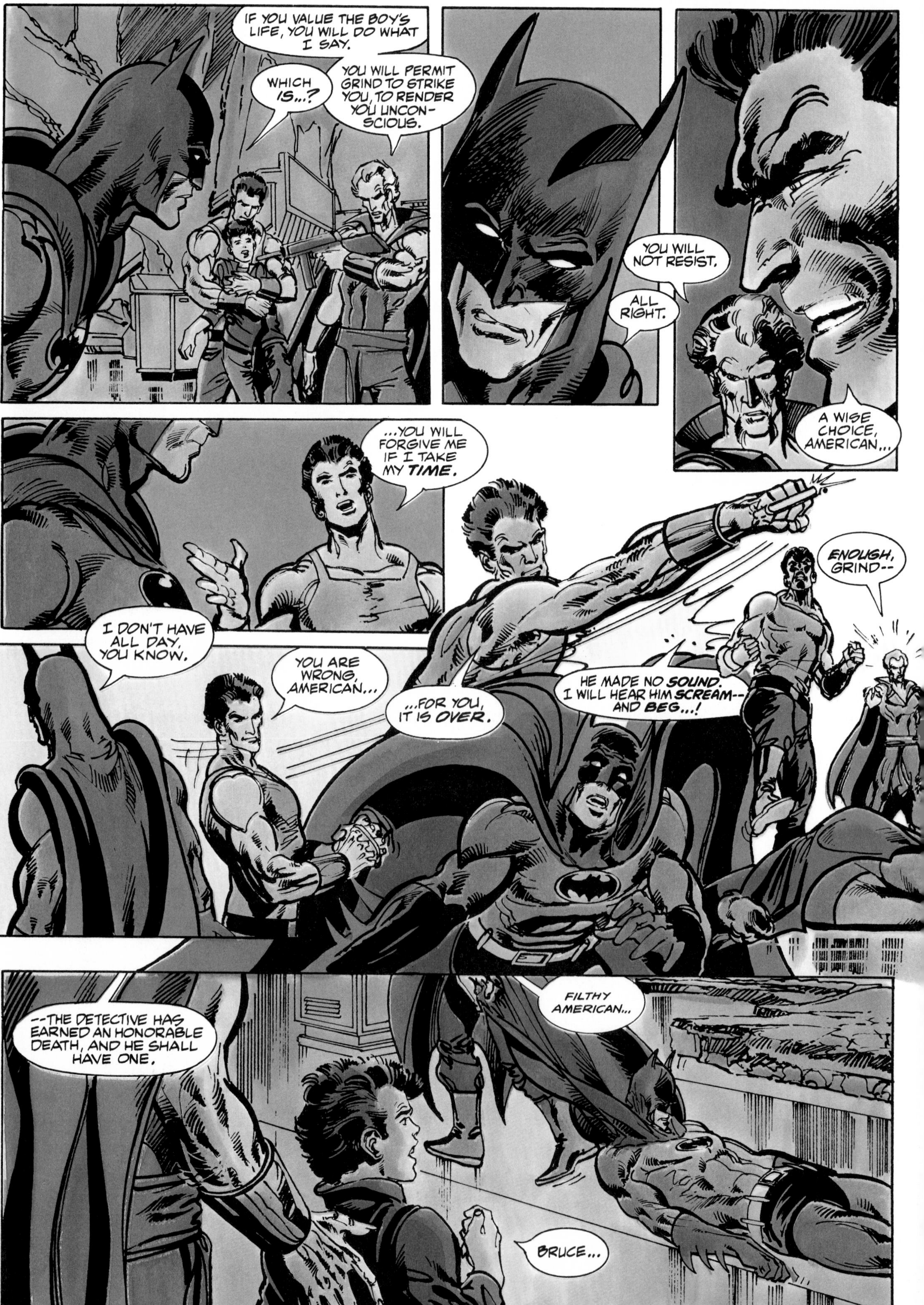
IF YOU VALUE THE BOY'S LIFE, YOU WILL DO WHAT I SAY.
WHICH IS...?
YOU WILL PERMIT GRIND TO STRIKE YOU, TO RENDER YOU UNCONSCIOUS.
YOU WILL NOT RESIST.
ALL RIGHT.
A WISE CHOICE, AMERICAN...
...YOU WILL FORGIVE ME IF I TAKE MY TIME.
I DON'T HAVE ALL DAY, YOU KNOW.
YOU ARE WRONG, AMERICAN...
...FOR YOU, IT IS OVER.
HE MADE NO SOUND. I WILL HEAR HIM SCREAM-- AND BEG...!
ENOUGH, GRIND--
--THE DETECTIVE HAS EARNED AN HONORABLE DEATH, AND HE SHALL HAVE ONE.
FILTHY AMERICAN...
BRUCE...

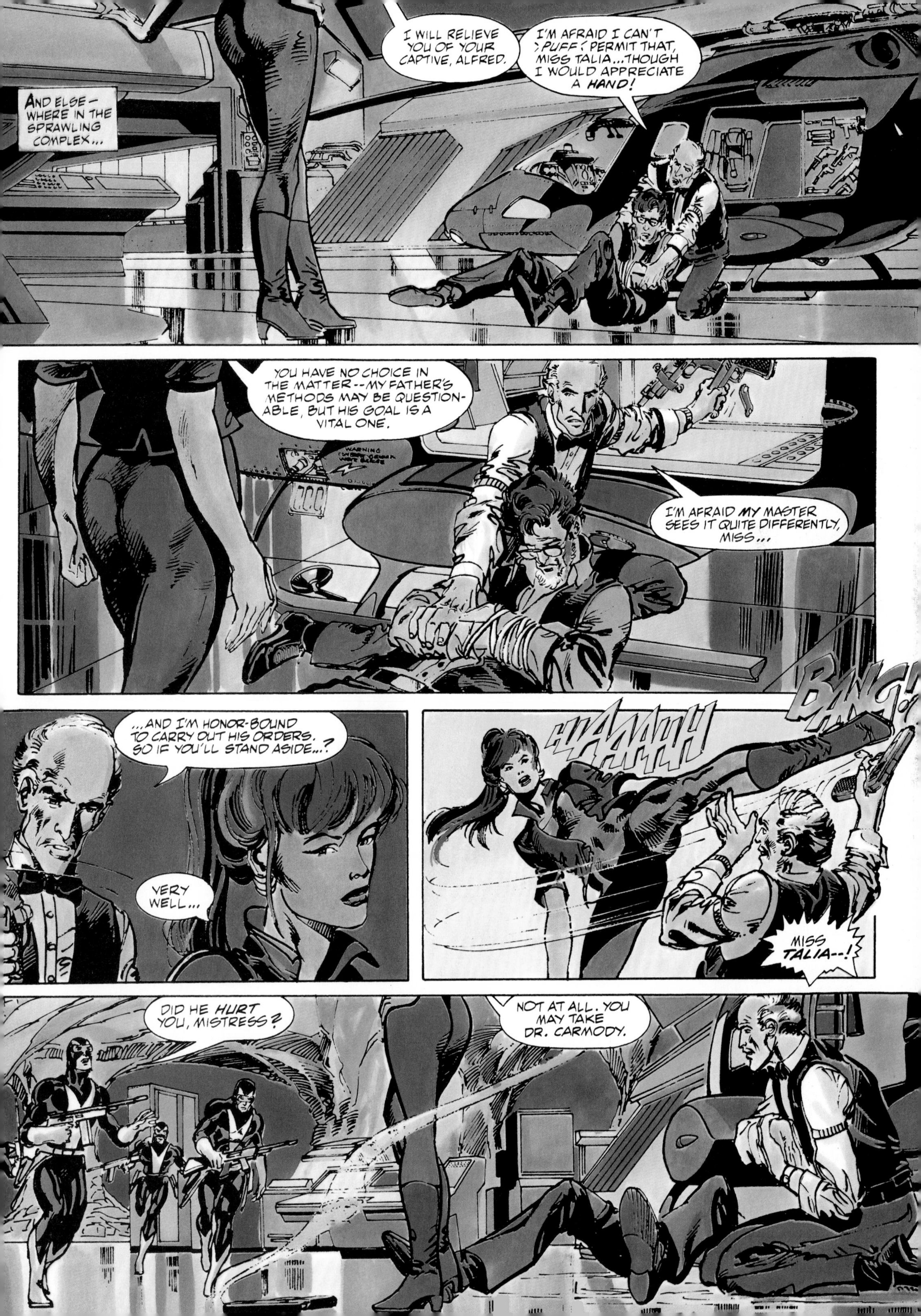

AND ELSE-WHERE IN THE SPRAWLING COMPLEX...
I WILL RELIEVE YOU OF YOUR CAPTIVE, ALFRED.
I'M AFRAID I CAN'T >PUFF< PERMIT THAT, MISS TALIA...THOUGH I WOULD APPRECIATE A HAND!
YOU HAVE NO CHOICE IN THE MATTER--MY FATHER'S METHODS MAY BE QUESTION-ABLE, BUT HIS GOAL IS A VITAL ONE.
I'M AFRAID MY MASTER SEES IT QUITE DIFFERENTLY, MISS...
...AND I'M HONOR-BOUND TO CARRY OUT HIS ORDERS. SO IF YOU'LL STAND ASIDE...?
VERY WELL...
HWAAAHH
BANG!
MISS TALIA--!
DID HE HURT YOU, MISTRESS?
NOT AT ALL. YOU MAY TAKE DR. CARMODY.

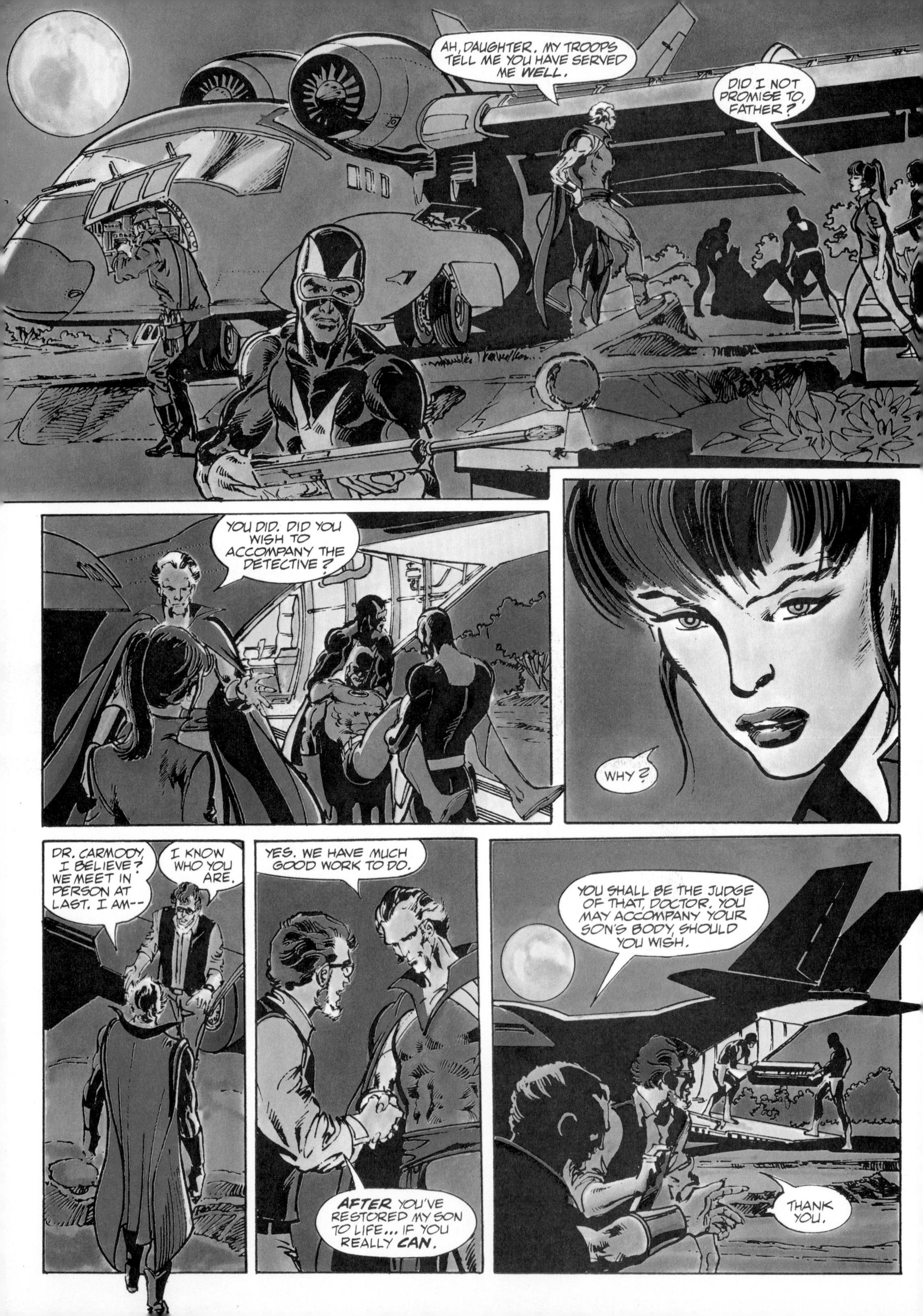
AH, DAUGHTER. MY TROOPS TELL ME YOU HAVE SERVED ME WELL.
DID I NOT PROMISE TO, FATHER?
YOU DID. DID YOU WISH TO ACCOMPANY THE DETECTIVE?
WHY?
DR. CARMODY, I BELIEVE? WE MEET IN PERSON AT LAST. I AM--
I KNOW WHO YOU ARE.
YES. WE HAVE MUCH GOOD WORK TO DO.
AFTER YOU'VE RESTORED MY SON TO LIFE... IF YOU REALLY CAN.
YOU SHALL BE THE JUDGE OF THAT, DOCTOR. YOU MAY ACCOMPANY YOUR SON'S BODY, SHOULD YOU WISH.
THANK YOU.

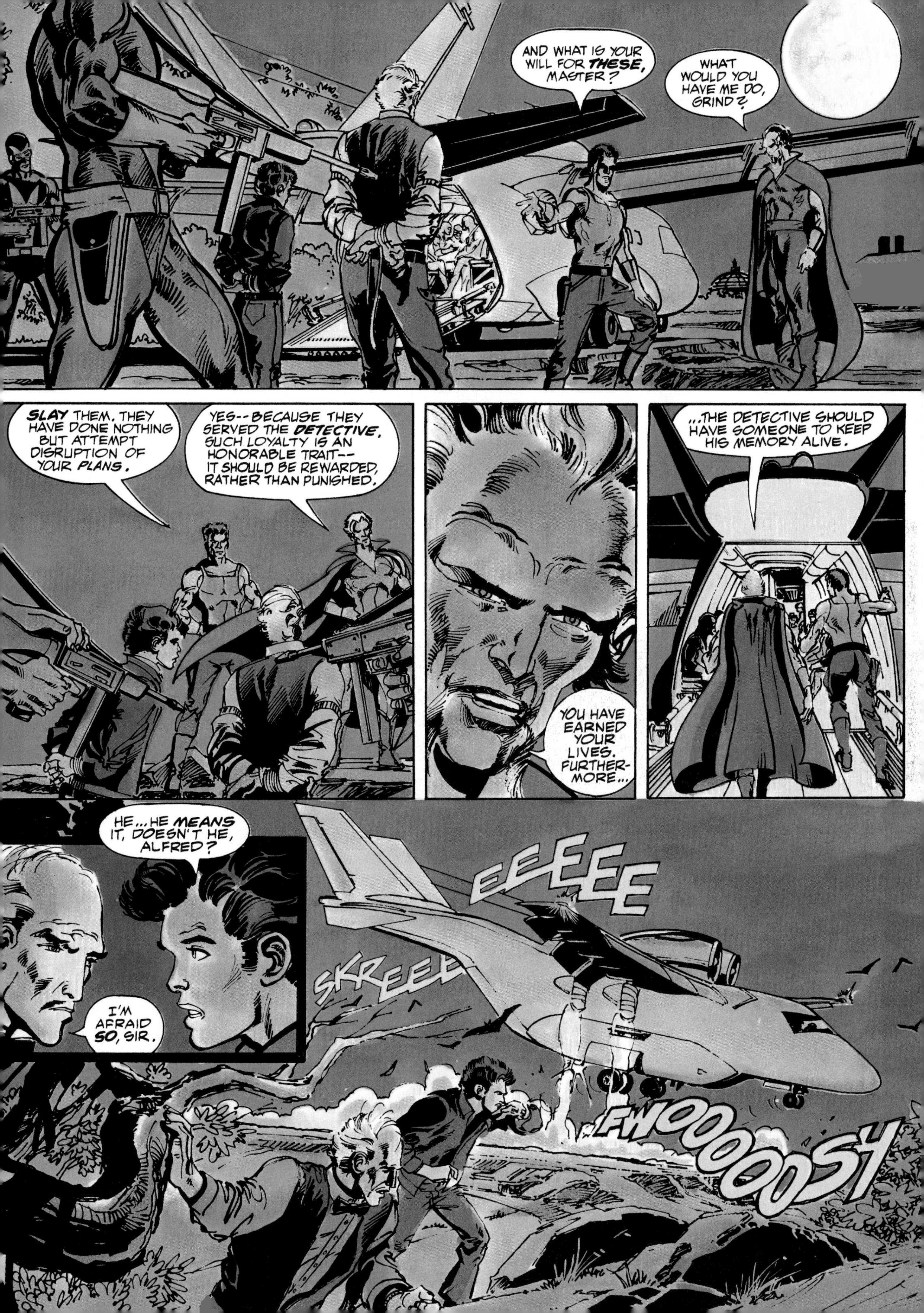
AND WHAT IS YOUR WILL FOR THESE, MASTER?
WHAT WOULD YOU HAVE ME DO, GRIND?
SLAY THEM. THEY HAVE DONE NOTHING BUT ATTEMPT DISRUPTION OF YOUR PLANS.
YES--BECAUSE THEY SERVED THE DETECTIVE. SUCH LOYALTY IS AN HONORABLE TRAIT--IT SHOULD BE REWARDED, RATHER THAN PUNISHED.
YOU HAVE EARNED YOUR LIVES. FURTHER-MORE...
...THE DETECTIVE SHOULD HAVE SOMEONE TO KEEP HIS MEMORY ALIVE.
HE...HE MEANS IT, DOESN'T HE, ALFRED?
I'M AFRAID SO, SIR.
EEEEEE
SKREEEE
FWOOOOOOSH

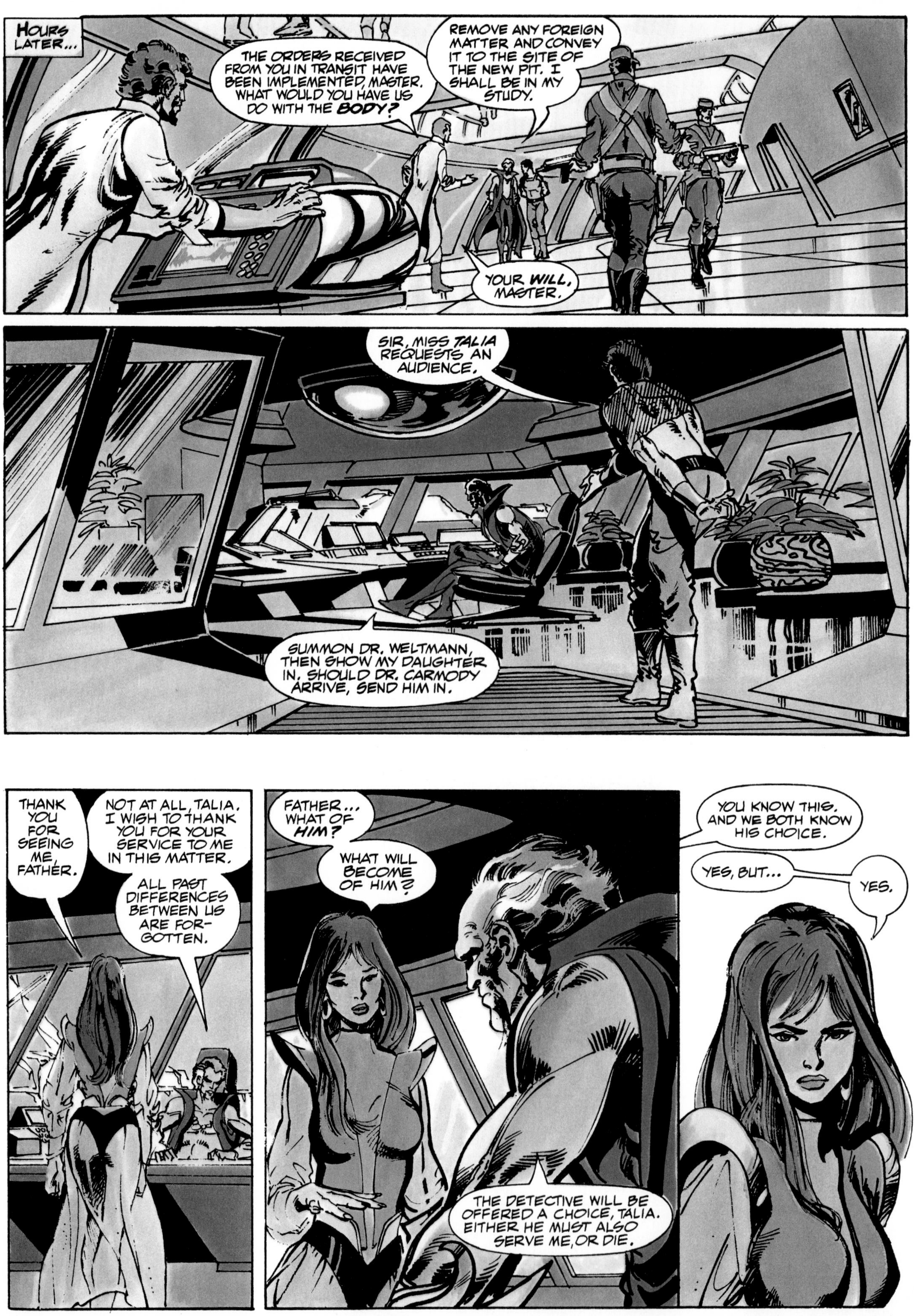
HOURS LATER...
THE ORDERS RECEIVED FROM YOU IN TRANSIT HAVE BEEN IMPLEMENTED, MASTER. WHAT WOULD YOU HAVE US DO WITH THE BODY?
REMOVE ANY FOREIGN MATTER AND CONVEY IT TO THE SITE OF THE NEW PIT. I SHALL BE IN MY STUDY.
YOUR WILL, MASTER.
SIR, MISS TALIA REQUESTS AN AUDIENCE.
SUMMON DR. WELTMANN, THEN SHOW MY DAUGHTER IN. SHOULD DR. CARMODY ARRIVE, SEND HIM IN.
THANK YOU FOR SEEING ME, FATHER.
NOT AT ALL, TALIA. I WISH TO THANK YOU FOR YOUR SERVICE TO ME IN THIS MATTER.
ALL PAST DIFFERENCES BETWEEN US ARE FORGOTTEN.
FATHER... WHAT OF HIM?
WHAT WILL BECOME OF HIM?
THE DETECTIVE WILL BE OFFERED A CHOICE, TALIA. EITHER HE MUST ALSO SERVE ME, OR DIE.
YOU KNOW THIS. AND WE BOTH KNOW HIS CHOICE.
YES, BUT...
YES.

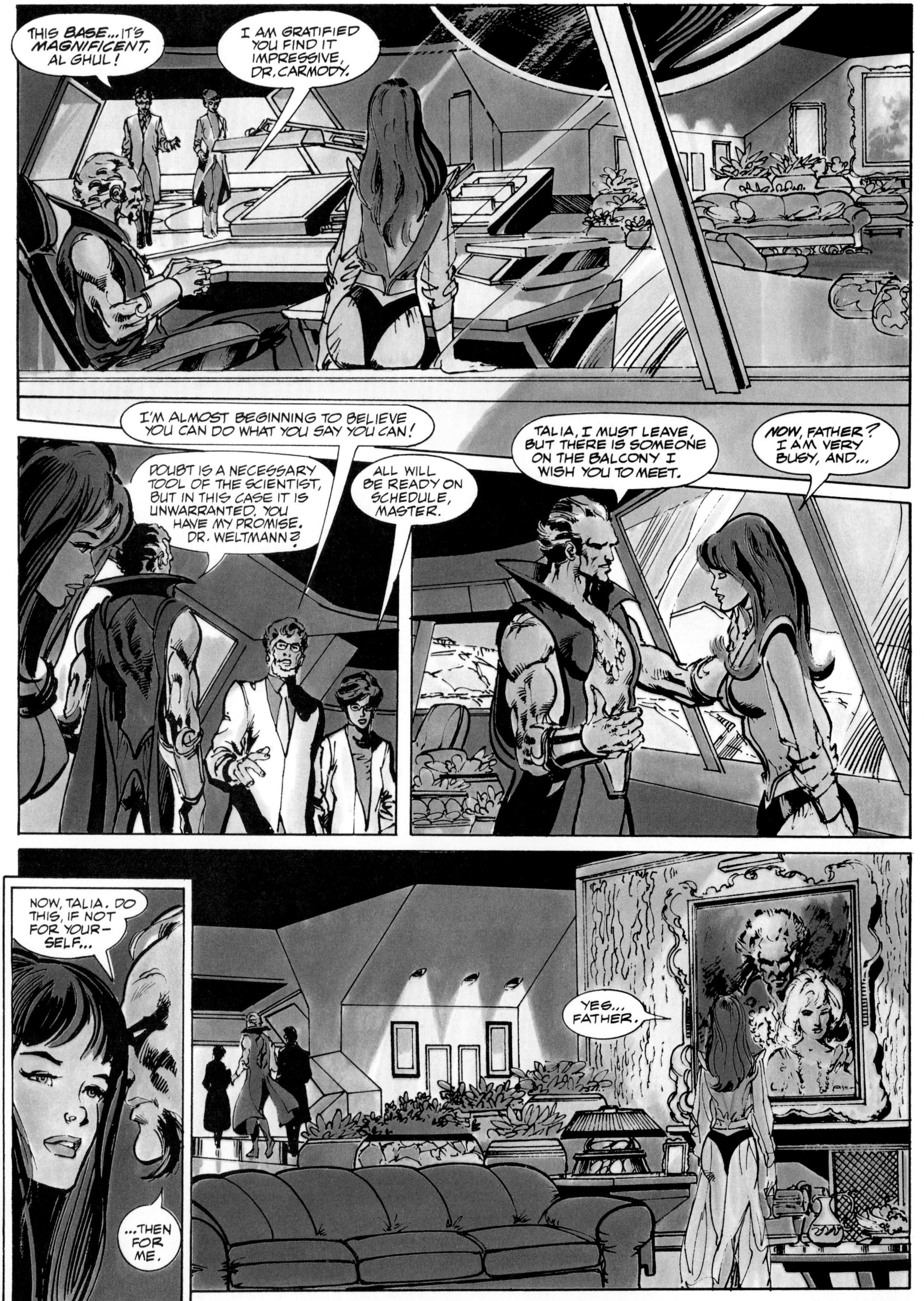
THIS BASE... IT'S MAGNIFICENT, AL GHUL!
I AM GRATIFIED YOU FIND IT IMPRESSIVE, DR. CARMODY.
I'M ALMOST BEGINNING TO BELIEVE YOU CAN DO WHAT YOU SAY YOU CAN!
DOUBT IS A NECESSARY TOOL OF THE SCIENTIST, BUT IN THIS CASE IT IS UNWARRANTED. YOU HAVE MY PROMISE. DR. WELTMANN?
ALL WILL BE READY ON SCHEDULE, MASTER.
TALIA, I MUST LEAVE, BUT THERE IS SOMEONE ON THE BALCONY I WISH YOU TO MEET.
NOW, FATHER? I AM VERY BUSY, AND...
NOW, TALIA. DO THIS, IF NOT FOR YOUR-SELF...
...THEN FOR ME.
YES... FATHER.

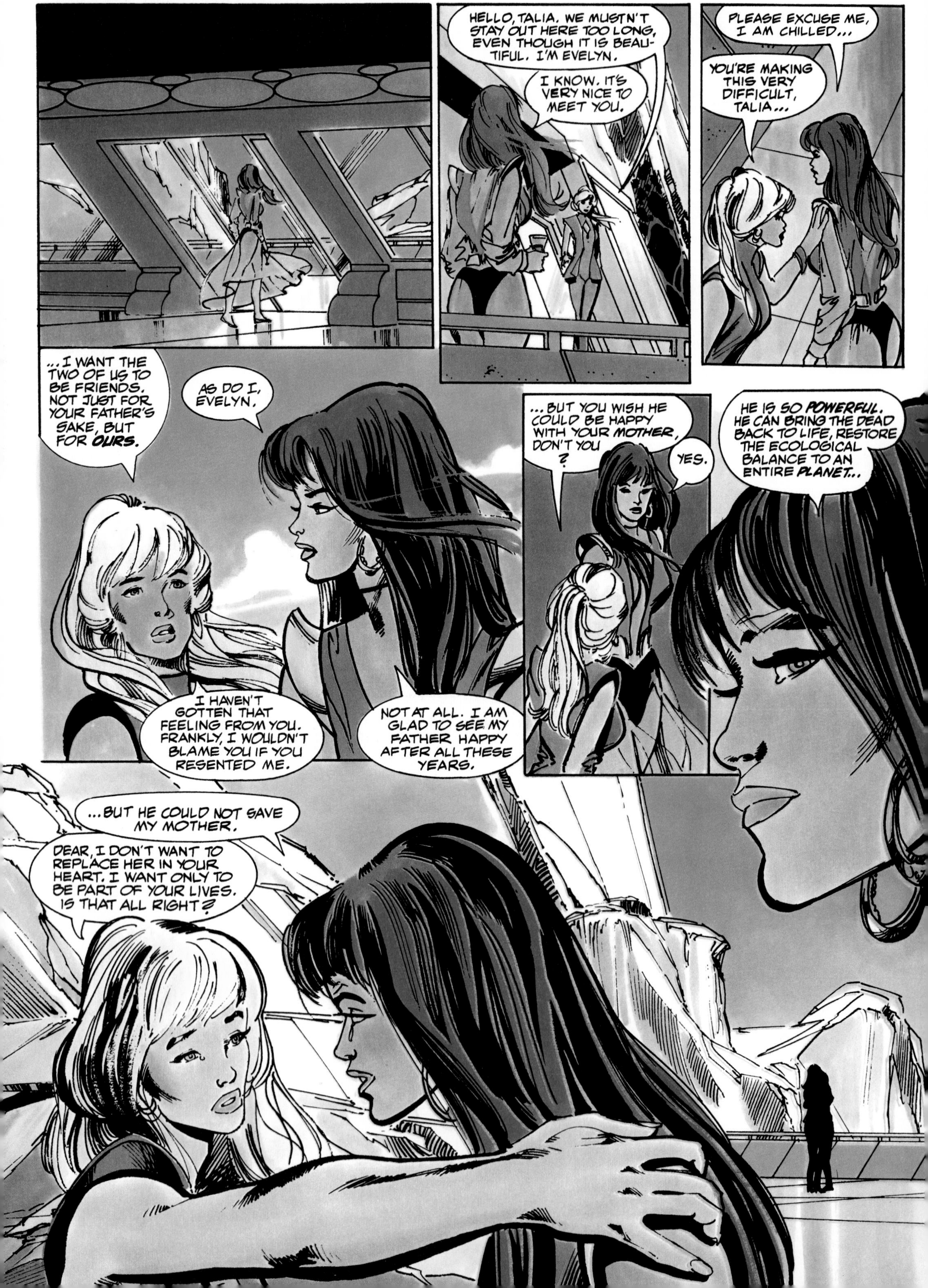

HELLO, TALIA. WE MUSTN'T STAY OUT HERE TOO LONG, EVEN THOUGH IT IS BEAUTIFUL. I'M EVELYN.
I KNOW. IT'S VERY NICE TO MEET YOU.
PLEASE EXCUSE ME, I AM CHILLED...
YOU'RE MAKING THIS VERY DIFFICULT, TALIA...
...I WANT THE TWO OF US TO BE FRIENDS. NOT JUST FOR YOUR FATHER'S SAKE, BUT FOR OURS.
AS DO I, EVELYN.
I HAVEN'T GOTTEN THAT FEELING FROM YOU. FRANKLY, I WOULDN'T BLAME YOU IF YOU RESENTED ME.
NOT AT ALL. I AM GLAD TO SEE MY FATHER HAPPY AFTER ALL THESE YEARS.
...BUT YOU WISH HE COULD BE HAPPY WITH YOUR MOTHER, DON'T YOU?
YES.
HE IS SO POWERFUL. HE CAN BRING THE DEAD BACK TO LIFE, RESTORE THE ECOLOGICAL BALANCE TO AN ENTIRE PLANET...
...BUT HE COULD NOT SAVE MY MOTHER.
DEAR, I DON'T WANT TO REPLACE HER IN YOUR HEART. I WANT ONLY TO BE PART OF YOUR LIVES. IS THAT ALL RIGHT?

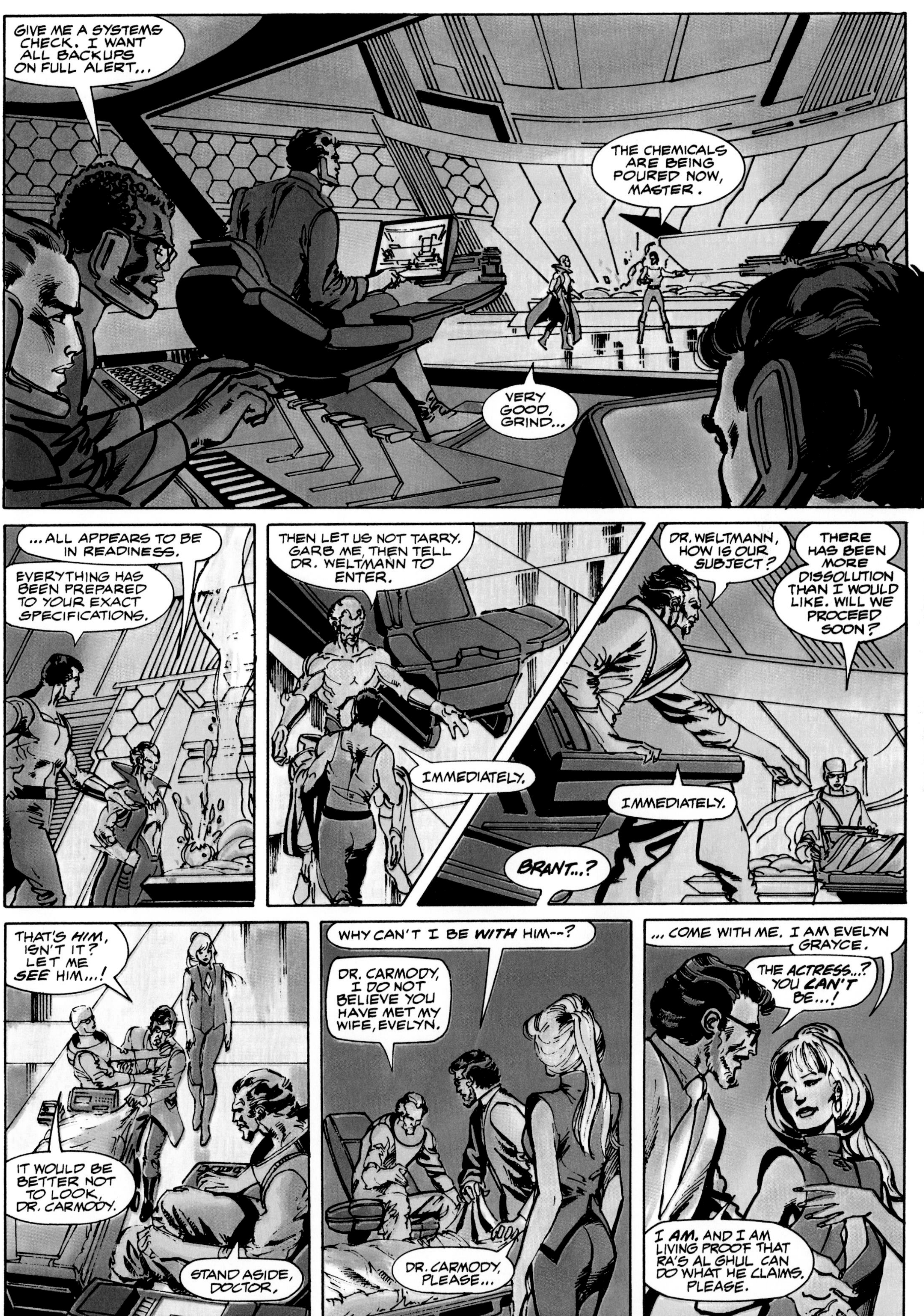
GIVE ME A SYSTEMS CHECK. I WANT ALL BACKUPS ON FULL ALERT...
THE CHEMICALS ARE BEING POURED NOW, MASTER.
VERY GOOD, GRIND...
...ALL APPEARS TO BE IN READINESS.
EVERYTHING HAS BEEN PREPARED TO YOUR EXACT SPECIFICATIONS.
THEN LET US NOT TARRY. GARB ME, THEN TELL DR. WELTMANN TO ENTER.
IMMEDIATELY.
DR. WELTMANN, HOW IS OUR SUBJECT?
THERE HAS BEEN MORE DISSOLUTION THAN I WOULD LIKE. WILL WE PROCEED SOON?
IMMEDIATELY.
BRANT...?
THAT'S HIM, ISN'T IT? LET ME SEE HIM...!
IT WOULD BE BETTER NOT TO LOOK, DR. CARMODY.
STAND ASIDE, DOCTOR.
WHY CAN'T I BE WITH HIM--?
DR. CARMODY, I DO NOT BELIEVE YOU HAVE MET MY WIFE, EVELYN.
DR. CARMODY, PLEASE...
...COME WITH ME. I AM EVELYN GRAYCE.
THE ACTRESS...? YOU CAN'T BE...!
I AM. AND I AM LIVING PROOF THAT RA'S AL GHUL CAN DO WHAT HE CLAIMS. PLEASE.

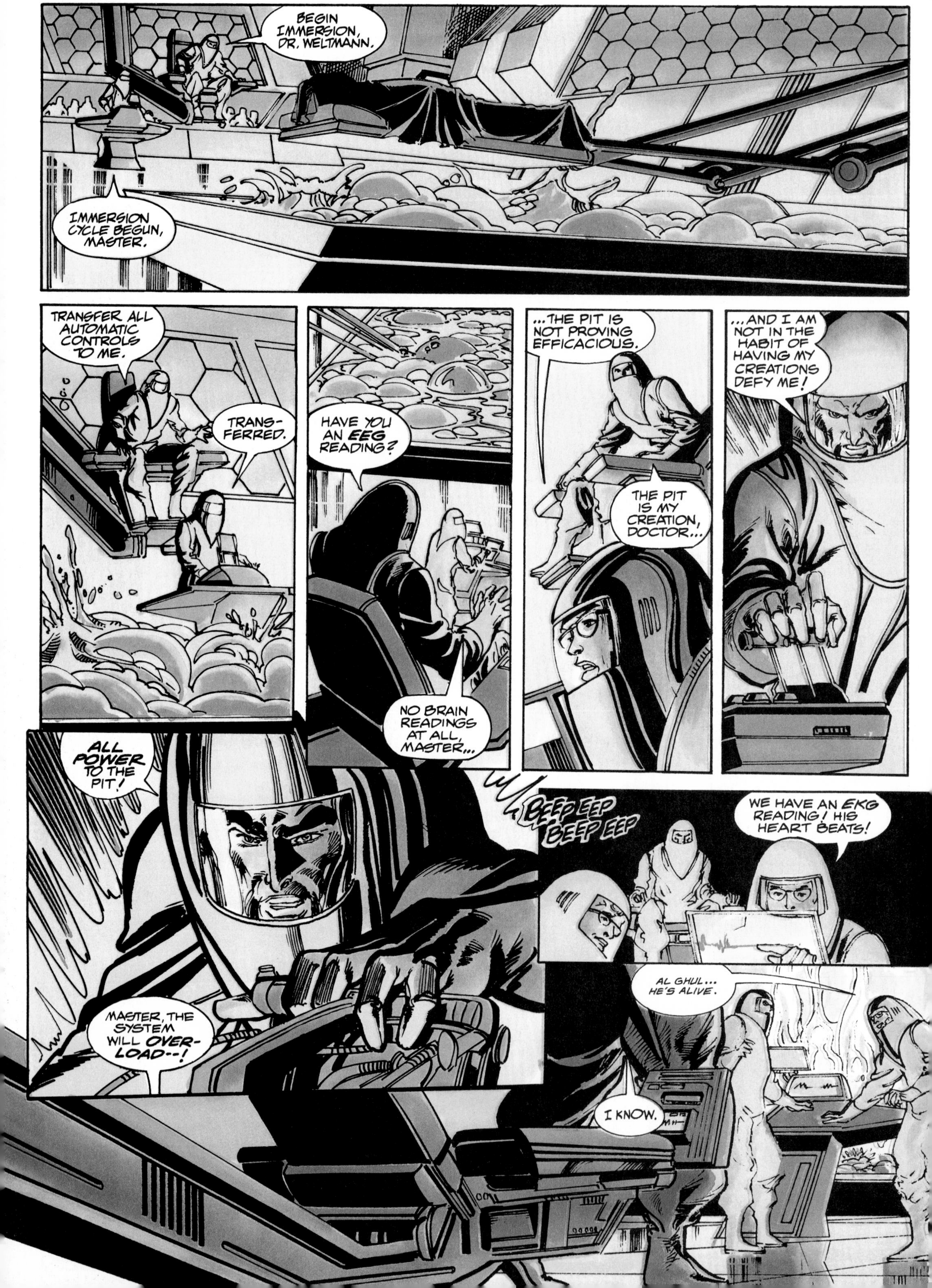
BEGIN IMMERSION, DR. WELTMANN.
IMMERSION CYCLE BEGUN, MASTER.
TRANSFER ALL AUTOMATIC CONTROLS TO ME.
TRANS-FERRED.
HAVE YOU AN EEG READING?
NO BRAIN READINGS AT ALL, MASTER...
...THE PIT IS NOT PROVING EFFICACIOUS.
THE PIT IS MY CREATION, DOCTOR...
...AND I AM NOT IN THE HABIT OF HAVING MY CREATIONS DEFY ME!
ALL POWER TO THE PIT!
MASTER, THE SYSTEM WILL OVER-LOAD--!
BEEP EEP BEEP EEP
WE HAVE AN EKG READING! HIS HEART BEATS!
AL GHUL... HE'S ALIVE.
I KNOW.

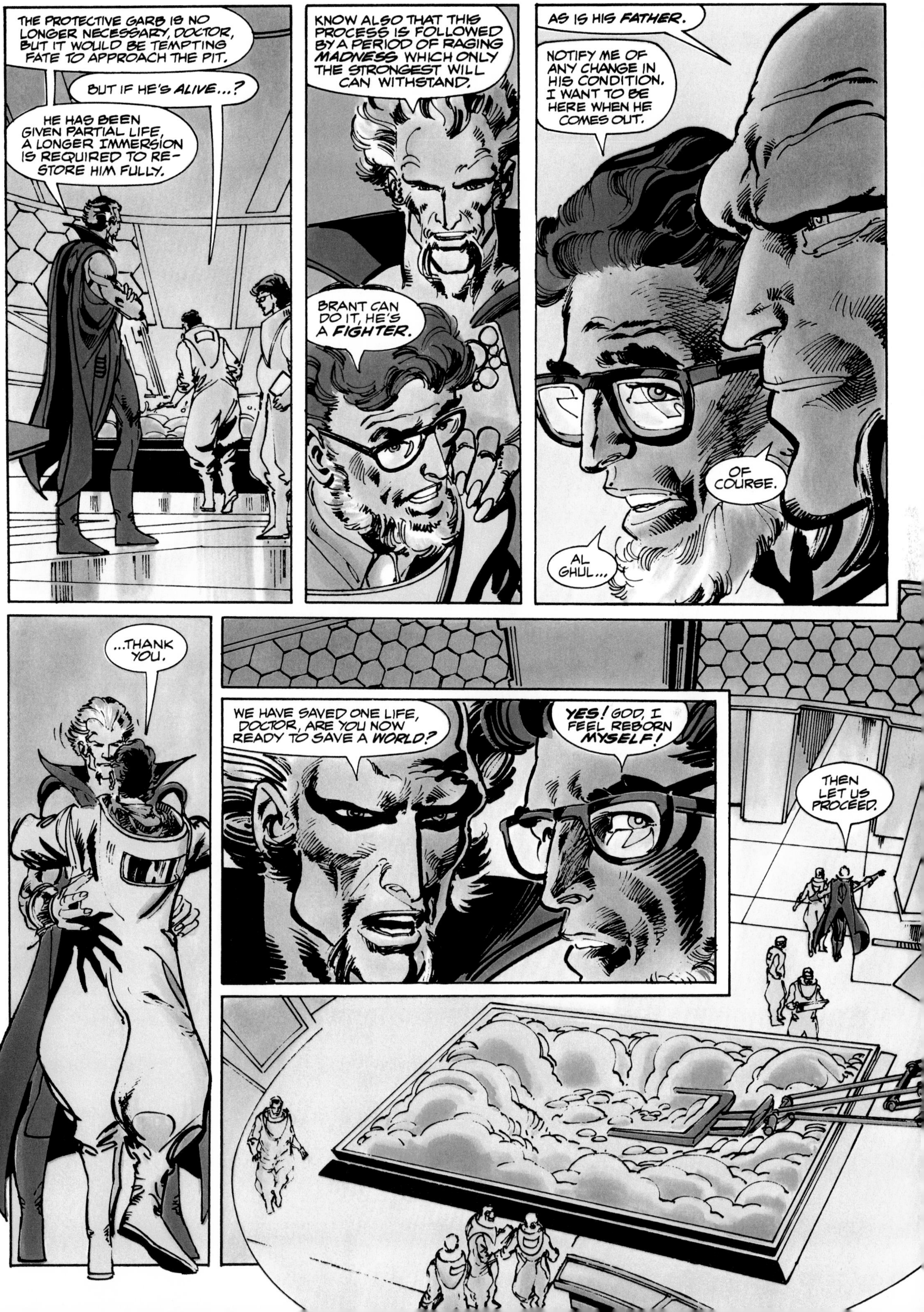
THE PROTECTIVE GARB IS NO LONGER NECESSARY, DOCTOR, BUT IT WOULD BE TEMPTING FATE TO APPROACH THE PIT.
BUT IF HE'S ALIVE...?
HE HAS BEEN GIVEN PARTIAL LIFE, A LONGER IMMERSION IS REQUIRED TO RE-STORE HIM FULLY.
KNOW ALSO THAT THIS PROCESS IS FOLLOWED BY A PERIOD OF RAGING MADNESS WHICH ONLY THE STRONGEST WILL CAN WITHSTAND.
BRANT CAN DO IT, HE'S A FIGHTER.
AS IS HIS FATHER.
NOTIFY ME OF ANY CHANGE IN HIS CONDITION. I WANT TO BE HERE WHEN HE COMES OUT.
OF COURSE.
AL GHUL...
...THANK YOU.
WE HAVE SAVED ONE LIFE, DOCTOR, ARE YOU NOW READY TO SAVE A WORLD?
YES! GOD, I FEEL REBORN MYSELF!
THEN LET US PROCEED.

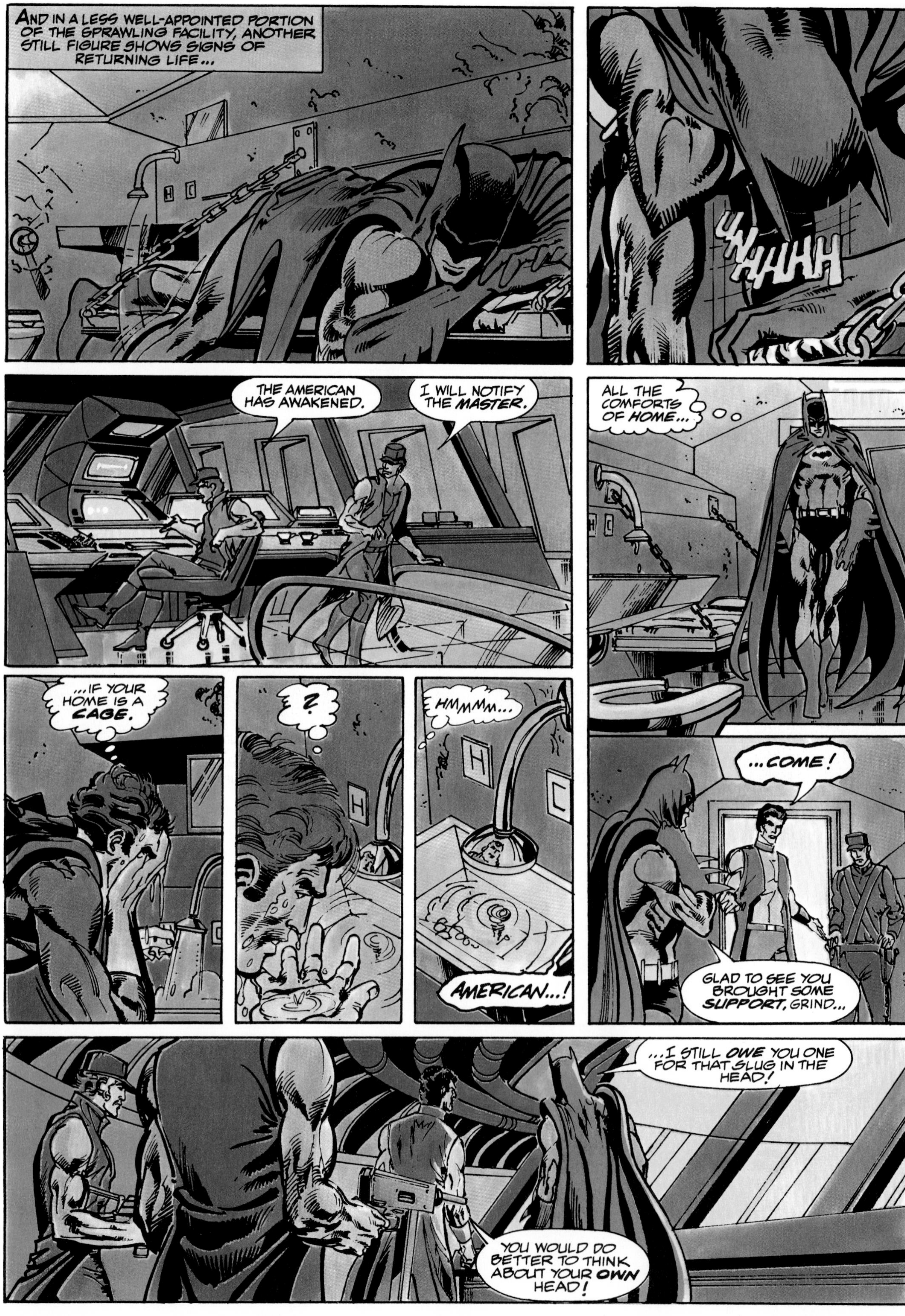

AND IN A LESS WELL-APPOINTED PORTION OF THE SPRAWLING FACILITY, ANOTHER STILL FIGURE SHOWS SIGNS OF RETURNING LIFE...
UNHHHHH
THE AMERICAN HAS AWAKENED.
I WILL NOTIFY THE MASTER.
ALL THE COMFORTS OF HOME...
...IF YOUR HOME IS A CAGE.
?
HMMMMM...
AMERICAN...!
...COME!
GLAD TO SEE YOU BROUGHT SOME SUPPORT, GRIND...
...I STILL OWE YOU ONE FOR THAT SLUG IN THE HEAD!
YOU WOULD DO BETTER TO THINK ABOUT YOUR OWN HEAD!

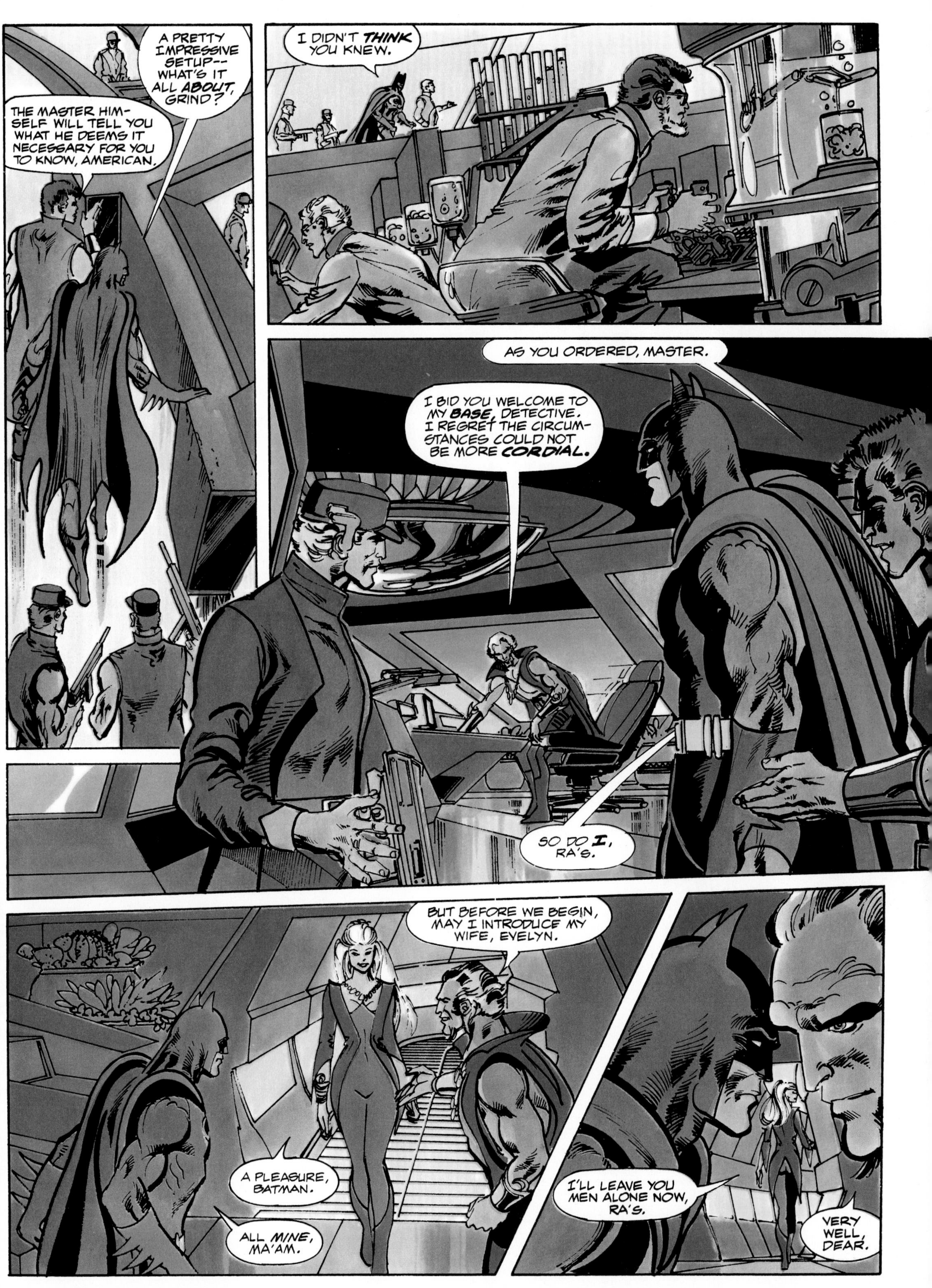
A PRETTY IMPRESSIVE SETUP-- WHAT'S IT ALL ABOUT, GRIND?
THE MASTER HIMSELF WILL TELL YOU WHAT HE DEEMS IT NECESSARY FOR YOU TO KNOW, AMERICAN.
I DIDN'T THINK YOU KNEW.
AS YOU ORDERED, MASTER.
I BID YOU WELCOME TO MY BASE, DETECTIVE. I REGRET THE CIRCUMSTANCES COULD NOT BE MORE CORDIAL.
SO DO I, RA'S.
BUT BEFORE WE BEGIN, MAY I INTRODUCE MY WIFE, EVELYN.
A PLEASURE, BATMAN.
ALL MINE, MA'AM.
I'LL LEAVE YOU MEN ALONE NOW, RA'S.
VERY WELL, DEAR.

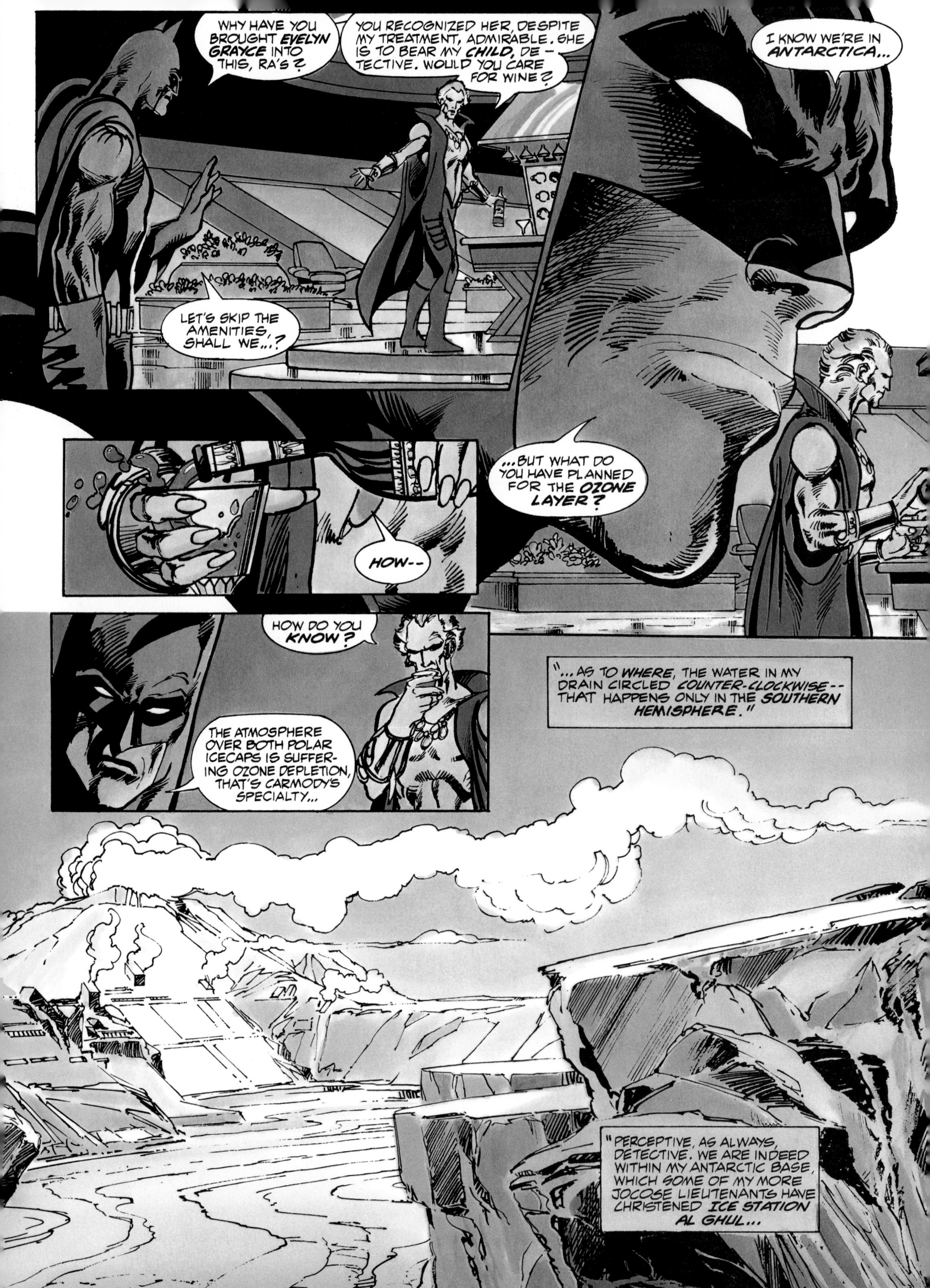
WHY HAVE YOU BROUGHT EVELYN GRAYCE INTO THIS, RA'S?
YOU RECOGNIZED HER, DESPITE MY TREATMENT, ADMIRABLE. SHE IS TO BEAR MY CHILD, DETECTIVE. WOULD YOU CARE FOR WINE?
LET'S SKIP THE AMENITIES, SHALL WE...?
I KNOW WE'RE IN ANTARCTICA...
...BUT WHAT DO YOU HAVE PLANNED FOR THE OZONE LAYER?
HOW--
HOW DO YOU KNOW?
THE ATMOSPHERE OVER BOTH POLAR ICECAPS IS SUFFERING OZONE DEPLETION, THAT'S CARMODY'S SPECIALTY...
"...AS TO WHERE, THE WATER IN MY DRAIN CIRCLED COUNTER-CLOCKWISE--THAT HAPPENS ONLY IN THE SOUTHERN HEMISPHERE."
"PERCEPTIVE, AS ALWAYS, DETECTIVE. WE ARE INDEED WITHIN MY ANTARCTIC BASE, WHICH SOME OF MY MORE JOCOSE LIEUTENANTS HAVE CHRISTENED ICE STATION AL GHUL...

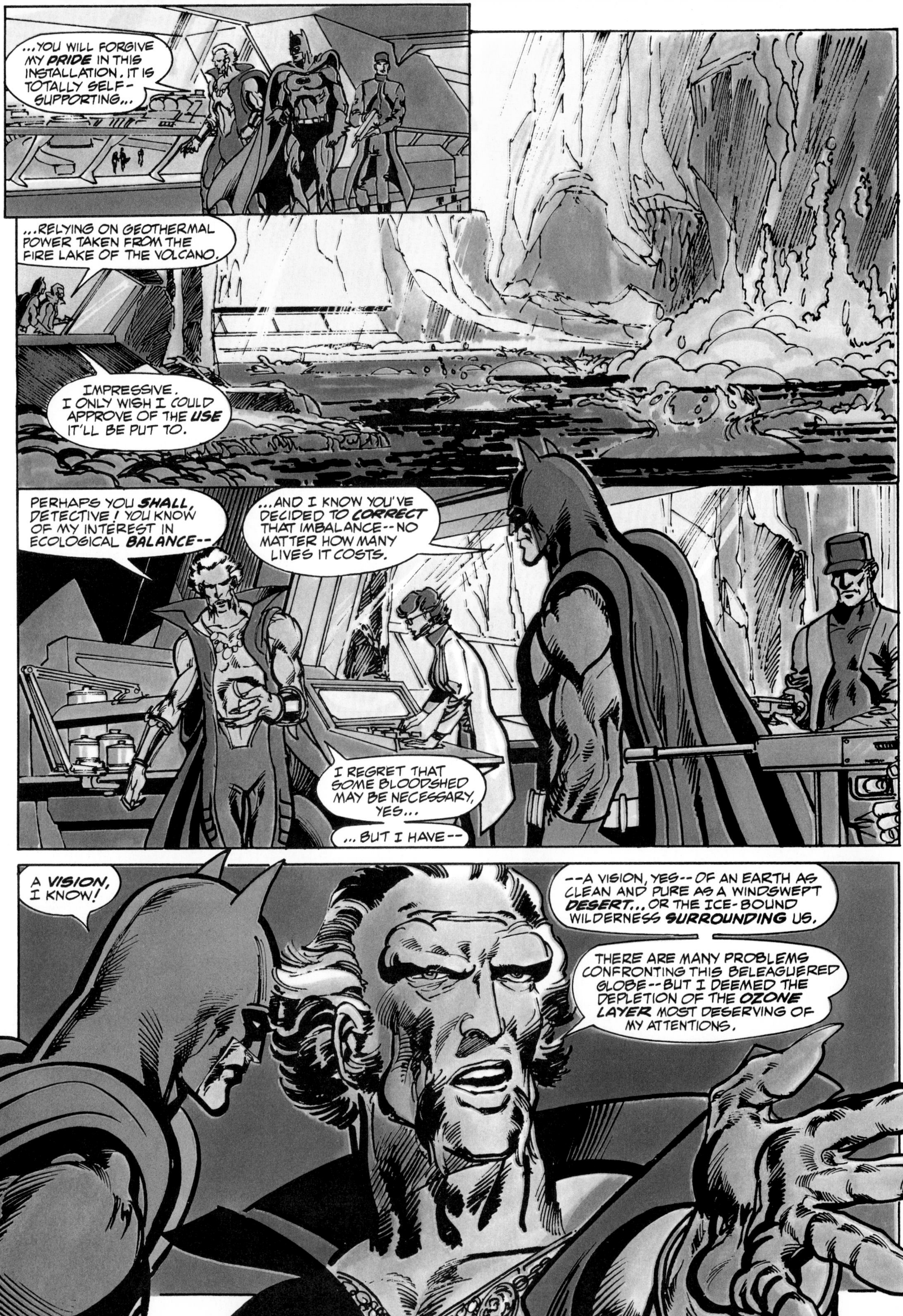
...YOU WILL FORGIVE MY PRIDE IN THIS INSTALLATION. IT IS TOTALLY SELF-SUPPORTING...
...RELYING ON GEOTHERMAL POWER TAKEN FROM THE FIRE LAKE OF THE VOLCANO.
IMPRESSIVE. I ONLY WISH I COULD APPROVE OF THE USE IT'LL BE PUT TO.
PERHAPS YOU SHALL, DETECTIVE! YOU KNOW OF MY INTEREST IN ECOLOGICAL BALANCE--
...AND I KNOW YOU'VE DECIDED TO CORRECT THAT IMBALANCE--NO MATTER HOW MANY LIVES IT COSTS.
I REGRET THAT SOME BLOODSHED MAY BE NECESSARY, YES...
...BUT I HAVE--
A VISION, I KNOW!
--A VISION, YES--OF AN EARTH AS CLEAN AND PURE AS A WINDSWEPT DESERT... OR THE ICE-BOUND WILDERNESS SURROUNDING US.
THERE ARE MANY PROBLEMS CONFRONTING THIS BELEAGUERED GLOBE--BUT I DEEMED THE DEPLETION OF THE OZONE LAYER MOST DESERVING OF MY ATTENTIONS.

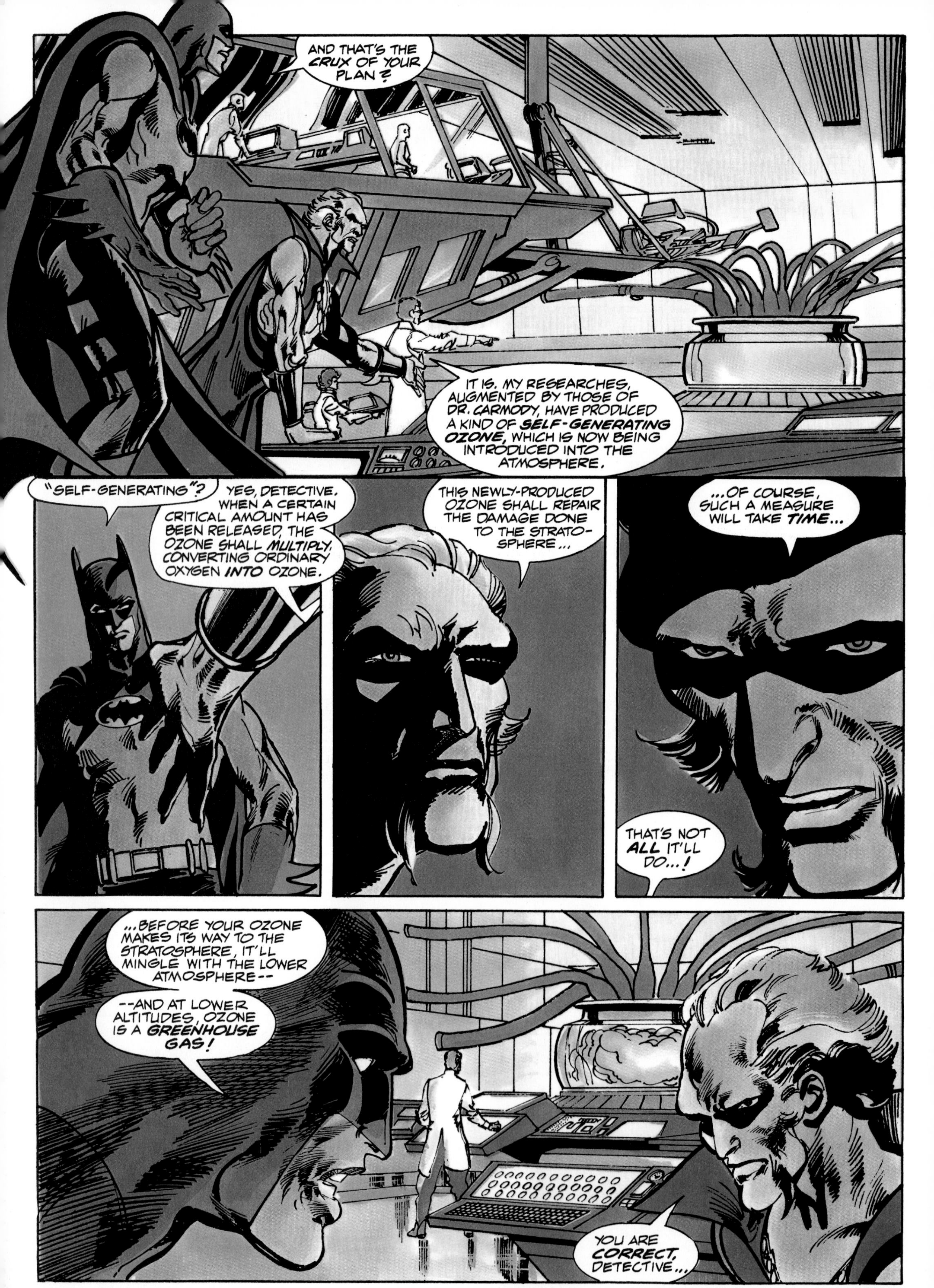

AND THAT'S THE CRUX OF YOUR PLAN?
IT IS. MY RESEARCHES, AUGMENTED BY THOSE OF DR. CARMODY, HAVE PRODUCED A KIND OF SELF-GENERATING OZONE, WHICH IS NOW BEING INTRODUCED INTO THE ATMOSPHERE.
"SELF-GENERATING"?
YES, DETECTIVE. WHEN A CERTAIN CRITICAL AMOUNT HAS BEEN RELEASED, THE OZONE SHALL MULTIPLY, CONVERTING ORDINARY OXYGEN INTO OZONE.
THIS NEWLY-PRODUCED OZONE SHALL REPAIR THE DAMAGE DONE TO THE STRATOSPHERE...
...OF COURSE, SUCH A MEASURE WILL TAKE TIME...
THAT'S NOT ALL IT'LL DO...!
...BEFORE YOUR OZONE MAKES ITS WAY TO THE STRATOSPHERE, IT'LL MINGLE WITH THE LOWER ATMOSPHERE--
--AND AT LOWER ALTITUDES, OZONE IS A GREENHOUSE GAS!
YOU ARE CORRECT, DETECTIVE...

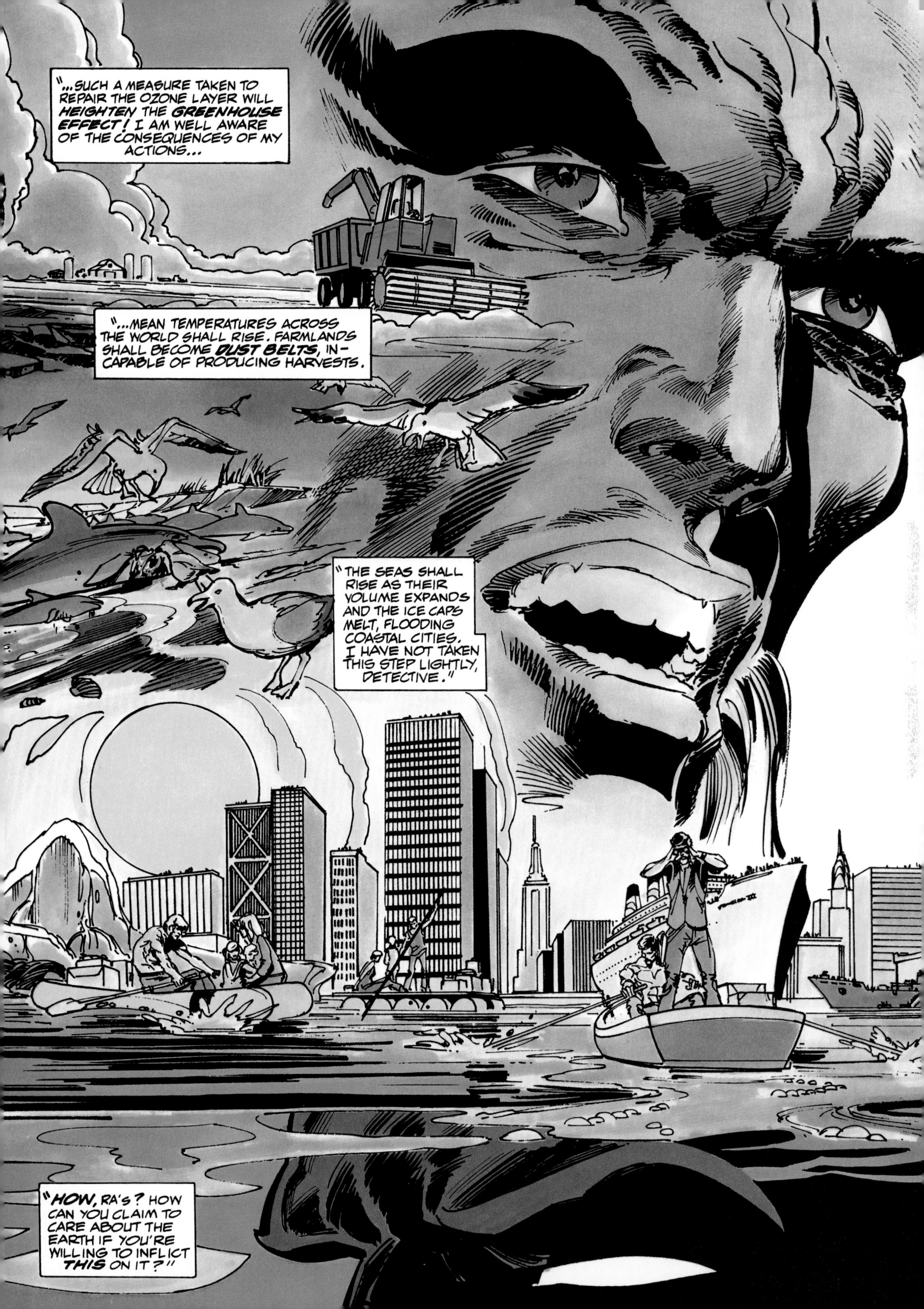
"...SUCH A MEASURE TAKEN TO REPAIR THE OZONE LAYER WILL HEIGHTEN THE GREENHOUSE EFFECT! I AM WELL AWARE OF THE CONSEQUENCES OF MY ACTIONS...
"...MEAN TEMPERATURES ACROSS THE WORLD SHALL RISE. FARMLANDS SHALL BECOME DUST BELTS, INCAPABLE OF PRODUCING HARVESTS.
"THE SEAS SHALL RISE AS THEIR VOLUME EXPANDS AND THE ICE CAPS MELT, FLOODING COASTAL CITIES. I HAVE NOT TAKEN THIS STEP LIGHTLY, DETECTIVE."
"HOW, RA'S? HOW CAN YOU CLAIM TO CARE ABOUT THE EARTH IF YOU'RE WILLING TO INFLICT THIS ON IT?"

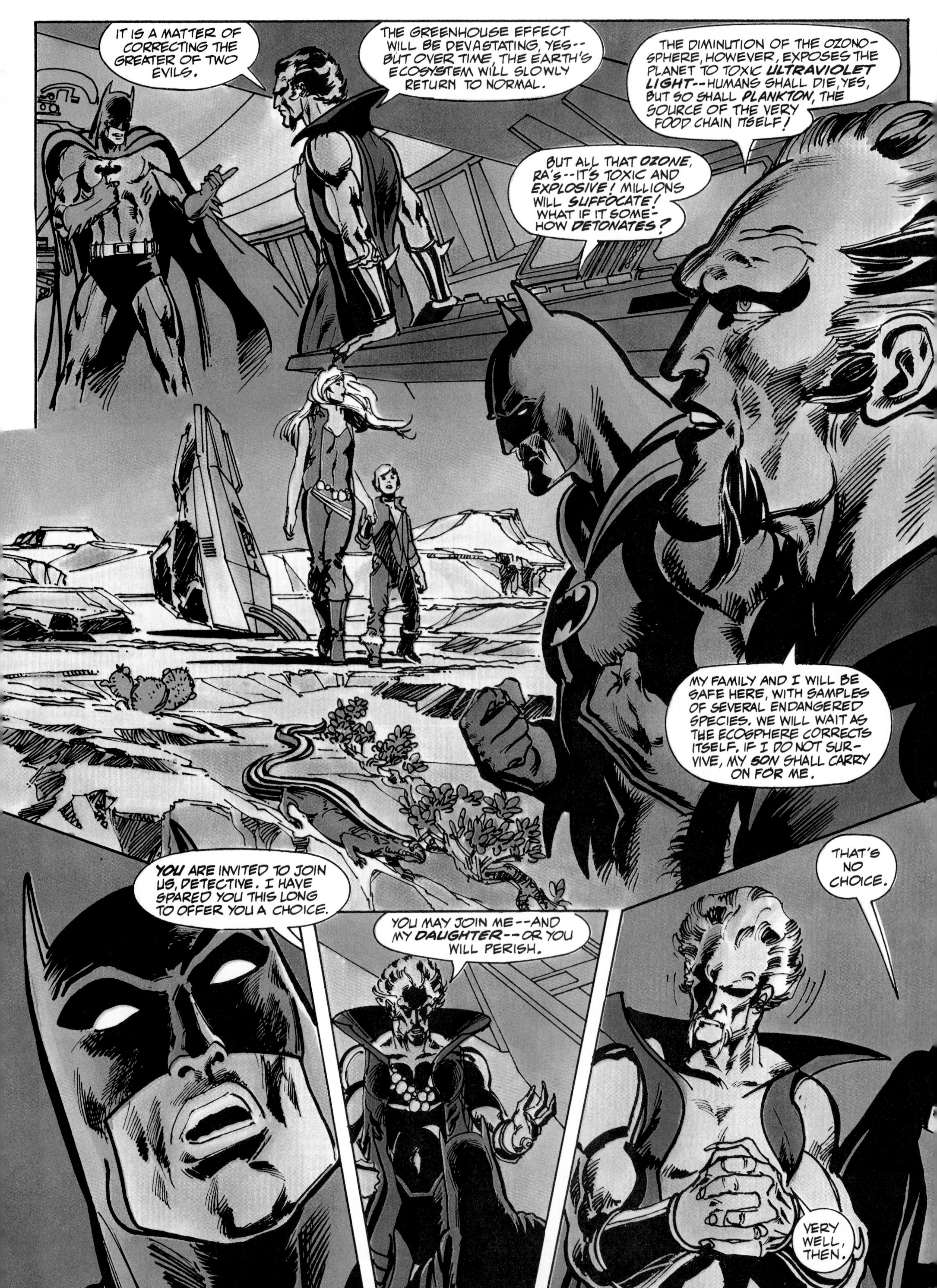
IT IS A MATTER OF CORRECTING THE GREATER OF TWO EVILS.
THE GREENHOUSE EFFECT WILL BE DEVASTATING, YES--BUT OVER TIME, THE EARTH'S ECOSYSTEM WILL SLOWLY RETURN TO NORMAL.
THE DIMINUTION OF THE OZONOSPHERE, HOWEVER, EXPOSES THE PLANET TO TOXIC ULTRAVIOLET LIGHT--HUMANS SHALL DIE, YES, BUT SO SHALL PLANKTON, THE SOURCE OF THE VERY FOOD CHAIN ITSELF!
BUT ALL THAT OZONE, RA'S--IT'S TOXIC AND EXPLOSIVE! MILLIONS WILL SUFFOCATE! WHAT IF IT SOMEHOW DETONATES?
MY FAMILY AND I WILL BE SAFE HERE, WITH SAMPLES OF SEVERAL ENDANGERED SPECIES. WE WILL WAIT AS THE ECOSPHERE CORRECTS ITSELF. IF I DO NOT SURVIVE, MY SON SHALL CARRY ON FOR ME.
YOU ARE INVITED TO JOIN US, DETECTIVE. I HAVE SPARED YOU THIS LONG TO OFFER YOU A CHOICE.
YOU MAY JOIN ME--AND MY DAUGHTER--OR YOU WILL PERISH.
THAT'S NO CHOICE.
VERY WELL, THEN.

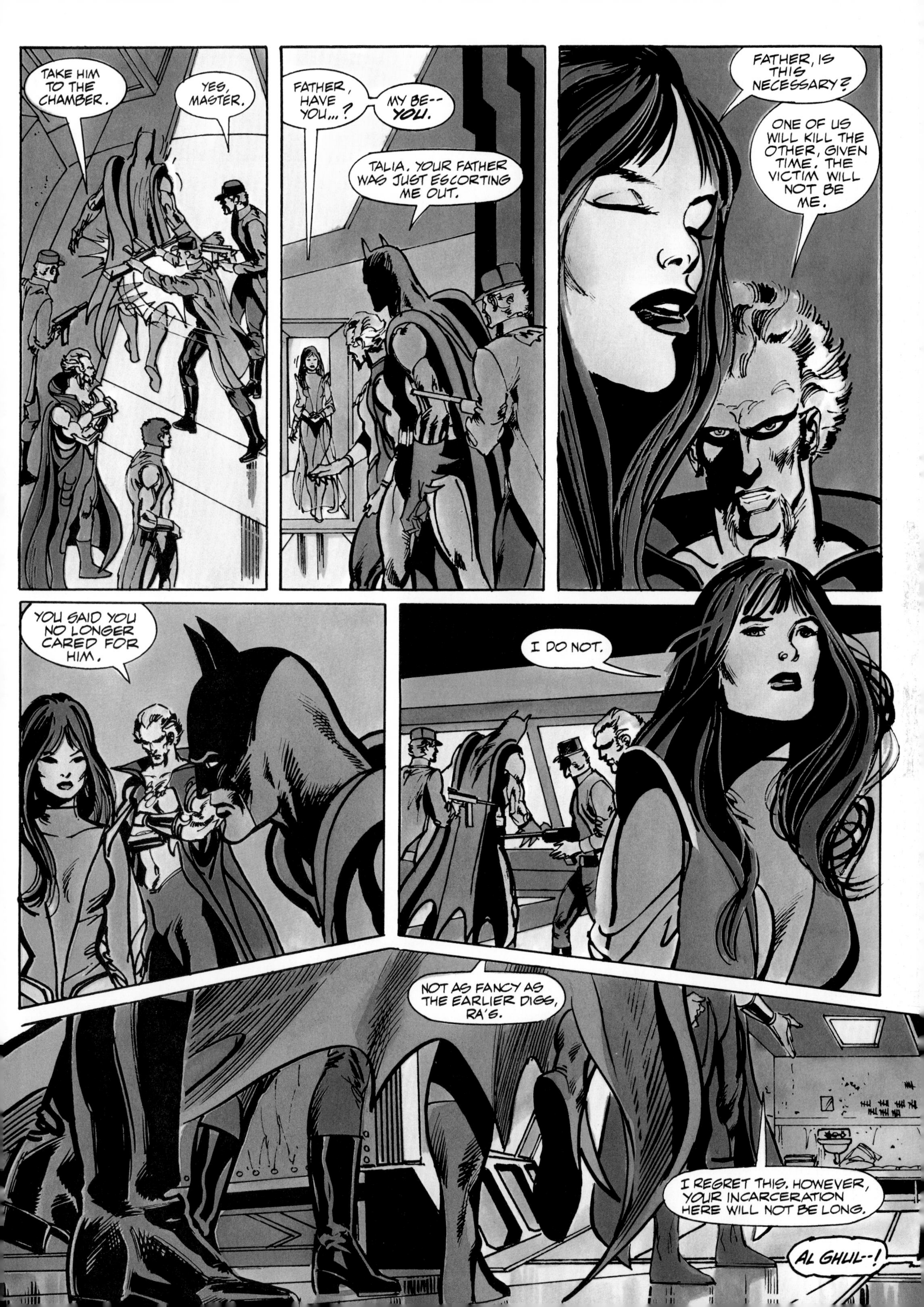
TAKE HIM TO THE CHAMBER.
YES, MASTER.
FATHER, HAVE YOU...?
MY BE-- YOU.
TALIA. YOUR FATHER WAS JUST ESCORTING ME OUT.
FATHER, IS THIS NECESSARY?
ONE OF US WILL KILL THE OTHER, GIVEN TIME. THE VICTIM WILL NOT BE ME.
YOU SAID YOU NO LONGER CARED FOR HIM.
I DO NOT.
NOT AS FANCY AS THE EARLIER DIGS, RA'S.
I REGRET THIS. HOWEVER, YOUR INCARCERATION HERE WILL NOT BE LONG.
AL GHUL--!

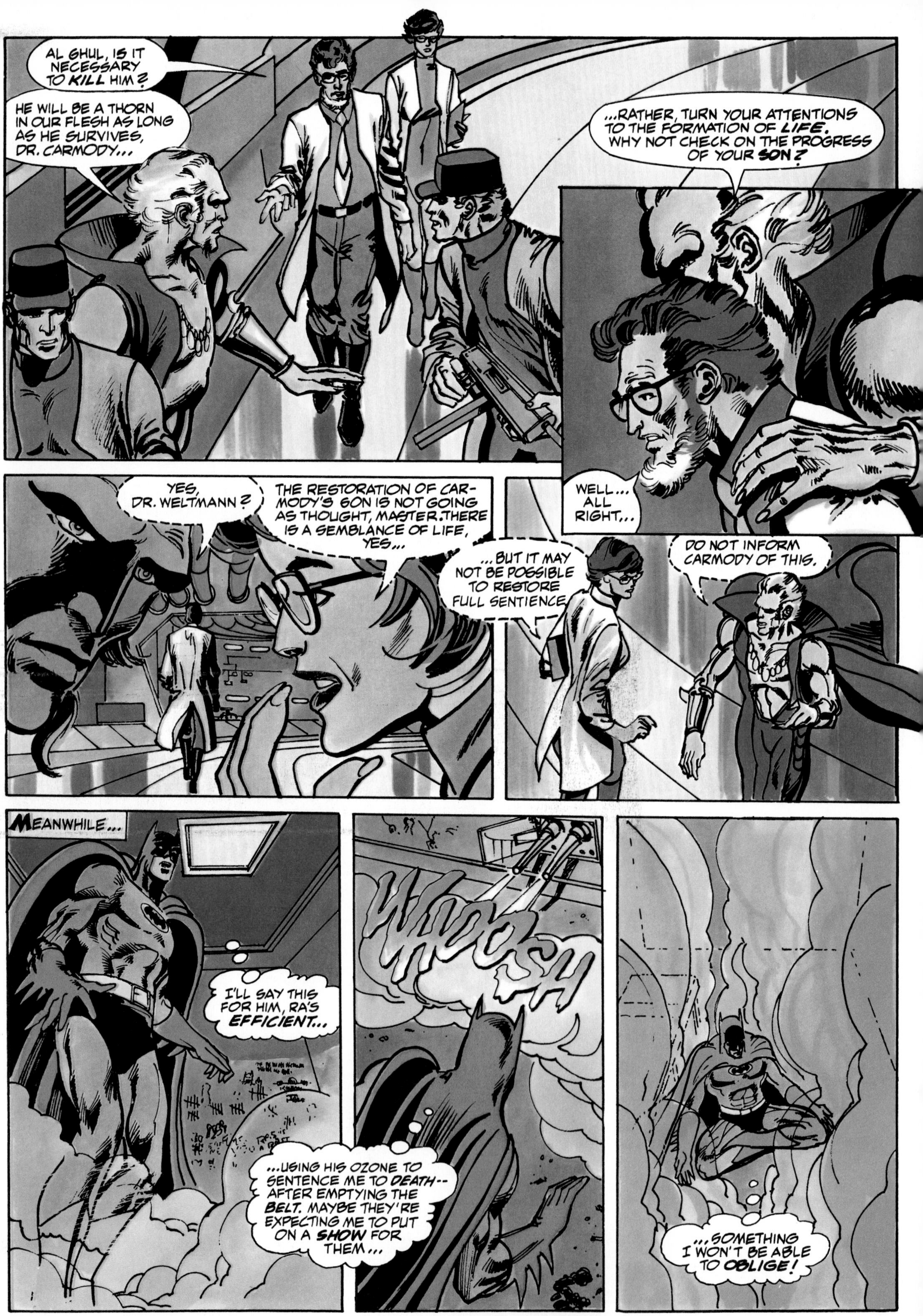
AL GHUL, IS IT NECESSARY TO KILL HIM?
HE WILL BE A THORN IN OUR FLESH AS LONG AS HE SURVIVES, DR. CARMODY...
...RATHER, TURN YOUR ATTENTIONS TO THE FORMATION OF LIFE. WHY NOT CHECK ON THE PROGRESS OF YOUR SON?
WELL... ALL RIGHT,...
YES, DR. WELTMANN?
THE RESTORATION OF CARMODY'S SON IS NOT GOING AS THOUGHT, MASTER. THERE IS A SEMBLANCE OF LIFE, YES...
...BUT IT MAY NOT BE POSSIBLE TO RESTORE FULL SENTIENCE.
DO NOT INFORM CARMODY OF THIS.
MEANWHILE...
I'LL SAY THIS FOR HIM, RA'S EFFICIENT...
WHOOSH
...USING HIS OZONE TO SENTENCE ME TO DEATH-- AFTER EMPTYING THE BELT. MAYBE THEY'RE EXPECTING ME TO PUT ON A SHOW FOR THEM...
...SOMETHING I WON'T BE ABLE TO OBLIGE!

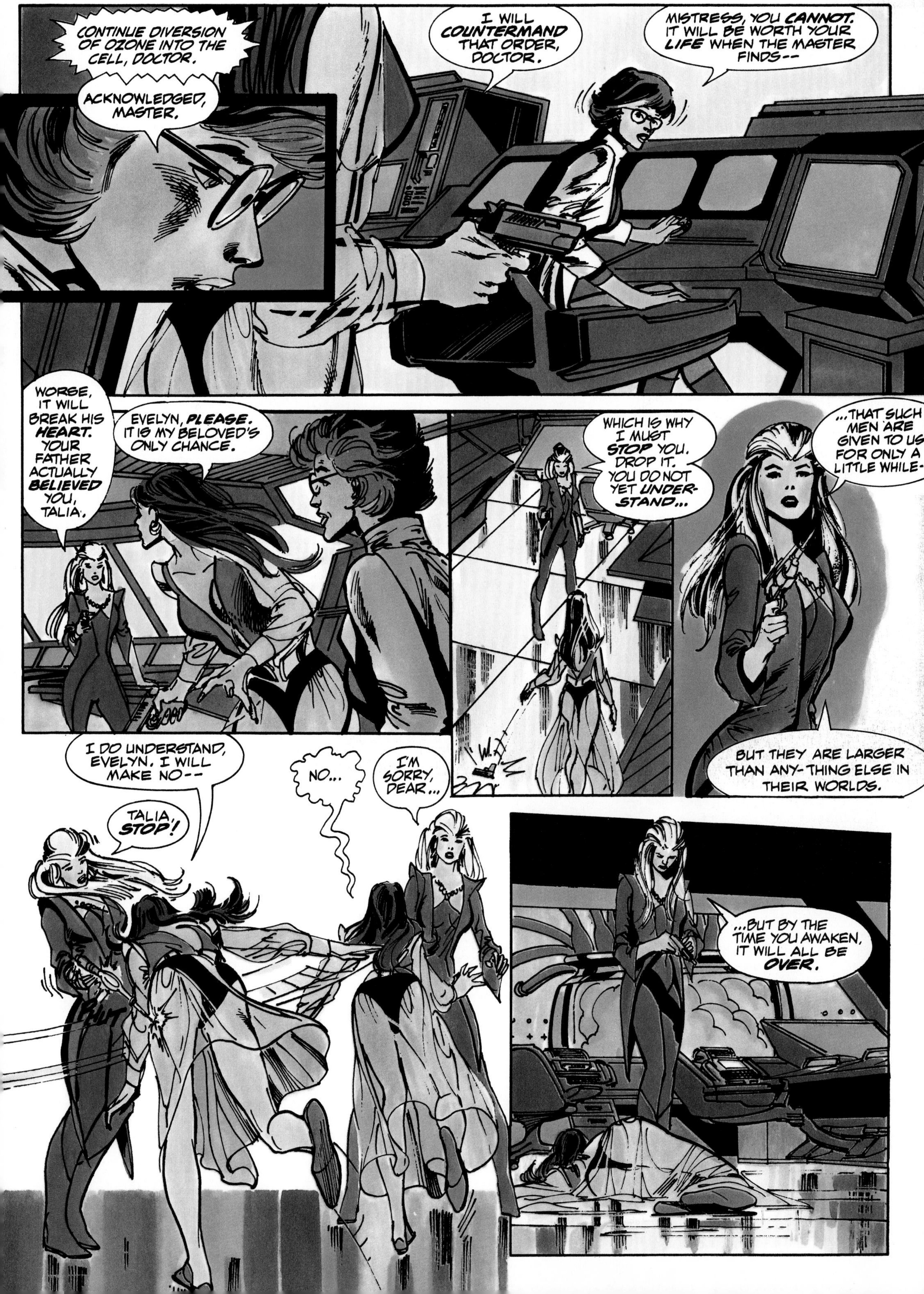
CONTINUE DIVERSION OF OZONE INTO THE CELL, DOCTOR.
ACKNOWLEDGED, MASTER.
I WILL COUNTERMAND THAT ORDER, DOCTOR.
MISTRESS, YOU CANNOT. IT WILL BE WORTH YOUR LIFE WHEN THE MASTER FINDS--
WORSE, IT WILL BREAK HIS HEART. YOUR FATHER ACTUALLY BELIEVED YOU, TALIA.
EVELYN, PLEASE. IT IS MY BELOVED'S ONLY CHANCE.
WHICH IS WHY I MUST STOP YOU. DROP IT. YOU DO NOT YET UNDER-STAND...
...THAT SUCH MEN ARE GIVEN TO US FOR ONLY A LITTLE WHILE--
BUT THEY ARE LARGER THAN ANY- THING ELSE IN THEIR WORLDS.
I DO UNDERSTAND, EVELYN. I WILL MAKE NO--
TALIA, STOP!
PHUT
NO...
I'M SORRY, DEAR...
...BUT BY THE TIME YOU AWAKEN, IT WILL ALL BE OVER.

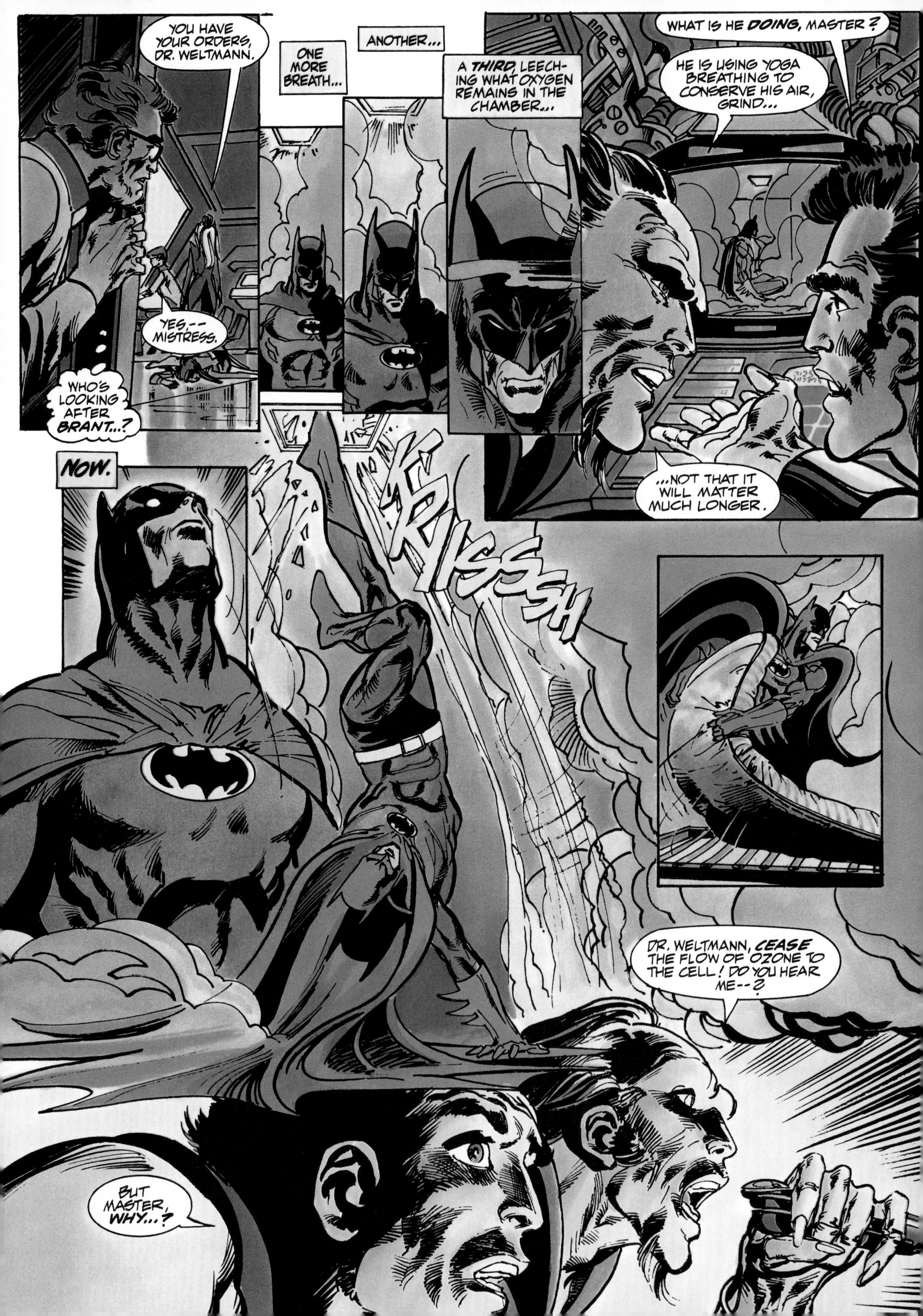
YOU HAVE YOUR ORDERS, DR. WELTMANN.
YES,-- MISTRESS.
WHO'S LOOKING AFTER BRANT...?
ONE MORE BREATH...
ANOTHER...
A THIRD, LEECHING WHAT OXYGEN REMAINS IN THE CHAMBER...
WHAT IS HE DOING, MASTER?
HE IS USING YOGA BREATHING TO CONSERVE HIS AIR, GRIND...
...NOT THAT IT WILL MATTER MUCH LONGER.
NOW.
KRASSSH
DR. WELTMANN, CEASE THE FLOW OF OZONE TO THE CELL! DO YOU HEAR ME--?
BUT MASTER, WHY...?

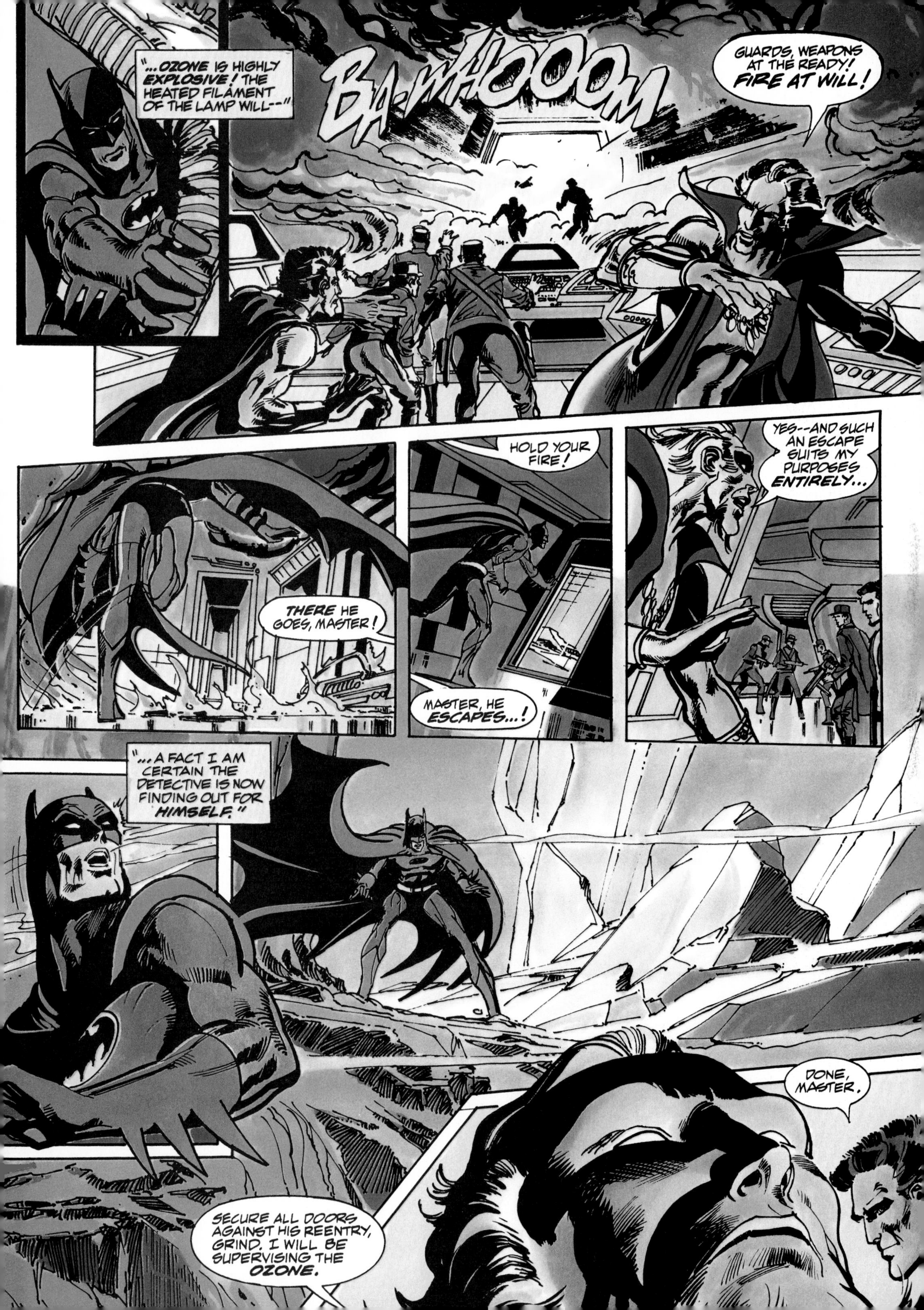
"...OZONE IS HIGHLY EXPLOSIVE! THE HEATED FILAMENT OF THE LAMP WILL--"
BA-WHOOOM
GUARDS, WEAPONS AT THE READY! FIRE AT WILL!
THERE HE GOES, MASTER!
HOLD YOUR FIRE!
MASTER, HE ESCAPES...!
YES--AND SUCH AN ESCAPE SUITS MY PURPOSES ENTIRELY...
"...A FACT I AM CERTAIN THE DETECTIVE IS NOW FINDING OUT FOR HIMSELF."
DONE, MASTER.
SECURE ALL DOORS AGAINST HIS REENTRY, GRIND. I WILL BE SUPERVISING THE OZONE.

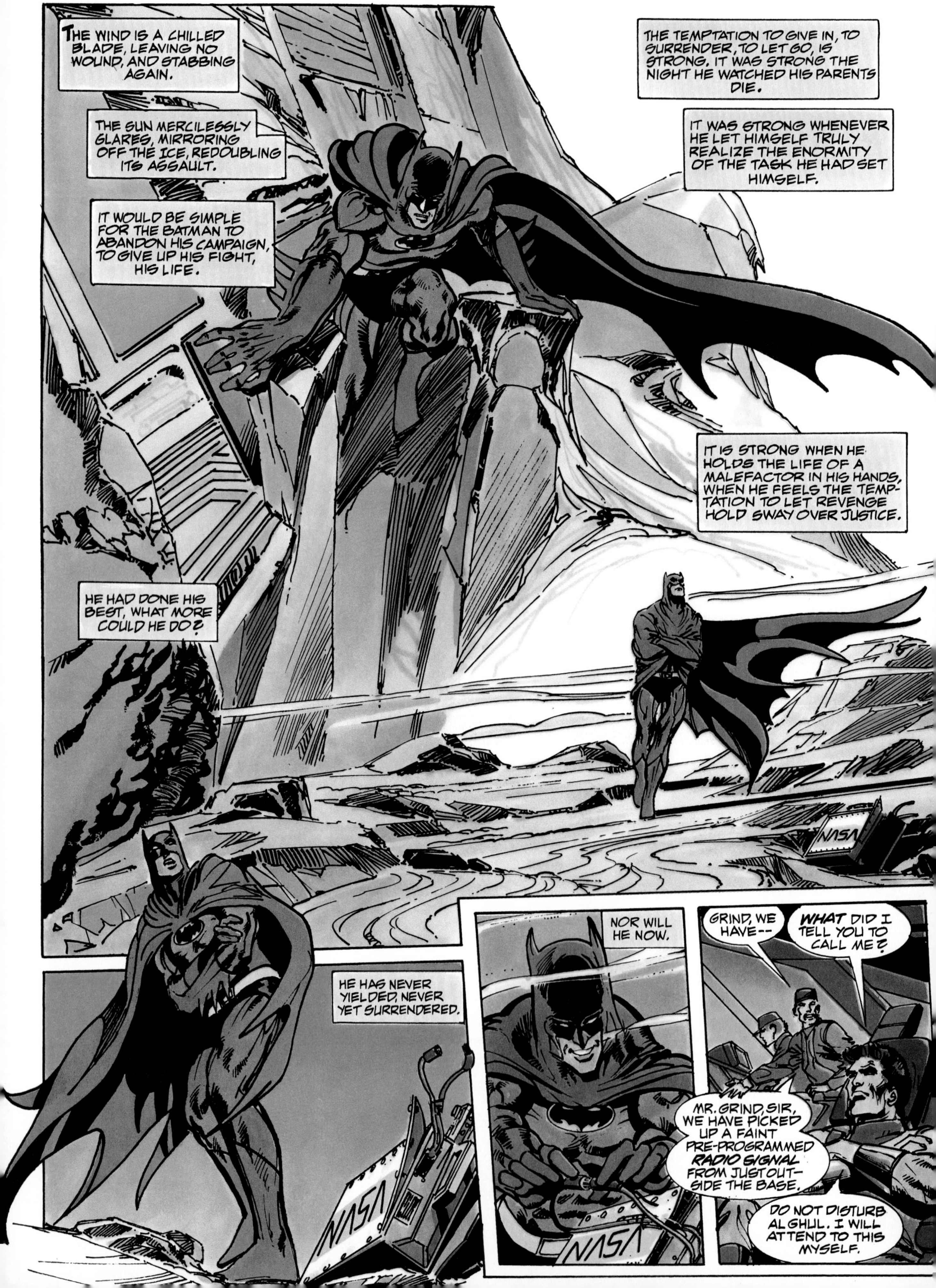

THE WIND IS A CHILLED BLADE, LEAVING NO WOUND, AND STABBING AGAIN.
THE SUN MERCILESSLY GLARES, MIRRORING OFF THE ICE, REDOUBLING ITS ASSAULT.
IT WOULD BE SIMPLE FOR THE BATMAN TO ABANDON HIS CAMPAIGN, TO GIVE UP HIS FIGHT, HIS LIFE.
THE TEMPTATION TO GIVE IN, TO SURRENDER, TO LET GO, IS STRONG. IT WAS STRONG THE NIGHT HE WATCHED HIS PARENTS DIE.
IT WAS STRONG WHENEVER HE LET HIMSELF TRULY REALIZE THE ENORMITY OF THE TASK HE HAD SET HIMSELF.
IT IS STRONG WHEN HE HOLDS THE LIFE OF A MALEFACTOR IN HIS HANDS, WHEN HE FEELS THE TEMPTATION TO LET REVENGE HOLD SWAY OVER JUSTICE.
HE HAD DONE HIS BEST, WHAT MORE COULD HE DO?
NASA
HE HAS NEVER YIELDED, NEVER YET SURRENDERED.
NOR WILL HE NOW.
NASA
NASA
GRIND, WE HAVE--
WHAT DID I TELL YOU TO CALL ME?
MR. GRIND, SIR, WE HAVE PICKED UP A FAINT PRE-PROGRAMMED RADIO SIGNAL FROM JUST OUTSIDE THE BASE.
DO NOT DISTURB AL GHUL. I WILL ATTEND TO THIS MYSELF.

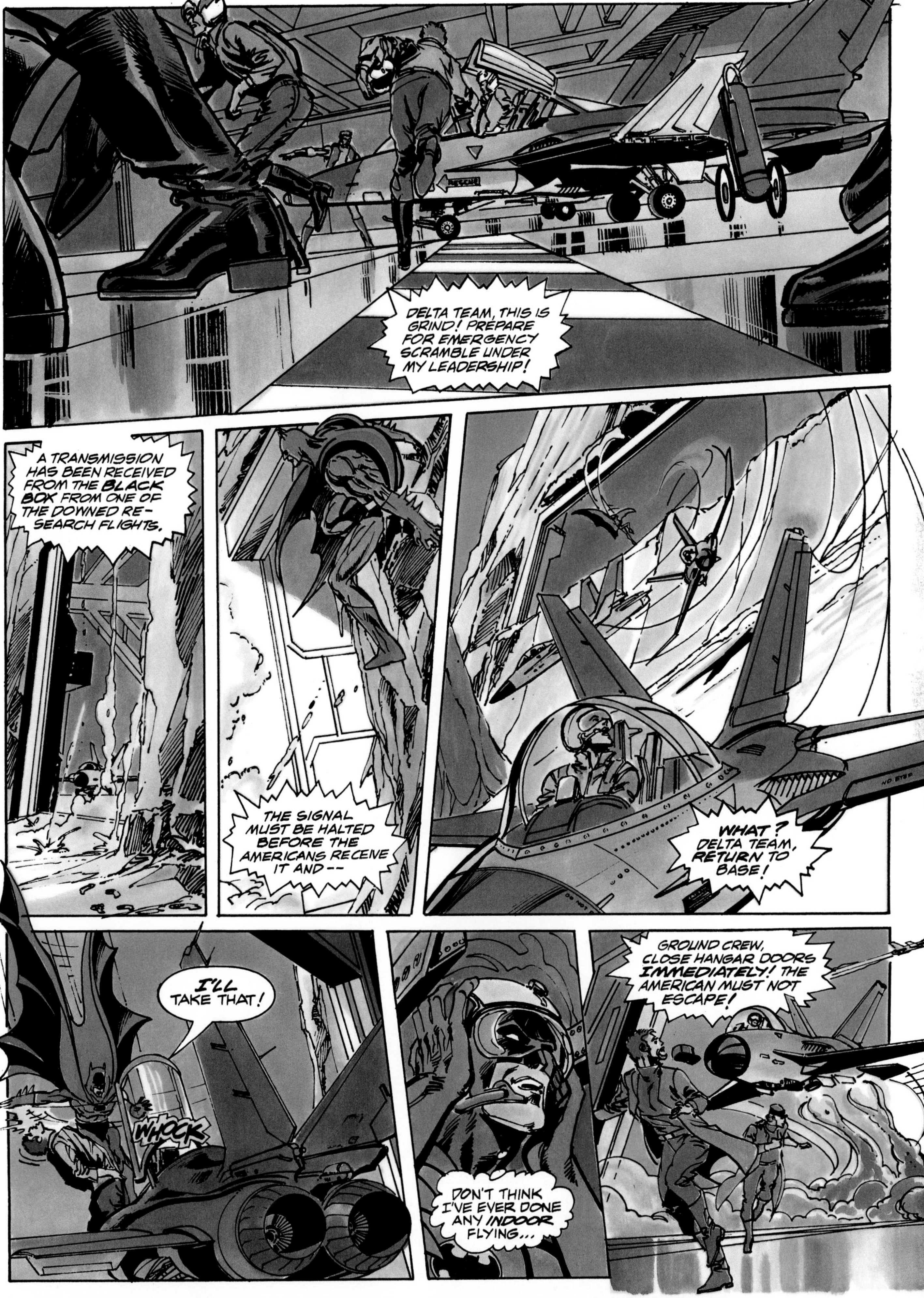
DELTA TEAM, THIS IS GRIND! PREPARE FOR EMERGENCY SCRAMBLE UNDER MY LEADERSHIP!
A TRANSMISSION HAS BEEN RECEIVED FROM THE BLACK BOX FROM ONE OF THE DOWNED RE-SEARCH FLIGHTS.
THE SIGNAL MUST BE HALTED BEFORE THE AMERICANS RECEIVE IT AND --
WHAT? DELTA TEAM, RETURN TO BASE!
I'LL TAKE THAT!
WHOCK
DON'T THINK I'VE EVER DONE ANY INDOOR FLYING...
GROUND CREW, CLOSE HANGAR DOORS IMMEDIATELY! THE AMERICAN MUST NOT ESCAPE!

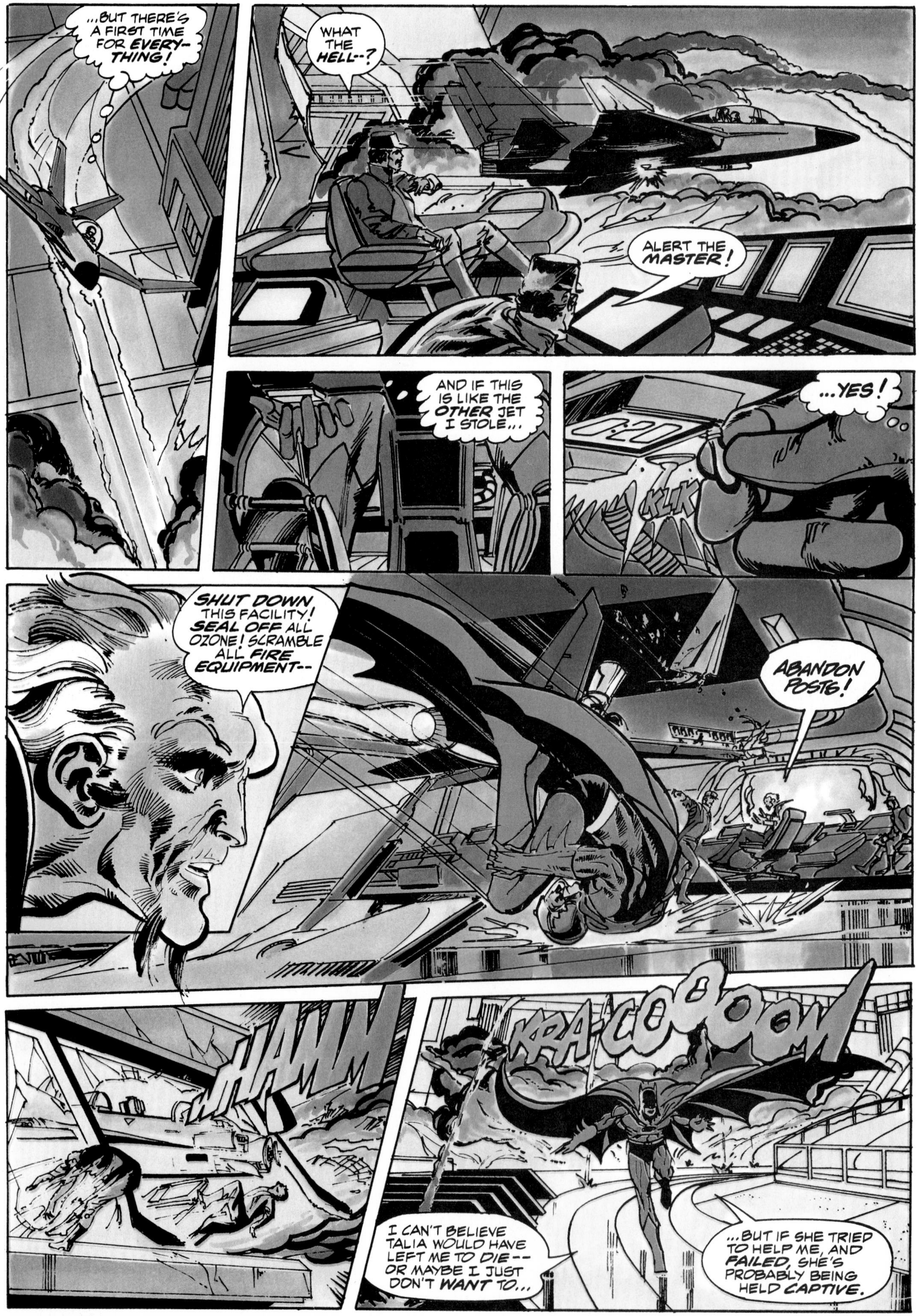
...BUT THERE'S A FIRST TIME FOR EVERYTHING!
WHAT THE HELL--?
ALERT THE MASTER!
AND IF THIS IS LIKE THE OTHER JET I STOLE...
...YES!
KLIK
SHUT DOWN THIS FACILITY! SEAL OFF ALL OZONE! SCRAMBLE ALL FIRE EQUIPMENT--
ABANDON POSTS!
HAMM
KRA-COOOOOM
I CAN'T BELIEVE TALIA WOULD HAVE LEFT ME TO DIE -- OR MAYBE I JUST DON'T WANT TO...
...BUT IF SHE TRIED TO HELP ME, AND FAILED, SHE'S PROBABLY BEING HELD CAPTIVE.

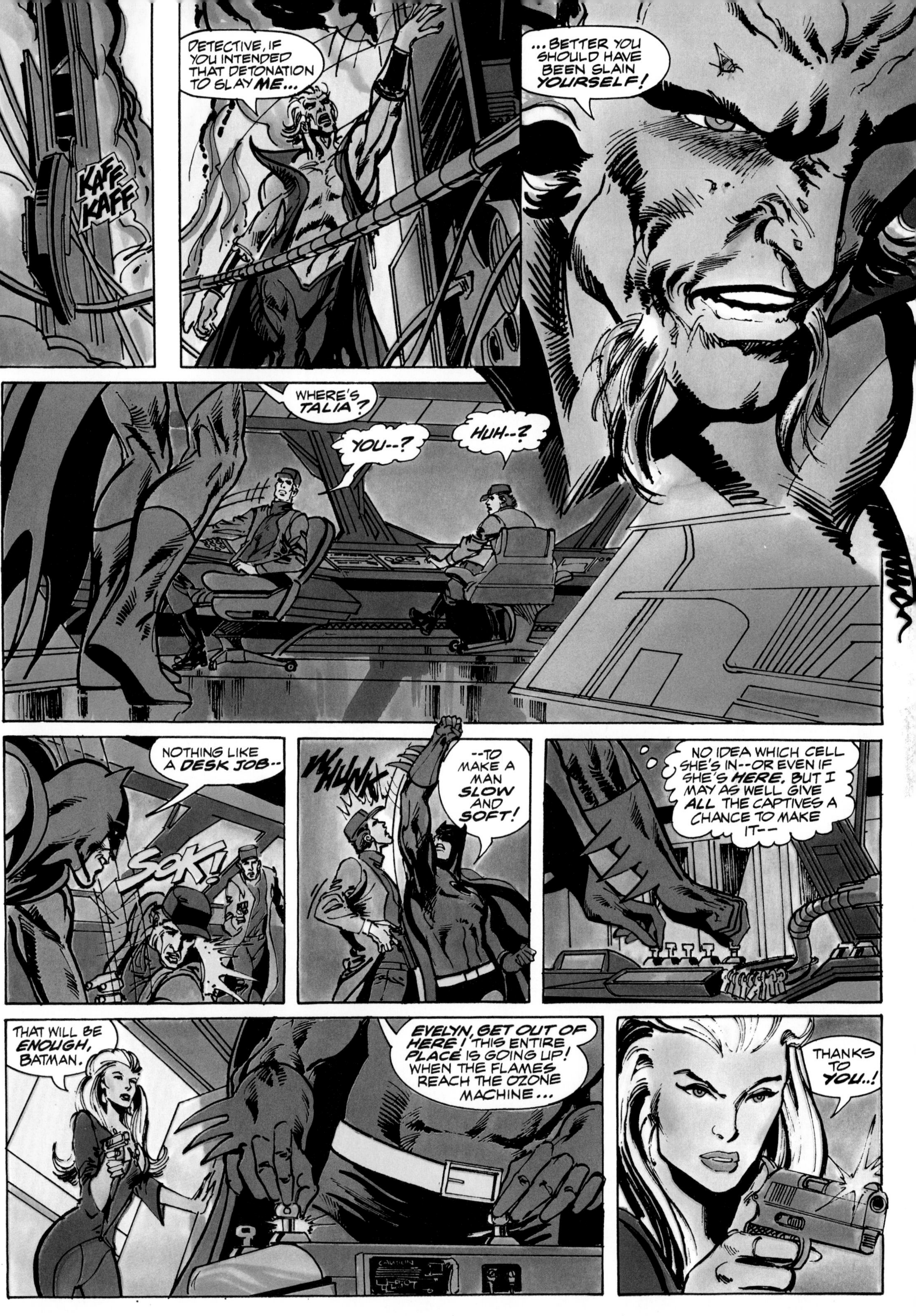
KAFF KAFF
DETECTIVE, IF YOU INTENDED THAT DETONATION TO SLAY ME...
...BETTER YOU SHOULD HAVE BEEN SLAIN YOURSELF!
WHERE'S TALIA?
YOU--?
HUH--?
NOTHING LIKE A DESK JOB--
SOK!
WHUNK
--TO MAKE A MAN SLOW AND SOFT!
NO IDEA WHICH CELL SHE'S IN--OR EVEN IF SHE'S HERE. BUT I MAY AS WELL GIVE ALL THE CAPTIVES A CHANCE TO MAKE IT--
THAT WILL BE ENOUGH, BATMAN.
EVELYN, GET OUT OF HERE! THIS ENTIRE PLACE IS GOING UP! WHEN THE FLAMES REACH THE OZONE MACHINE...
THANKS TO YOU..!

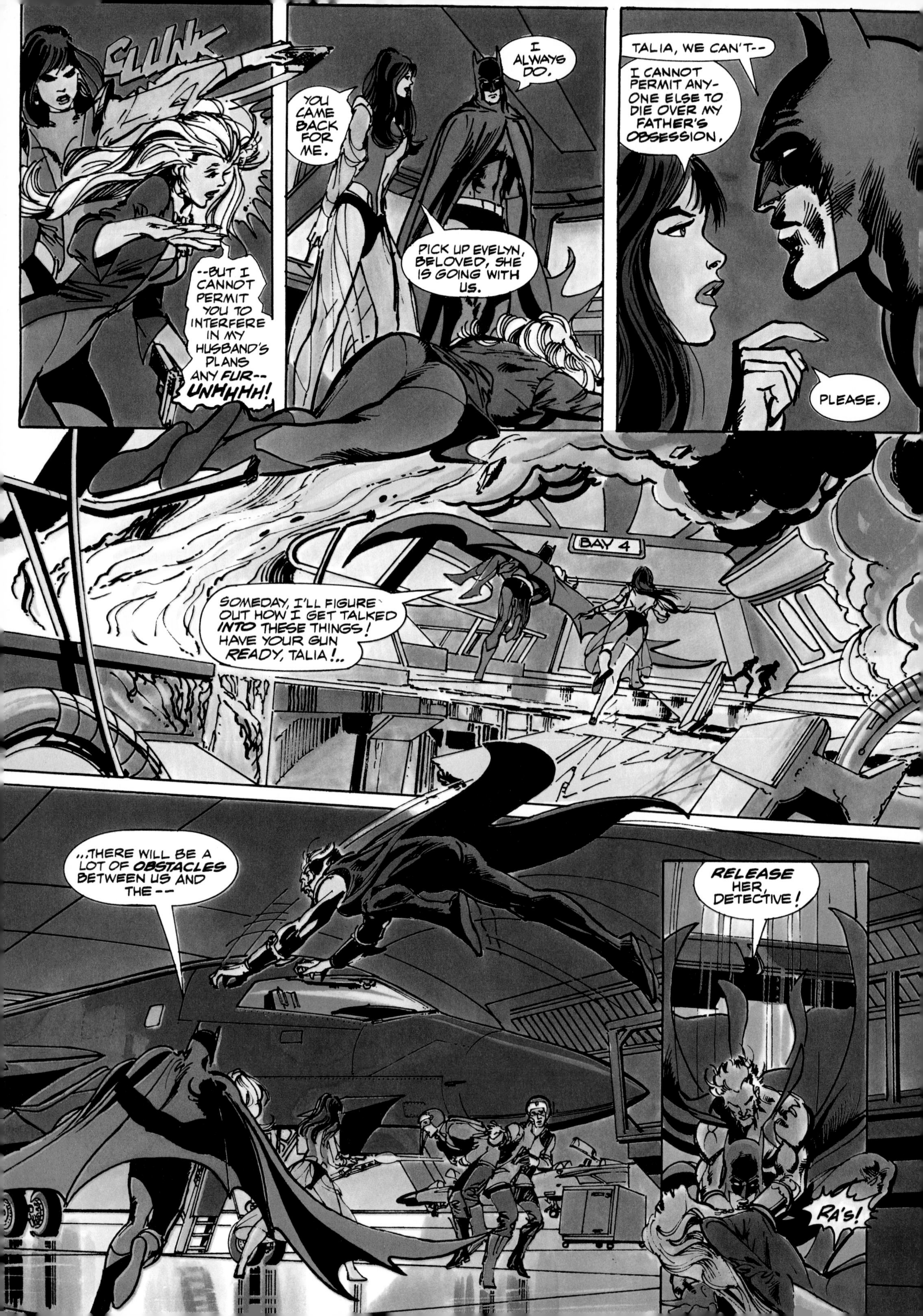
CLUNK
--BUT I CANNOT PERMIT YOU TO INTERFERE IN MY HUSBAND'S PLANS ANY FUR-- UNHHHH!
YOU CAME BACK FOR ME.
I ALWAYS DO.
PICK UP EVELYN, BELOVED, SHE IS GOING WITH US.
TALIA, WE CAN'T--
I CANNOT PERMIT ANY-ONE ELSE TO DIE OVER MY FATHER'S OBSESSION.
PLEASE.
BAY 4
SOMEDAY, I'LL FIGURE OUT HOW I GET TALKED INTO THESE THINGS! HAVE YOUR GUN READY, TALIA!..
..THERE WILL BE A LOT OF OBSTACLES BETWEEN US AND THE--
RELEASE HER, DETECTIVE!
RA'S!

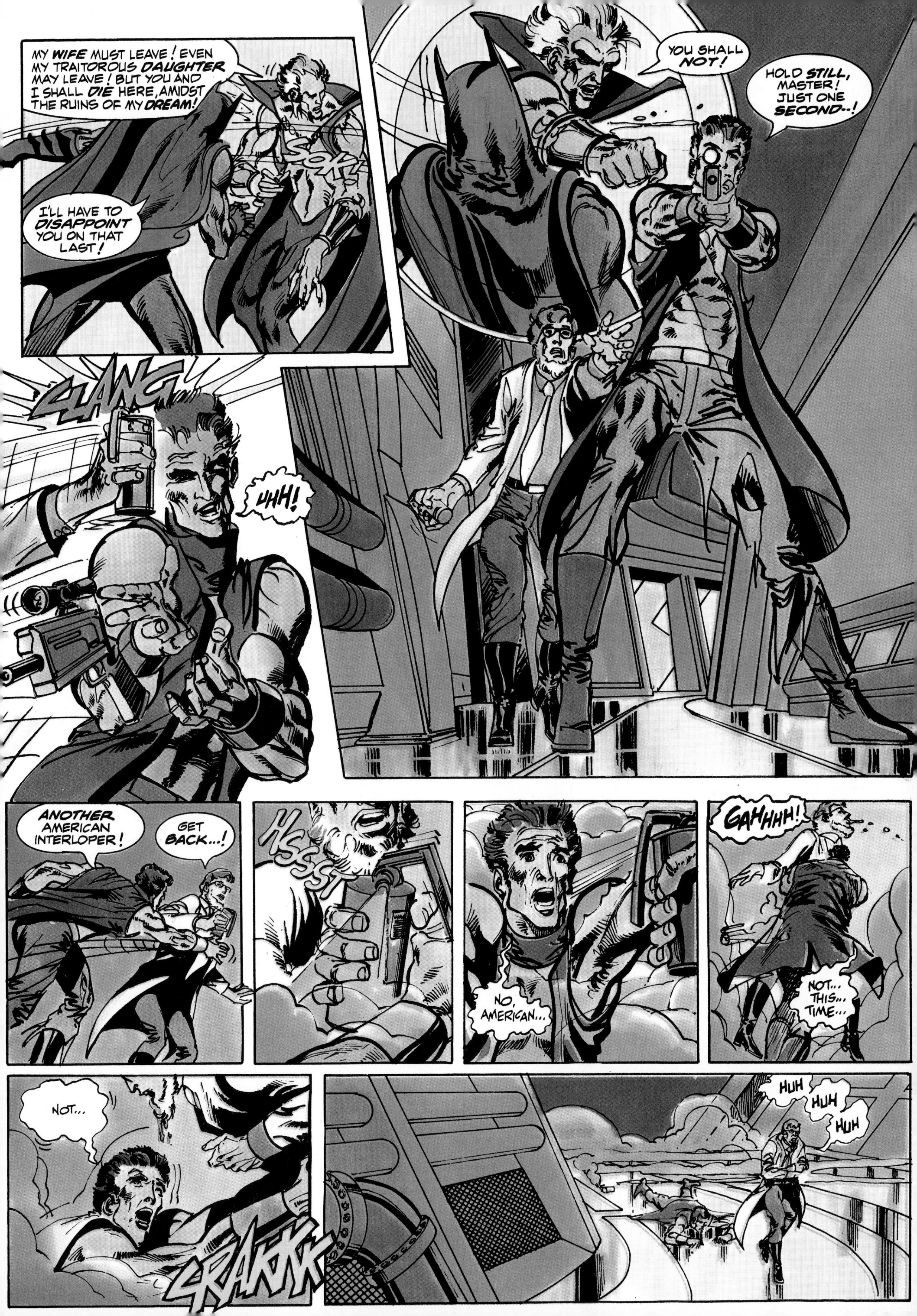

MY WIFE MUST LEAVE! EVEN MY TRAITOROUS DAUGHTER MAY LEAVE! BUT YOU AND I SHALL DIE HERE, AMIDST THE RUINS OF MY DREAM!
SOK!
I'LL HAVE TO DISAPPOINT YOU ON THAT LAST!
YOU SHALL NOT!
HOLD STILL, MASTER! JUST ONE SECOND..!
CLANG
UHH!
ANOTHER AMERICAN INTERLOPER!
GET BACK...!
HSSSST
NO, AMERICAN...
GAHHHH!
NOT... THIS... TIME...
NOT...
CRAKKK
HUH
HUH
HUH

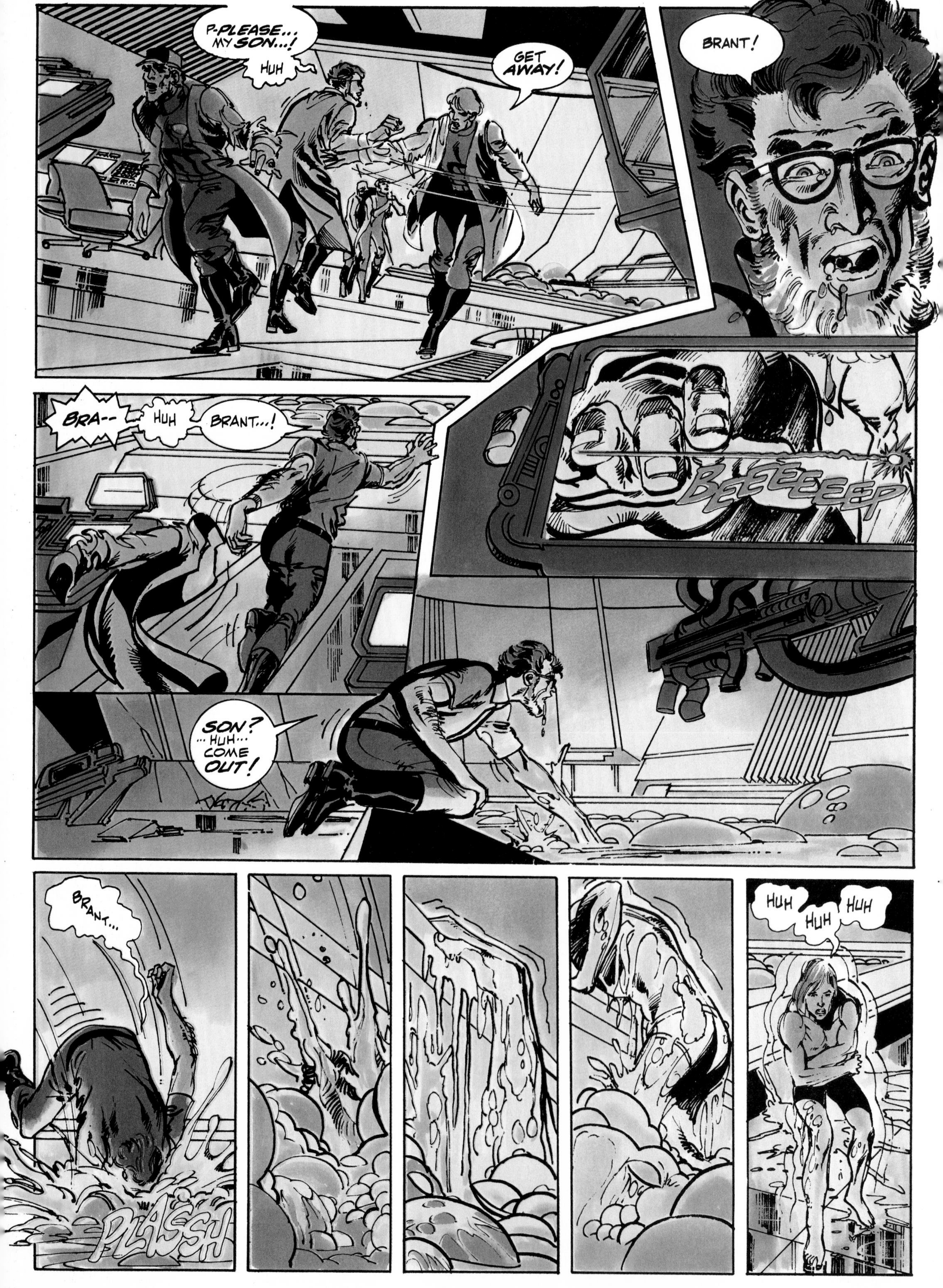
P-PLEASE... MY SON...!
HUH
GET AWAY!
BRANT!
BRA--
HUH
BRANT...!
BEEEEEEP
SON? ...HUH... COME OUT!
BRANT...
PLASSH
HUH
HUH
HUH

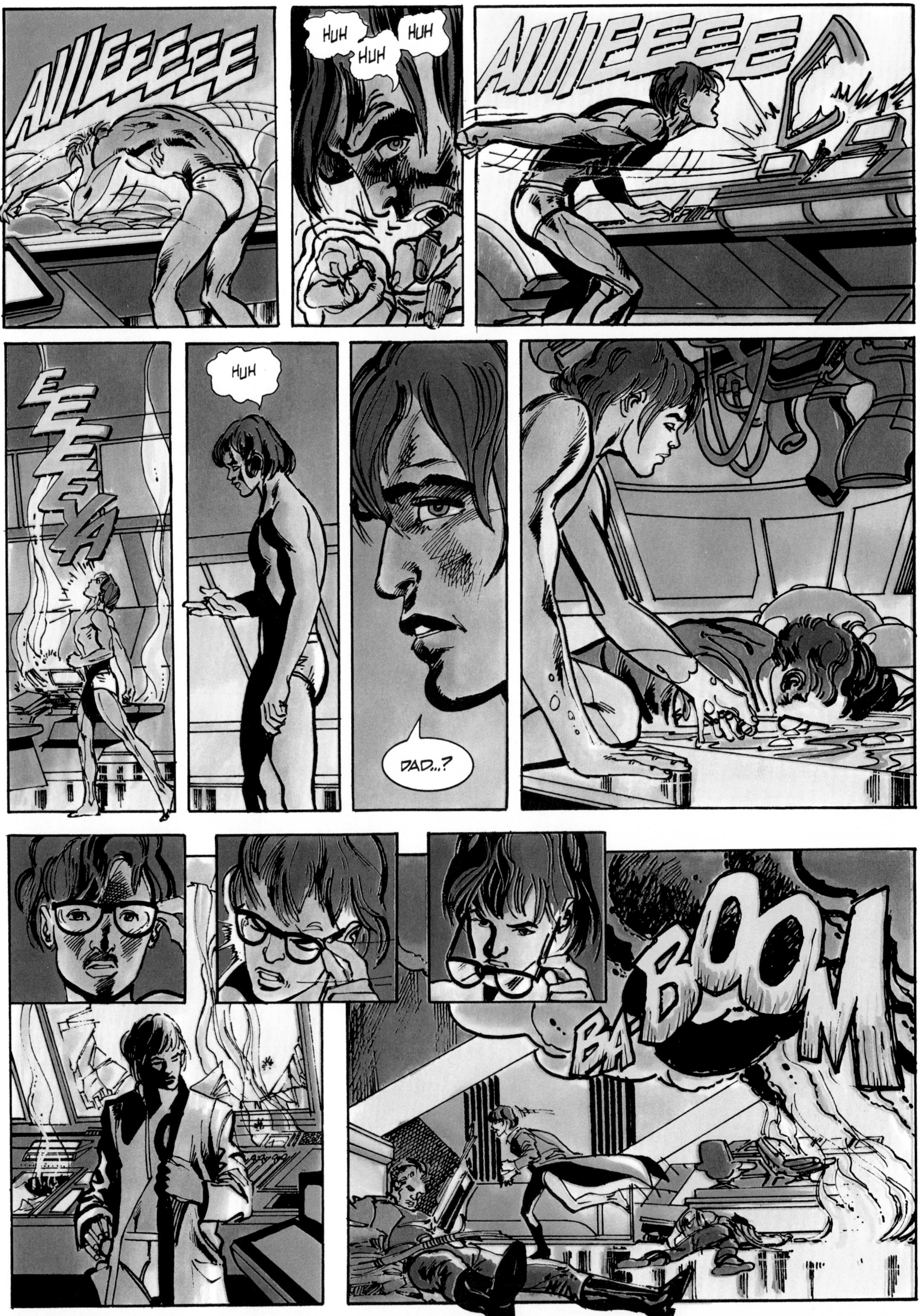
AIIIEEEEEE
HUH
HUH
HUH
AIIIEEEEE
EEEEYA
HUH
DAD...?
BA BOOM

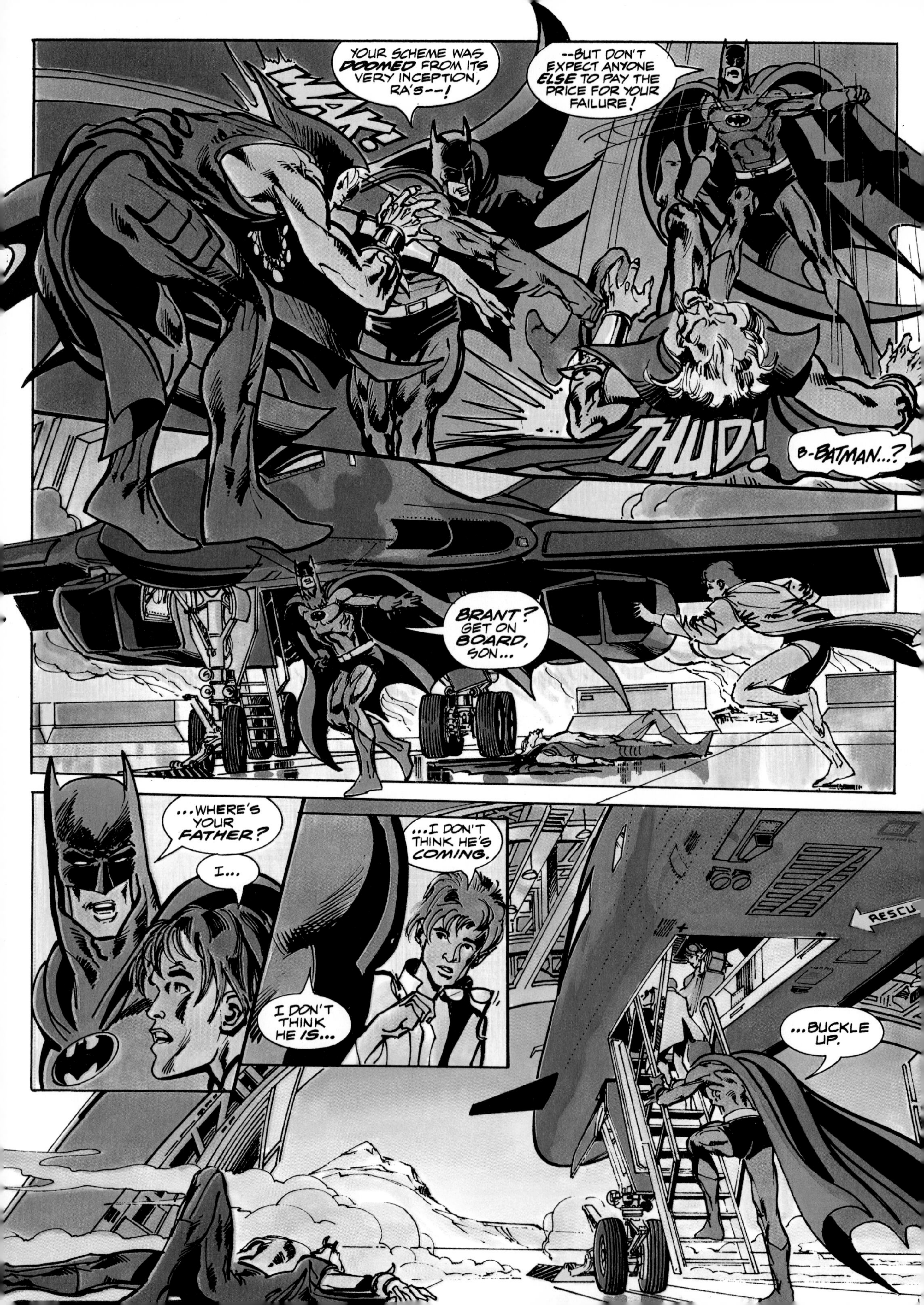
WAK!
YOUR SCHEME WAS DOOMED FROM ITS VERY INCEPTION, RA'S--!
--BUT DON'T EXPECT ANYONE ELSE TO PAY THE PRICE FOR YOUR FAILURE!
THUD!
B-BATMAN...?
BRANT? GET ON BOARD, SON...
...WHERE'S YOUR FATHER?
I...
...I DON'T THINK HE'S COMING.
I DON'T THINK HE IS...
RESCU
...BUCKLE UP.

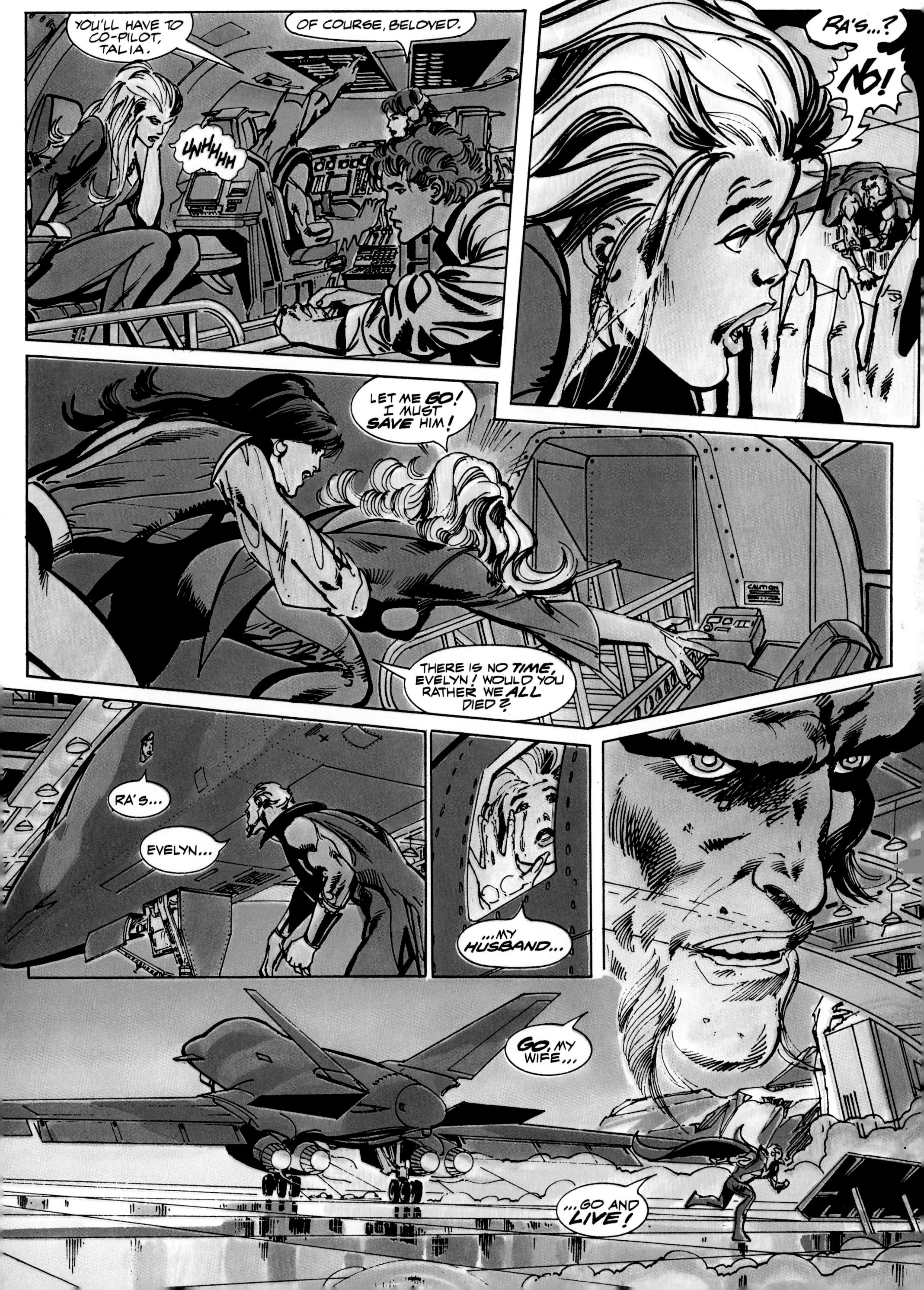
YOU'LL HAVE TO CO-PILOT, TALIA.
OF COURSE, BELOVED.
UNHHHH
RA'S...?
NO!
LET ME GO! I MUST SAVE HIM!
THERE IS NO TIME, EVELYN! WOULD YOU RATHER WE ALL DIED?
RA'S...
EVELYN...
...MY HUSBAND...
GO, MY WIFE...
...GO AND LIVE!

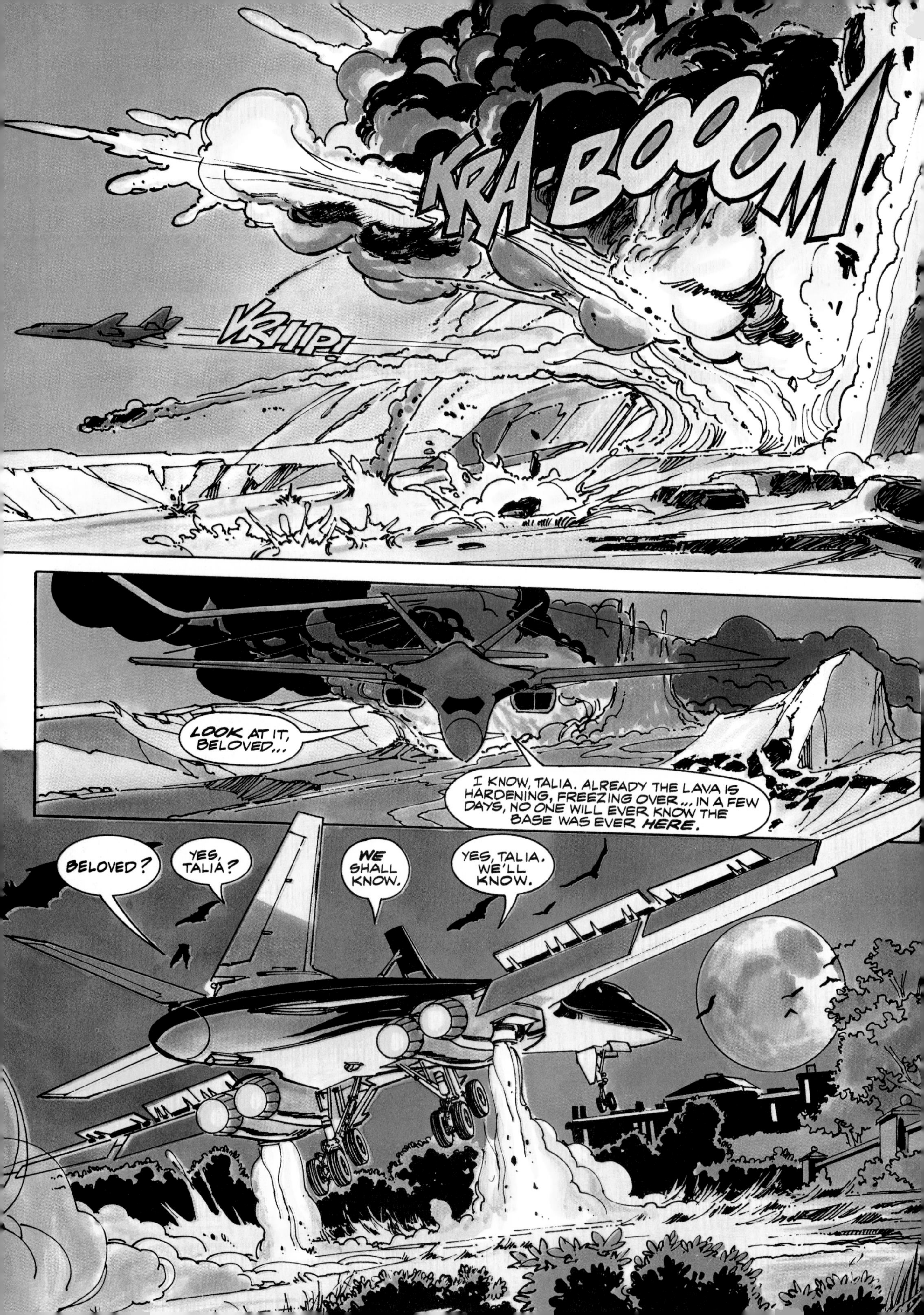
KRA-BOOOOM!
VRHIP!
LOOK AT IT, BELOVED...
I KNOW, TALIA. ALREADY THE LAVA IS HARDENING, FREEZING OVER... IN A FEW DAYS, NO ONE WILL EVER KNOW THE BASE WAS EVER HERE.
BELOVED?
YES, TALIA?
WE SHALL KNOW.
YES, TALIA. WE'LL KNOW.

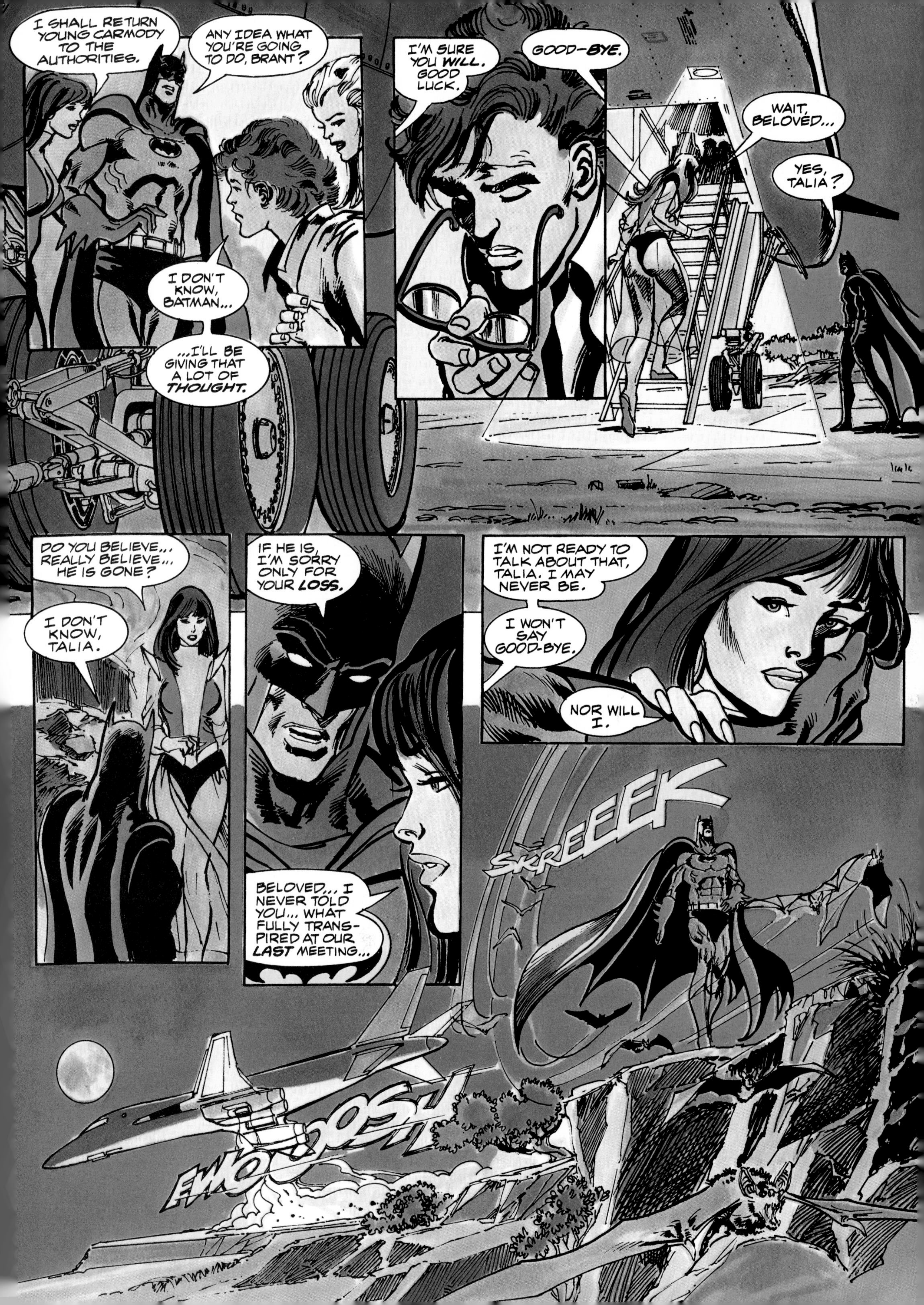
I SHALL RETURN YOUNG CARMODY TO THE AUTHORITIES.
ANY IDEA WHAT YOU'RE GOING TO DO, BRANT?
I DON'T KNOW, BATMAN...
...I'LL BE GIVING THAT A LOT OF THOUGHT.
I'M SURE YOU WILL. GOOD LUCK.
GOOD-BYE.
WAIT, BELOVÉD...
YES, TALIA?
DO YOU BELIEVE... REALLY BELIEVE... HE IS GONE?
I DON'T KNOW, TALIA.
IF HE IS, I'M SORRY ONLY FOR YOUR LOSS.
BELOVED... I NEVER TOLD YOU... WHAT FULLY TRANSPIRED AT OUR LAST MEETING...
I'M NOT READY TO TALK ABOUT THAT, TALIA. I MAY NEVER BE.
I WON'T SAY GOOD-BYE.
NOR WILL I.
SKREEEEK
FWOOOOSH

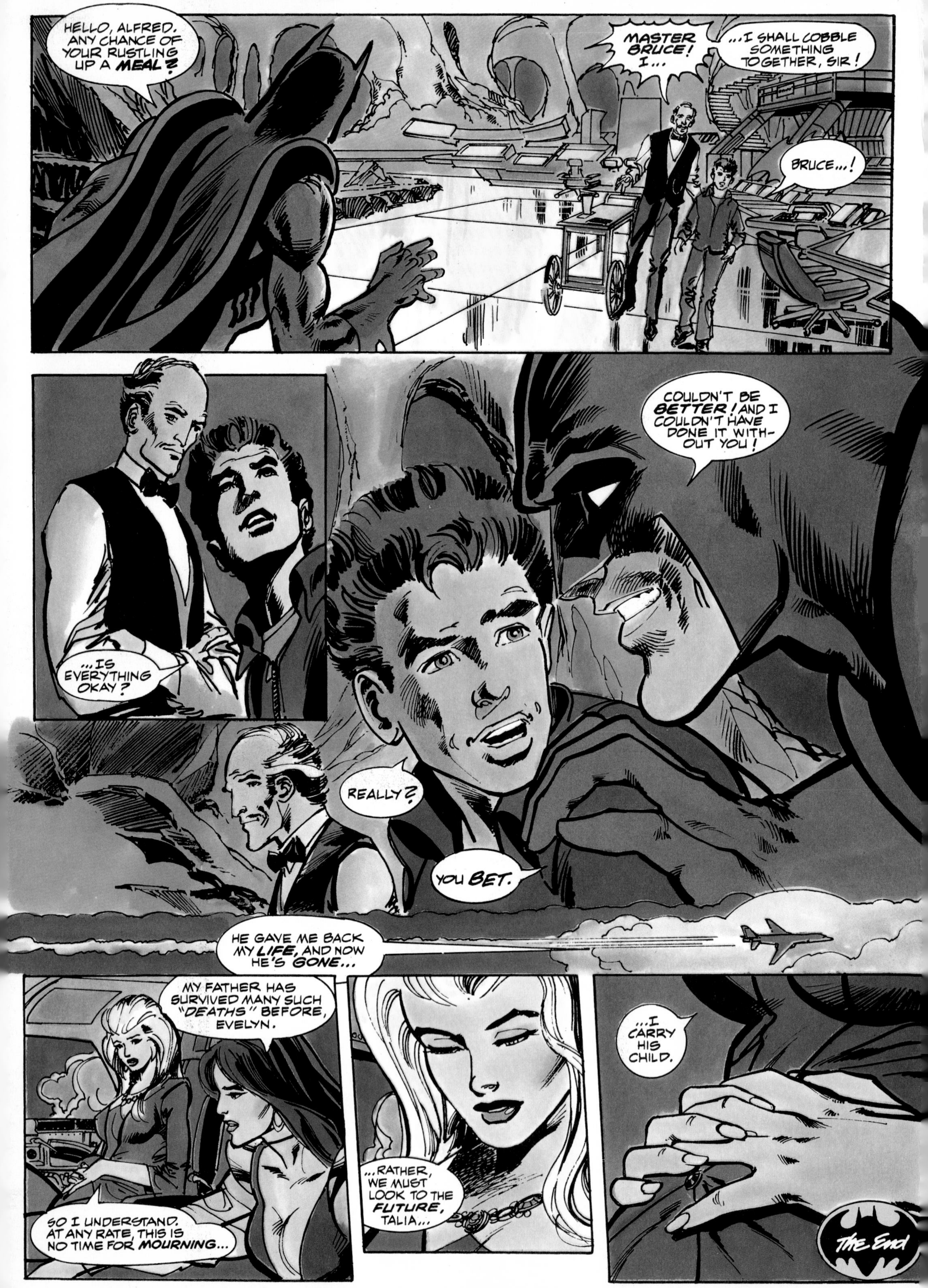
HELLO, ALFRED. ANY CHANCE OF YOUR RUSTLING UP A MEAL?
MASTER BRUCE! I...
...I SHALL COBBLE SOMETHING TOGETHER, SIR!
BRUCE...!
...IS EVERYTHING OKAY?
COULDN'T BE BETTER! AND I COULDN'T HAVE DONE IT WITH-OUT YOU!
REALLY?
YOU BET.
HE GAVE ME BACK MY LIFE, AND NOW HE'S GONE...
MY FATHER HAS SURVIVED MANY SUCH "DEATHS" BEFORE, EVELYN.
SO I UNDERSTAND. AT ANY RATE, THIS IS NO TIME FOR MOURNING...
...RATHER, WE MUST LOOK TO THE FUTURE, TALIA...
...I CARRY HIS CHILD.
The End